WITHDRAWN

WITHDRAWN

The Jossey-Bass
Higher and Adult Education Series

Dialogue Education at Work

A Case Book

Jane Vella and Associates
Foreword by Margaret Wheatley

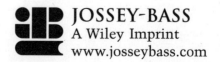

JOSSEY-BASS
A Wiley Imprint
www.josseybass.com

35.00

Jossey-Bass books and products are available through most bookstores. To contact Jossey-
Bass directly call our Customer Care Department within the U.S. at 800-956-7739, outside
the U.S. at 317-572-3986 or fax 317-572-4002.

Jossey-Bass also publishes its books in a variety of electronic formats. Some content that
appears in print may not be available in electronic books.

Library of Congress Cataloging-in-Publication Data

Vella, Jane Kathryn, 1931–
  Dialogue education at work : a casebook / Jane Vella and associates ;
foreword by Margaret Wheatley.— 1st ed.
    p. cm. — (The Jossey-Bass higher and adult education series)
Includes bibliographical references (p.   ) and index.
  ISBN 0-7879-6473-5 (alk. paper)
  1. Popular education—Case studies. 2. Adult learning—Case studies.
3. Adult education teachers—Training of—Case studies. I. Title. II.
Series.
  LC196.V45 2003
  370.11'5—dc1`
                              2003012215

Printed in the United States of America
FIRST EDITION
HB Printing   10 9 8 7 6 5 4 3 2 1

Contents

Part II: The Public Sector and Not-for-Profit Organizations

Part III: International Education

Foreword

Margaret Wheatley

This book is filled with treasures, many different ways to use dialogue in settings as varied and interesting as the whole wide world. This should not come as a surprise—to realize that dialogue works everywhere, in such diverse places. The reason it is no surprise is that conversation is the most fundamental of human pleasures, no matter our culture or upbringing. Conversation has always been the primary way we humans come together, think together, plan together, dream together. It is what we like to do most.

It is hard to look past the complicated processes of our time to this simple truth. We live in an age when there is a specific technique for almost everything. We have to learn a sophisticated process for setting goals, for strategic planning, for communicating, for thinking creatively. We have allowed basic human capacities, skills possessed by humans everywhere, to be taken from us. We have decided that experts and complex techniques are absolutely necessary if we need to plan, set goals, communicate, be creative, or change the world. Far too many of us have forgotten that we already know how to do these things; far too many of us have been separated from our basic human competencies. Even dialogue has become too technical a term for me, insofar as it becomes specialized and requires expert facilitators. I value most the work of those who have written these pages, those who make dialogue simple and accessible once again.

Everyone I know who has been engaged in dialogue work eventually admits that people do not need as much instruction in dialogue as they need encouragement *to remember it*. The more you do dialogue work, the more you learn to trust that all of us, by virtue of being human, carry a deep, primal memory of being together and talking to one another.

This species memory goes far back in time. The earliest archeological record of humans sitting in a circle goes back nearly five hundred million years, perhaps even before there were *Homo sapiens*. (These circles may have been created by *Homo erectus*.) Whoever they were, they sat around fires, and the need to keep warm was the reason why they formed into circles. Had they sat in rectangular fashion, some of them would have frozen!

Today when we sit together and engage in real conversation, talking about the things that matter most to us, we can trust that we are evoking this collective memory. In our bright, artificially lit offices and rooms, something, someone, is speaking to us from the flickering firelight shadows of history. Perhaps they knew more than we do these days. They knew they had to be together, that without one another they would perish. They knew that by gathering together they would find warmth and comfort from the terrors of the dark. It would be good for us to realize that five hundred million years later, we still have the same basic needs; we still face the same perils if we try and go it alone.

The great Chilean biologist Humberto Maturana has speculated that humans developed the capacity for language when we moved into family groups. Living intimately, we became curious about one another. We wanted to know who the other was, and so we invented language—words and concepts that would help us describe the world we were feeling and experiencing.

We have journeyed too far from that initial curiosity and love that led us to create language. Today we struggle to hide our thoughts, to live inside our own version of reality, and to avoid the explorations that once were so fascinating to us as a species. We have become more afraid of each other than curious, and we have retreated into cold, dark places of isolation and fear.

But we can get out of those places. Nearly every human being has the desire for connection. We still want to find each other at the fire, share our experiences, think about how we might live together so that more may benefit. In this volume, you will read the records of those who dared to re-create the fire and were courageous enough to call us together in the darkness. They tell their stories so that we too might remember: humans want to be together to dream a better world into existence.

*This book is dedicated to the memory of
Darryl Burrows of New Orleans,
a great friend of dialogue education.*

Preface

What is dialogue education? It is a finely structured system of learning-focused teaching rooted in a research-based set of principles and practices. I have been doing dialogue education since meeting Paulo Freire in 1968. I have been writing about it since 1986. In 2002 I read a request from one of the professional readers of the manuscript of the revised edition of my book *Learning to Listen, Learning to Teach*: "I would love to see a set of data telling how dialogue education is being used in diverse settings." That was my dream, too! I presented a proposal to Jossey-Bass, which had, in 1984, published a casebook prepared by Malcolm Knowles, *Andragogy in Action: Applying Modern Principles of Adult Learning*. That casebook has been a useful model for the construction of this one.

Why a Case Book?

A case book is a presentation of action research. Each story tells what happened in a learning event, the preparation and design of it, a sample of the learning tasks, indicators of learning, transfer, and impact. The model of dialogue education presented in this casebook is highly structured, with a rigorous design tool and explicit principles and practices. That structure looks different in diverse situations, and all of the authors bring their unique perspectives to the description. Our purpose in designing and constructing this volume is to give readers examples of dialogue education in practice. Reading twenty-three cases showing how your peers designed and led and evaluated adult learning can be useful to you, especially if you use the open questions for analysis and synthesis accompanying each story.

What Is Here for You

After an introduction that describes dialogue education today, the casebook is organized into three parts. In Part One, "University Education," Jane Connor, an experienced psychology professor, shows how she redesigned her undergraduate multicultural psychology course at the State University of New York-Binghamton. Elena Carbone, a nutritionist, describes her efforts at designing and leading an undergraduate nutrition course for young professionals at another state university. Meredith Pearson, with long experience in the Cooperative Extension Service of land-grant universities, shows how she used dialogue education to design a training program for the Extended Food and Nutrition Program (EFNEP). Marianne Reiff, professor of education, describes her work not only using dialogue education in a weekend college setting but also teaching it there. Steve Stahl tells the story of a college-based videoconference undergraduate course for child care providers in Vermont. Three educators—Jay Ekleberry, Mary Hoddy, and Tara Cordes—describe the gradual transformation of all the education programs and systems at the Wisconsin Union of the University of Wisconsin at Madison to effective adult learning through dialogue. Sarah Gravett offers the story of her efforts teaching dialogue education principles and practices to educators at three colleges in Johannesburg, South Africa.

In Part Two, "The Public Sector and Not-for-Profit Organizations," we hear from educators designing community education and training. Cynthia Bizzell shows how the training of volunteers in the National Court-Appointed Special Advocate (CASA) program was improved by the use of dialogue. Three other adult educators—Valerie Uccellani, Jyaphia Christos-Rodgers, and Mack Slan—

describe the genesis, design, and daily operation of the New Orleans Jobs Initiative (NOJI), which uses dialogue education for instructor training. Greg Walker-Wilson and Joye Norris share the story of how dialogue was used to revitalize a flagging adult education program for new entrepreneurs in the mountains of North Carolina. Barbara Gassner tells the story of a group of welfare mothers who, through dialogue and friendship, learned how to work together to form a bakery business. Darlene Goetzman shows how dialogue education and appreciative inquiry enhanced a strategic planning session for the board of a branch of Literacy Volunteers of America in New York State. Michael Culliton describes a national workshop series of NET-WORK, the social justice lobby, aimed at moving citizens to work for congressional reauthorization of legislation to serve welfare mothers. Jean Anliker shows how the training curriculum for a national, federally funded nutrition program was reshaped through dialogue education. Kathy Johnson, Peter Perkins, and Nicole Saginor, from the Vermont Institutes, demonstrate the use of dialogue education with math and science teachers in their statewide program. Karen Ridout shows how dialogue informs strategic planning for boards of directors of not-for-profit groups. Valerie Uccellani describes the use of dialogue education to train professional staff in the California Women, Infants, and Children (WIC) program.

Part Three, "International Education," introduces Robb Davis, Ellen Vor der Bruegge, and Jeanette Treiber, from the organization Freedom from Hunger, who show how their adult education program on microfinancing for small entrepreneurs worldwide has been designed with dialogue. Linda Gershuny describes how dialogue education informs teacher training in Haiti. Gail von Hahmann describes the use of dialogue in a World Education program in Cambodia. Peter Perkins and Michaela Stickney show how dialogue education worked in Russia with teams of professionals at the Volgograd Center for Environmental Training. Klaus Püschel, a physician at the School of Medicine of the Catholic University of Chile, tells the story of the transformation of primary health care in Santiago when dialogue education was introduced in a new residency program titled Family and Community Medicine. Peter Noteboom describes the use of dialogue in the design of an antiracism program for churches in Canada.

We have a wide stream of evidence for you. Each case offers a set of open questions for analysis and synthesis, inviting readers to identify the design principles perceived and exploring cross-case connection. A concluding chapter looks at lessons learned from all the stories and the issues raised for dialogue education. There is also an appendix with an updated description of selected principles and practices of dialogue education.

Who Will Find This Case Book Useful?

Adult educators, undergraduate and graduate students in adult education, trainers, program and curriculum designers, health educators, board members of not-for-profit groups, and university and college professors may be moved by these stories to examine their work in terms of dialogue education. Although this is a practical case book, it is also meant to invite reflection on the philosophical and epistemological questions raised in every case. Readers will no doubt go to the stories that most readily relate to their own work.

I assume that many readers will have met dialogue education through my other Jossey-Bass books and know of the courses offered through Global Learning Partners, Inc. (www.globalearning.com). I welcome your responses to these stories at jane@janevella.com.

The poet Rumi captures the heart of dialogue education for me: "You think because you understand one you understand two, because one and one are two. But you must understand *and*" (Wheatley, 1999, p. 10). We work through dialogue, as Paulo Freire (1972) put it, to create a world where it is easier to love.

Jane Vella
Raleigh, North Carolina
August 2003

References

Freire, P. *Pedagogy of the Oppressed*. New York: Herder & Herder, 1972.

Knowles, M. *Andragogy in Action: Applying Modern Principles of Adult Learning*. San Francisco: Jossey-Bass, 1984.

Vella, J. *Learning to Listen, Learning to Teach: The Power of Dialogue in Educating Adults*. San Francisco: Jossey-Bass, 2002. (Originally published 1994.)

Wheatley, M. *Leadership and the New Science*. San Francisco: Berrett-Koehler, 1999.

The Authors

Jane Vella is an educator who began teaching fifty years ago. After meeting Paulo Freire in Tanzania in 1970, Vella began her exploration of dialogue as a new way of designing and offering adult education. In 1981 she founded the Jubilee Popular Education Center, now Global Learning Partners, Inc. Vella is the author of *Learning to Listen, Learning to Teach, Training Through Dialogue, How Do They Know They Know?* (with Paula Berardinelli and Jim Burrow), and *Taking Learning to Task*, all published by Jossey-Bass. She has also contributed to two recent volumes of the Jossey-Bass journal series New Directions for Adult and Continuing Education. Vella is an adjunct professor at the School of Public Health of the University of North Carolina at Chapel Hill. Now semi-retired, she lives in Raleigh, North Carolina, where she continues her research on adult learning. Janevella@globalearning.com; www.janevella.com

Jean A. Anliker has designed, delivered, and tested nutrition education interventions for low-income, culturally diverse audiences for more than twenty-five years. She earned her Ph.D. in nutrition at the University of Massachusetts and her M.S. in preventive medicine from the University of Iowa. She also completed a dietetic internship at the University of Iowa hospitals. She works as research associate professor at the University of Massachusetts-Amherst, adjunct associate professor at the University of Maryland-Baltimore, and consultant for The Johns Hopkins University in Baltimore. janliker@nutrition.umass.edu

Cynthia Bizzell, having completed fifteen years as an administrator in the North Carolina Guardian ad Litem Program, now designs and teaches employee development courses for the judicial branch of state government. She coaches managers and work teams on communication and performance issues. As an adjunct faculty member of the University of North Carolina at Chapel Hill, she teaches professional communication to graduate students in the master of public administration program. Bizzell certifies training facilitators in not-for-profit and government settings across the country. She directs a performing women's choral group, where she explores the use of dialogue education in teaching music to adults. She earned a M.Ed. in higher education student personnel services and counseling at North Carolina State University and a B.Mus.Ed. at Meredith College. She is an associate of Global Learning Partners and a certified integrative coach. Bizzell@ipass.net

Elena T. Carbone earned her doctorate in health behavior and health education at the University of North Carolina, Chapel Hill. Earlier, she served for six years as nutrition education adviser with the U.S. Public Health Service, Office of Disease Prevention and Health Promotion, in Washington, D.C. She worked for several years as a clinical dietitian at the Massachusetts General Hospital in Boston. She is a registered dietitian with a master of science degree in nutrition communications from Boston University and a bachelor of science degree in nutritional sciences from the University of New Hampshire. She completed her internship at Yale-New Haven Hospital. She is an associate of Global Learning Partners, and is currently professor of nutrition at the University of Massachusetts-Amherst. ecarbone@nutrition.umass.edu

Jyaphia Christos-Rodgers is director of information systems and program development at the New Orleans Jobs Initiative (NOJI). She is a community builder and sociologist who has a long history as an antiracist community organizer, researcher, and facilitator. She works as an antiracism trainer for the People's Institute for Survival and Beyond and the Unitarian Universalist Association's Journey Towards Wholeness Anti-Racism/Anti-Oppression Initiative. Since 1998, when she first encountered the learning-centered approach to adult education, Christos-Rodgers has found the principles and practices to be invaluable in all of her work. Jyaphia@aol.com

Jane Marantz Connor earned her doctorate in psychology from the University of Wisconsin at Madison. She has taught in Guatemala and at Tennessee State University and Vanderbilt University. Since 1973 she has been a teacher and researcher in the psychology department of the State University of New York at Binghamton. She developed a new course in multicultural psychology using the principles of dialogue education and has seen its enrollment grow in three years from thirty-five to four hundred students. Jconnor@binghamton.edu

Tara Cordes is the assistant director of staff education and training at the Wisconsin Union. Besides coordinating workshops for approximately one thousand new employees each year, she is working to bring a dialogue approach to on-line learning opportunities. Cordes has an M.B.A. and an M.S. in information and communication technology. tcordes@uwisc.edu

Michael A. Culliton is coordinator of NETWORK Education Program (NEP), the educational partner of NETWORK, a national Catholic social justice lobby. He is an associate of Global Learning Partners and has taught Learning to Listen, Learning to Teach courses in the United States, Thailand, and Romania. Mculliton@networklobby.org

Robb Davis earned a master of public health degree and a Ph.D. from the Johns Hopkins University School of Public Health. He joined Freedom from Hunger in 1999. He has extensive experience in participatory learning methods and training, specifically in West Africa. He is an associate of Global Learning Partners, Inc. Rdavis@freefromhunger.org

Jay Ekleberry is director of Wisconsin Union Mini-Courses and a member of the program staff at the University of Wisconsin-Madison's Wisconsin Union. He has an M.S. in continuing and vocational education from the University of Wisconsin, and is an associate of Global Learning Partners. jpeklebe@facstaff.wisc.edu

Barbara Gassner works in the fields of delinquency prevention, substance abuse prevention, and adult education. She is also a visual artist and is currently studying meditation and healing practices. Her work with families and communities integrates substance abuse prevention strategies and education. She is an associate of Global Learning Partners and an associate of the Northeast Center for the Application of Prevention Technology, an affiliate of the Center for Substance Abuse Prevention. bgassner@vtadultlearning.org

Linda Gershuny is an associate of Global Learning Partners. She has facilitated the Learning to Listen, Learning to Teach course several times in French and Haitian Creole, and has co-facilitated the advanced design and evaluation courses. Gershuny completed her master of education degree in adult education at the University of Toronto (OISE). Her formal teaching experience includes preschool (Montessori), primary, secondary, and university levels. In Haiti since 1976, she has developed and conducted training courses for community development workers, teachers, and rural women as peer health educators. She is currently the director of the Center for Learning, Training, and Transformation (CAFT), where she works with a team of Haitian educators specializing in participatory research and training. Lgershuny@hotmail.com

Darlene Goetzman has combined her love of questions, dialogue education, and organization development to work with organizations and groups who seek to be enlivened by and accountable for their work. She specializes in organization recovery work. Most recently, her consulting work has led her to the Pfeiffer Nature Center in Portville, New York, where she is serving as acting director. Goetzman is the founder of New Visions Consulting and is an associate of Global Learning Partners. She earned her M.A. in human and organizational transformation at the California Institute of Integral Studies. darlene@blumenthals.com

Sarah Gravett is professor of higher and adult education and chair of the Department of Educational Sciences at Rand Afrikaans University in Johannesburg, South Africa. Her research interests are the advancement of teaching and learning in higher education, adult learning, and faculty development. Sjg@edcur.rau.ac.za

Mary Hoddy coordinates staff education and training at the University of Wisconsin-Madison's Wisconsin Union, where she develops and facilitates programs in communication skills, coaching, management, learning styles, and workshop design. She has an M.S. in adult education from that university, and is an associate of Global Learning Partners. Mhoddy@wisc.edu

Kathy A. Johnson is Director of Equity Initiatives at the Vermont Institutes (formerly the Vermont Institute for Science, Math, & Technology). She is a senior associate with Global Learning Partners as well as a consultant and teacher on equity and diversity issues in education. Johnson has worked with schools and colleges, state governmental departments, the Vermont Governor's Commission on Women, the Center for the Study of Social Policy, and other organizations. kjohnson@vermontinstitutes.org

Joye A. Norris is an adult educator and curriculum design consultant from Myrtle Beach, South Carolina. She has her own adult education company called Learning by Dialogue and runs the Sun-Coast Adult Education Center in North Myrtle Beach. Since studying with Jane Vella in the early 1990s, Norris has devoted her career to introducing educators in dozens of organizations to a "raising all voices" dialogue approach to teaching. She has coauthored two books on adult education, including *Developing Literacy Programs for Homeless Adults* and *Maximizing Paraprofessional Potential*. She does extensive work for the Cooperative Extension and WIC nutrition education programs, helping their educators become more effective, more interesting, and more inspired. Norris is a senior associate of Global Learning Partners with a particular focus on advanced learning design. Docnj@aol.com; www.learningbydialogue.com

Peter Noteboom is managing director of Global Learning Partners, the education and consulting company founded by Jane Vella that teaches the principles and practices of dialogue education and specializes in the assessment, design, teaching, and evaluation of learning. He works in the fields of social justice, organizational and community development, and international relations. Besides working with various institutions in North America, he has extensive experience working overseas in South and East Asia, West Africa, and Europe. Pnoteboom@globalearning.com; www.globalearning.com

Meredith Pearson earned a master's degree in nutrition in 1983 and a Ph.D. in curriculum and instruction in 1988, both from Kansas State University. She is the director of the Maryland Food Stamp Nutrition Education Program, providing nutrition education to limited-resource learners. mp221@umail.umd.edu

Peter J. Perkins. is the principle learning consultant, coach, and teacher with Five Dimensions, his own adult education company. He focuses on the facilitation of adolescent and adult learning, holistic adolescent development, organizational development, facilitation and community development. Perkins started the first college-level prevention and community development program in the nation. He has been nationally recognized twice for development of substance abuse programs. A senior associate with Global Learning Partners, he teaches dialogue education and evaluation throughout the world. He has a master of arts in human development. Perk5dim@together.com

Klaus Püschel was trained as a medical doctor at the School of Medicine of the Catholic University in Chile. He helped create the new Family and Community Medicine Program and was one of its first residents. From 1997 to 1999 he worked on and completed a master's degree in public health at the University of Washington. Currently, he combines a clinical practice with his work as assistant professor at the Catholic University's medical school. Püschel has long experience in health prevention and promotion in community settings, and his experience with many grassroots groups has allowed him to put many of the principles of dialogue education into practice. He is on the team that offers the Learning to Listen, Learning to Teach course at the medical school and also teaches a number of courses in preventive medicine and clinical decision making. Kpuschel@hotmail.com

Marianne Reiff earned her doctorate in education in 1992 at the University of California-Santa Barbara, where she focused on adults as learners. She continues that focus as an independent consultant working with faculty members and administrators. She teaches education and management at Lesley University in Massachusetts, and is a senior associate with Global Learning Partners. Mariannereiff@hotmail.com

Karen G. Ridout, a graduate of Coach U, is a consultant and coach with Wellspring Consulting. In addition, she trains trainers in effective adult learning theory and is an associate of Global Learning Partners. She is immediate past chair of the southeast region of the Association for Psychological Type. Ridout holds a degree in political science from the University of Nebraska. For the past eight years she has worked as a consultant and coach, using her twenty-five years experience in both business and nonprofit arenas. Kgr@mindspring.com; www.wellspring-consulting.com

Nicole Saginor, associate executive director of the Vermont Institutes, is a former teacher, curriculum coordinator, principal, and superintendent. As director of leadership initiatives at the Vermont Institute for Science, Math, & Technology (VISMT) from 1998 to 2002, she directed the teacher associate program, a program of teacher leadership aimed at raising the quality of science, math, and technology instruction in the state. She has also worked to build a partnership of organizations whose focus is to strengthen school leadership at all levels. She earned her doctorate in educational leadership and policy development at the University of Vermont. nsaginor@vermontinstitutes.org

Mack M. Slan is the deputy CEO of the New Orleans Jobs Initiative. He is a business manager who has worked in both the private and public sectors. He has managed national and international training programs as well as the development of NOJIS's Twenty-First-Century Success Principles curriculum. His experience working with both the private and public sectors has given him a deeper insight and appreciation for building working relationships between both business worlds. He also does community organizing that focuses on building a community's capacity to become self-sufficient and self-sustaining. Nojislan@aol.com

Steven Stahl has a doctorate in instructional technology and distance education from NOVA Southeastern University. He is an associate of Global Learning Partners, and president of Consultants for Innovative Instruction, which supports distance education for business and educational institutions. sstahl@InnovativeInstruction.com; www.InnovativeInstruction.com

Michaela B. Stickney specializes in watershed planning, sustainable development, and community-based natural resource protection. She has experience in twenty local Vermont communities, four U.S. states, and Russia, Macedonia, Albania, Bulgaria, Canada, Bolivia, and Japan. Currently, she is the state watershed coordinator for the transboundary Lake Champlain Basin Program, an international partnership between Vermont, New York, and Quebec. In Volgograd, she managed the Center for Environmental Training with the global NGO Institute for Sustainable Communities. She has a master of science degree in natural resources planning. michaela.stickney@anr.state.vt.us

Jeanette Treiber holds a Ph.D. in literature and has worked since 1977 as a program associate in communication, evaluation, and training coordination for Freedom from Hunger. She has extensive adult teaching experience and was trained in the Global Learning Partners' method. Jtreiber@freefromhunger.org

Valerie Uccellani owns Progressive Program Design, a consulting business. The focus of her work is on principles of adult learning and on using these principles to design and implement learning programs. Uccellani served as the director of program design and instructional quality for the New Orleans Jobs Initiative (NOJI). She is a senior associate of Global Learning Partners and project manager for its collaboration with the California WIC program. Her professional experience spans the fields of interpersonal communication, adult experiential learning, qualitative research, materials development, and vocational literacy in the United States, Latin America, and Africa. val@talk2val.com

Gail von Hahmann is a training specialist in participatory education methods. She works with educators in formal schools systems and with adult and nonformal programs in the United States, Africa, and Asia. She served as vice president of field services for Literacy

Volunteers of America and she has taught at the School for International Training, the University of Massachusetts at Amherst, and the State University of New York. She is an associate of Global Learning Partners. Gvonh@aol.com

Ellen Vor der Bruegge holds master's degrees in public health and education. She joined Freedom from Hunger in 1988. She designed the initial education component of the Credit with Education program and continues to refine and innovate the education component and to train trainers of the local practitioner organizations in dialogue education techniques and the various education topics. ellenvb@freefromhunger.org

Greg Walker-Wilson is executive director of the Mountain Microenterprise Fund in Asheville, North Carolina. He first worked with low-wealth entrepreneurs in Washington, D.C., and then in Bolivia. He has a master's degree in international development from American University. He has worked as a management consultant for Anderson Consulting and now serves on several boards, including Hand Made in America, Center for Participatory Change, and the Association for Enterprise Opportunity. He is a Friday Fellow with the Wildacres Leadership Initiative. greg@mtnmicro.org; www.mtnmicro.org

Introduction
Dialogue Education Today

Jane Vella

The structured system that we call *dialogue education* was designed to implement the ideas of Paulo Freire, Kurt Lewin, and many other teachers whose passion was for learning. I see dialogue education today as a viable and effective alternative to prevailing structures of formal and informal adult education.

Origins of Dialogue Education

Why does adult education need an alternative? Paulo Freire compared monologue—what he called the *banking system*—to problem-posing education, or dialogue. Freire's phrase referred to how the teacher deposited information into the minds of learners, who returned the information, with interest, on tests and examinations. In contrast, problem-posing education or dialogue meant that concepts, skills, or attitudes were presented as open questions for reflection and integration into a particular context (Freire, 1972). Monologue today is often seen in the lecture hall or conference center, where a teacher makes a presentation of information and data, with little or no engagement of learners, and little design for learning. It is also seen in lengthy presentations at training sessions and orientation programs in the public and not-for-profit sectors. It is experienced in international settings where hierarchical, colonial education processes persist.

The structured approach to dialogue presented in this volume focuses on learning, not teaching. This casebook offers twenty-three examples of significant learning. The purpose of this research is to turn our practice into praxis—reflection on action—so that readers can explore the possibility of using dialogue in their own educational context.

My History with Dialogue Education

In the late 1960s, I was a professor at the Institute of Education of the University of Dar es Salaam in Tanzania. Julius Nyerere, the nation's first president, was an advocate and articulate voice for authentic education. He urged the new nation to redesign the colonial system to fit the Tanzanian context. However, the educational practices at the university were far from what Nyerere intended. I was seriously considering a change of career: I could not continue in this domination system. Then, a friend told me about an exciting book she was reading: *The Pedagogy of the Oppressed,* by Paulo Freire (1972). I found in Freire's work a conceptual alternative to domination: problem-posing dialogue.

Bakhtin, the Russian philosopher and linguist, says of dialogue: "Life by its very nature is dialogic. To live means to participate in dialogue: to ask questions, to heed, to respond, to agree, and so forth. In this dialogue a person participates wholly and throughout his whole life: with his eyes, lips, hands, soul, spirit, with his whole body and deeds. He invests his entire self in discourse, and this discourse enters into the dialogic fabric of human life, into the world symposium" (Bakhtin, 1981, p. 293).

Dialogue education as described and analyzed in these stories is rooted in that position so clearly expressed by Bakhtin. It is based on the work of Paulo Freire, and the research of Kurt Lewin, who recognized the need for greater equity in the relationship of adult learners and teachers. This approach falls under the umbrella of *social constructivism*, and it can be a means toward transformational learning. We present here one format that uses the work of all these thinkers. That format is composed of a set of principles (Vella, 1995, 2002) and practices.

Anne Hope and Sally Timmell, authors of *Training for Transformation* (Hope, Timmell, and Hodzi, 1984), offered two-week courses in community education for dialogue in Nairobi, Kenya. I moved from the university into a community education setting, designing Community Education for Development, a leadership development program, with invaluable input from Hope and Timmell. That experience led to my doctoral dissertation (Vella, 1978), in which a structure of principles and specific practices began to emerge. As a professor at North Carolina State University, I organized these principles and practices into a system that I called *popular education*, after the model offered by Freire. The Jubilee Popular Education Center, which opened in 1981, was a source of action research as we taught this approach to teachers and trainers, health workers, and managers. From Freire's noble abstractions, an eclectic system of adult education based on dialogue developed.

One spring day in 1992 Malcolm Knowles, my colleague at North Carolina State University, and his wife, Hulda, sat at my dinner table. I confessed that I had a manuscript in the bottom drawer of my desk. . . . Malcolm smiled and kindly offered me a referral to the president of Jossey-Bass Publishers, Lyn Luckow, who had been a graduate student under Professor Knowles at the Fielding Graduate Institute. That was the beginning of a wonderful journey into this present research. The book that emerged from that garbled manuscript, *Learning to Listen, Learning to Teach*, originally published in 1994, is influencing adult educators around the world. Jossey-Bass published three later books: *Training Through Dialogue* (1995), *How Do They Know They Know?* (1998), and *Taking Learning to Task* (2000). Dialogue education now has a firm foothold as one form expressing adult learning theories of participation, constructivism, and transformational learning.

We teach the way we have been taught. All of the authors writing cases for this book have studied with Global Learning Partners, Inc. (formerly the Jubilee Popular Education Center). This is a set of first-generation evidence. Each person I invited to join this research said this: "Thank you for the invitation! Even if my work does not get published, I am excited about doing it. I am grateful for this chance to examine my educational work this way." These men and women show themselves to be not only good educators but also very good social scientists.

Principles and Practices

The model of dialogue education presented in this casebook is highly structured, but that structure looks different in different situations. Our hope is that the action research in this casebook can influence and develop that structure, those principles and practices, and the growing theory and practice of dialogue education. In the appendix you will find an updated summary of current principles and practices.

Dialogue education is holistic in that none of these principles and practices can be omitted with impunity. We have not yet named all the principles and practices that are at work in effective adult learning.

The evaluation concept of learning, transfer, and impact (Vella, Berardinelli, and Burrow, 1998) is central to dialogue education: learning occurs *within* the program, not in a study hall later on. What occurs after the learning event is transfer. This is what adult learners do with the learning in their context. Impact is the change that occurs in individuals or organizations as a function of the learning. Explicit indicators of learning, transfer, and impact are useful for evaluation.

The Seven Design Steps

The Seven Design Steps—based on the classic questions *who, why, when, where, what, what for,* and *how*—form a distinctive planning instrument in this model of dialogue education. *Who*—the participants—and *why*—the situation of this learning event— together provide an essential set of information for the designer.

The learning needs and resource assessment is designed and used to respond to those two opening questions. *When*—the time frame of the session—and *where*—the site—provide the parameters within which to design. *What*—the content of concepts, knowledge, skills, and behaviors manifesting attitudes—and *what for*—the distinctive achievement-based objectives of the learning session—set up the learning tasks. The *how*—the learning tasks and materials—presents the work of learners and teacher throughout. You will read about the Seven Design Steps in many of these chapters. They provide a vital instrument for creating a design that ensures accountability.

Assumptions

This model of dialogue education assumes that human beings come to learning with some appetite, and that they can and will make intelligent choices. The stories in this casebook bear out this assumption. We assume that folks come prepared to work hard, and to work together. We assume that adults come to a learning event with abundant life experience. We assume that levels of honesty can and will deepen as safety is established and meaning becomes clear. We assume that learners have and will take the time to reflect both during the course and during transfer. We assume that the resources provided for follow-up will be accessible and utilized. We assume that a process and protocols for leading dialogue can be learned and repeated with quality assurance. We assume that learning, transfer, and impact can be demonstrated through specific quantitative and qualitative indicators. These assumptions may seem naïve. The events described in this case book demonstrate how realistic they are.

Prospects for Dialogue Education

My friend's son is a Park Scholar at North Carolina State University. As a freshman, he took a history course on the Middle East taught by a visiting professor from that region. On the first day of the seminar, the professor came in with an armload of books.

He said to the twelve students: "We have fourteen weeks. Your task is to read all of these. I will help you understand them. Then, design a peace plan for the Middle East. I am going back to Jerusalem in June. If you have anything to offer, I will bring it to people who have power there."

Immediacy, engagement, respect, learning task, clear roles, safety, sequence, reinforcement—all were there! Look at his assumptions about those young students. This scholar was using dialogue education. He did so without even a glance at this model. It was simply good teaching and good learning!

It should be noted that good learning means there is a minimum of traditional "telling." Good teaching is the other side of the coin. Good teaching in this model is good design: doing a learning needs and resource assessment, using the Seven Design Steps, setting learning tasks with reinforcement, safety, accountability, respect for learners. It involves using all of the principles and practices. It is an implementation based on all of the assumptions named earlier.

This is our vision: readers of this book will experiment with forms of dialogue education in universities and colleges and in public and not-for-profit organizations all around the world.

References

Bakhtin, M. *The Dialogic Imagination*. Austin: University of Texas Press, 1981.

Freire, P. *Pedagogy of the Oppressed*. New York: Herder & Herder, 1972.

Hope, A., Timmell, S., and Hodzi, C. *Training for Transformation: A Handbook for Community Workers*. Harare, Zimbabwe: Mambo Press, 1984.

Vella, J. "Community Education for Self-Reliant Development." Unpublished doctoral dissertation, Center for International Education, University of Massachusetts, 1978.

Vella, J. *Training Through Dialogue: Promoting Effective Learning and Change with Adults*. San Francisco: Jossey-Bass, 1995.

Vella, J. *Taking Learning to Task: Creative Strategies for Teaching Adults*. San Francisco: Jossey-Bass, 2000.

Vella, J. *Learning to Listen, Learning to Teach: The Power of Dialogue in Educating Adults*. San Francisco: Jossey-Bass, 2002. (Originally published 1994.)

Vella, J., Berardinelli, P., and Burrow, J. *How Do They Know They Know? Evaluating Adult Learning*. San Francisco: Jossey-Bass, 1998.

Part I

University Education

"This can never happen at university!"

This was the response of a friend of mine, a professor at the University of North Carolina at Chapel Hill, when she started to learn about dialogue education. My own experience as a university professor since 1978 did not belie her observation. What I was doing to foster learning through dialogue in my university classroom was suspect. "Why are they always so excited?" asked the chairman of my department when he visited my classroom. Because of entrenched patterns of teaching and research that are naturally hierarchical, the university is often not a welcoming site for experiments in dialogue education. Students expect a professor to "cover" content in the textbook and are often the most resistant to effective learning. Small group work is precluded by the very physical layout of most university and college classrooms.

Where the principles and practices of dialogue education are used in university education, the results are notable in both students and professors. Jane Connor's students (Chapter One) told their friends: "You've got to take this course!" Registration went from 35 to 410 in three years. And that course is a very tough way for undergraduates to earn three credits in psychology. I am aware of an appetite, even a hunger, for demanding, challenging courses. The engagement in praxis in the undergraduate nutrition education courses given by Elena Carbone (Chapter Two) enhanced not only the learning of the young health educators, nurses, and nutritionists but also their experience of constructing theory. This is what they must do in future to educate their clients and patients. Such a transfer of knowledge, skills, and behaviors to the community is at the heart of the university-based, federally funded Extended Food and Nutrition Programs (EFNEP). A traditional university lecture to pregnant teenagers or busy mothers is clearly inappropriate. Meredith Pearson (Chapter Three) demonstrates how a community education model using dialogue struggled for a place in a university setting. We teach the way we were taught!

The weekend university or accelerated graduate program is a growing university offering in the United States. Marianne Reiff (Chapter Four) tells how shocked her students initially were when presented with more than a menu of information. She deals honestly with the resistance faced by professors who are adamant about designing for learning. Without a design formed by a set of strong principles, a twenty-one-hour weekend "course" can get very long indeed. When real learning and community occur, the participants can transfer both immediately into their world of work.

Distance learning through videoconferencing is another format that can use the learning-centered practices of dialogue education. Steven Stahl (Chapter Five) shows how a college-based videoconference training program for child care workers used dialogue throughout. When a group of educators uses the principles and practices of dialogue education, they can model dialogue among themselves. The team from the University of Wisconsin Student Union (Chapter Six) demonstrates how difficult it was initially to move those who taught short courses at the union to a new way of teaching. Sarah Gravett's report (Chapter Seven) on an action research project at three colleges in Johannesburg, South Africa, shows how vital continued reflection on the process of teaching is. Her conclusions about the need for a disciplined model and for ongoing support and collaborative research are compelling.

The challenge to us all is to make of every university classroom a research laboratory, invested in the examination of current theory and practice, and the discovery of meaning. We do that, as Sarah Gravett did, one college at a time! Reading a life of Thomas Alva Edison, I was inspired by the tenacity of the inventor in the face of numerous failures. I can hear him saying over and over again to his colleagues in that Menlo Park, New Jersey, laboratory: "Imagine this small bulb lighting up every home in the United States of America!" Imagine the principles and practices of dialogue education informing the classrooms and laboratories of universities and colleges around the world!

1

Dialogue Education Goes to College

Jane Marantz Connor

This chapter tells the story of an experienced university professor who transformed her undergraduate social psychology course, Multicultural Psychology, into dialogue education. Students and professors alike from the State University of New York at Binghamton tell us about how demanding such a transformation is.

"My high school of about nine hundred students was all white except for three Asians and one black student. The diversity in the student body that exists at this college was one of the things that attracted me to the school, but I really don't find myself getting to know persons from different backgrounds hardly at all. I want to be more knowledgeable about different groups. I don't like feeling that I have to walk on eggshells when I am around people who are different for fear of offending them."

"I feel much more comfortable with my Latino and black friends. We understand each other—it's just easier to be with them. But I know I need to get along with a wider range of people. I hope that this course will help me with that."

These statements of expectations, given by students at the beginning of my course, Multicultural Psychology, show their recognition of their need for multicultural competence. They know that great diversity exists in the United States when it comes to race, ethnicity, sexual orientation, religion, and socioeconomic background, but they often do not feel prepared to interact with persons from diverse backgrounds. Meeting this felt need, and helping students develop the skills and understanding that is important for them to live and work effectively in a multicultural society, are the purposes of this course.

Course Description and Methodology

This three-credit course meets for three hours a week for fourteen weeks in a large, traditional lecture hall. Although it is somewhat uncomfortable for students to turn around in their seats to communicate with team members in the row behind them, they willingly do so. Students also spend one hour a week in discussion sections of twenty-five, led by two undergraduate teaching assistants, both of whom took the course the preceding semester.

Research indicates that lecturing on tolerance and the importance of valuing others may affect what people *say* they believe, but it is likely to have little effect on true beliefs or behavior (Bligh, 2000). Bringing students from diverse groups together to talk is no guarantee that increased mutual understanding or decreased prejudice will result; in some cases prejudice can even increase (Allport, 1958).

After struggling and experimenting with a range of approaches and methodologies over the years, I have developed a set of learning practices and experiences that are firmly rooted in the principles of dialogue education (Vella, 2002). This program has had an effect greater than I could ever have imagined possible in my earlier years as a teacher. It is a multifaceted course incorporating a wide variety of teaching styles. Here are some of the important concepts and principles that guide the design.

Engagement in the Process

Learning from other students is at least as important to students as learning from the instructor. Students learn best when they are actively engaged in the learning process, doing learning tasks and experiencing events.

Use of Prior Knowledge

Personal experience can be profitably viewed in a historical, economic, political, and social context. It is vital for young people to understand the role of power and privilege in relationships and perceptions and to comprehend how society is hierarchically organized and the effects of this organization.

Listening Skills

Good listening skills and a willingness to avoid judging others while learning to understand deeply are core skills for multicultural competence. The ability to open up and share one's stories with others are skills to be developed. This is how we come to know one another. Learning new skills and acquiring new knowledge and diverse perspectives involves risk taking, a willingness to move out of one's "comfort zone."

Team Learning and the Readiness Assurance Process

"I thought I would dislike team learning, but I was proven wrong. It is amazing how much the 'quiet' kids in the class end up contributing in groups. They have vast amounts of information and opinions to provide if given a less threatening environment in which to do so."

"Team learning is a great way to initiate discussion and it's a way to help each other understand material. When working in groups you get to learn and understand a lot more perspectives than just your own. I never want to let my team down by being unprepared."

One of the most important techniques that I employ in this course is an instructional format called *team learning*, which was developed and refined over many years by Larry Michaelsen (1992). The first part of the team learning model is the Readiness Assurance Process (RAP), by which the students' mastery of basic concepts and principles (usually through their completing reading assignments) is assessed, and deficits in their understanding are addressed by the small group.

Here is how the RAP process works. First, the students individually take a brief multiple-choice test on the readings they have done, before any classroom instruction has occurred on the material. The answer sheets are collected. Next, the students immediately take the same test again as part of a team of four to six students. These teams remain constant for the semester. During the team test, each team must decide on the single best answer to each question. In order to reach a consensus on the single best answer, they must review their earlier, individual answers and discuss the possibilities. They learn to listen carefully and solicit everyone's input, because they often find that the student who talks the most is not necessarily the one who has the correct answer.

For the team test I have found it helpful to use a special "scratch-off" form called the IF AT (Immediate Feedback Assessment Technique) that has recently been invented by a professor, Michael Epstein. This form employs the gray material that is used on scratch-off-style lottery tickets. For example, if a team decides the correct answer to question 1 is *b*, they go to line 1 and scratch off the gray material in column *b*. If *b* is the correct answer, they will see an asterisk after they rub it off. If *b* is not correct, they must talk again and decide what their second-choice answer is. If they choose *a* as their second choice, they rub off the gray material under the *a* column to see if the asterisk is exposed. In this fashion the students receive immediate feedback on their choices and do not leave a question without discovering the correct answer. This process also allows the students to discuss among themselves why the designated answer is (or is not) the best alternative.

In a series of carefully controlled studies, Epstein and others have shown that learning and retention are higher and student attitudes more positive when they are tested with the IF AT as opposed to a traditional computer scan form (Epstein, Epstein, and Brosvic, 2001). These results make sense. At the time of greatest interest in the test question—that is, when they are trying to determine the correct answer—the students find out whether they are right. Students also appreciate receiving partial credit for their partial knowledge; the team gets some points for each question they answer correctly on the second or third attempt, although not as many as when they answer it correctly on the first attempt.

What is most significant, from my perspective, is the impact of the combination of the RAP and the IF AT on team dynamics. The group score on these tests is almost invariably higher than the individual scores. No one person has all the answers. It is easy to misread a question. The group discussion of the questions and potential answers allows the students to hear how each of them has read and understood the assigned material. Because the team members need to work together to come up with the best answers and they all benefit when the team does well, a very strong bond develops among them. We hear little cheers and expressions of joy from the teams when they find the asterisk and celebrate each victory; we hear their moans when they "strike out." It is clear to me that this procedure involves both cognitive and affective consequences.

Appeals

The next step in the RAP is the appeals procedure. If a team has made a choice I did not designate as correct, they have the option to appeal the answer. Appeals must be made as a team and can be based on alleged ambiguity in the question or in the text material. Allowing these appeals shows a respect for the fact that the students may have different interpretations, that the professor is not the only person whose perspective counts, and that the professor is not infallible. The students need to substantiate the basis for their appeal, either by citing relevant passages from the readings or analyzing the ambiguity in the question in order for the appeal to be approved. They know they will get credit for missed questions based on thoughtful appeals. The appeals procedure teaches the students to take the textual material seriously and shows that the professor is listening to them.

The adoption of the RAP has truly revolutionized my teaching. I cannot speak too highly of it. I do not need to lecture to "cover" the material. The students do that work through outside reading and in-class discussions of the test questions and answers. Because there is an individual administration of the test and their test grade is a weighted average of individual and team scores, I never hear students complain "I did all the reading and this other person did not, but we got the same grade. It's not fair!" It also becomes quickly evident when others have not done the work and are not contributing to the team effort. This gives the team the ability to address such issues directly.

Deepening Understanding with Learning Tasks

"If you want to know me, then you must know my story, for my story defines who I am. And if I want to know myself, to gain insight into the meaning of my own life, then I, too, must come to know my story" (McAdams, 1997, p. 11).

"We don't change people's minds. We change their hearts with personal stories of discrimination" (Brown and Mazza, 1998, p. 56).

Three different forms of learning tasks are used to involve learners with multicultural content: *Visitors and Voices, Narratives and Narrative Responses*, and *Out-of-Class Learning Experiences*.

Visitors and Voices

Visitors and Voices is one of the most popular of these learning tasks, which have a common theme of students learning the stories of others who are culturally different from them. Each week a different group of people is invited to talk with the class. The groups include both people from the community and students from different cultural backgrounds. This creates an important sense of immediacy in the classroom. We are not just talking and reading about issues such as racism, ageism, and anti-Semitism, but can see how these phenomena actually play out in people's lives and how their experiences reflect principles and concepts described in the readings.

As one student commented: "These are people not so different from me. They hurt and feel pain, the slings and arrows, just as I would."

We have heard the voices of people who identify, or are identified by others, as gay, lesbian, disabled, Native American, Latino, Jewish, white, black, Asian American, Muslim, drug-addicted or alcoholic, on welfare, consumer of mental health services, immigrant, and ex-convict. We learn their stories and find out about their experiences: What was it like for you to discover your identity as a gay person? How was it for you when you came out to your family, your friends? How has your experience as a disabled person been different from, and similar to, persons who are not disabled? What effect does anti-Semitism have on your perception of the world around you? How do you, as a Native American, view the world differently than a white person does?

At the beginning of class I often ask the students (in their teams) to write down briefly what they know or have heard about the group whose voices we will hear that day. Then, after they have listened to and talked with the speakers, I ask them to reflect on the extent to which their preconceptions were similar to or different from what they heard. The students especially value hearing the voices of student speakers who are the same age as themselves. I am respectful of the students' right to choose not to share about themselves in this very public manner, yet the class is very appreciative when individuals do. One young man who recently made a very strong impression on the class had suffered serious brain damage when he was hit by a car at three years of age. He really had to struggle to continue with his education. His thinking processes and speech are slower than that of other people, so it is easy to think that he doesn't understand what they are saying. He recounted his struggles, as well as his joy in becoming an emergency medical technician (EMT). There was not a dry eye in the room when he described what it meant to him the day his fellow EMTs stood up for him against a hostile and patronizing EMT instructor.

Narratives and Narrative Responses

In another weekly learning task, the students write a narrative or story describing some experience they have had that relates to the content of the week's readings. I tell them that they should not simply describe their thoughts or feelings about what they have read. Rather, they are to describe an experience or story that can help us understand where those thoughts or feelings come from. I suggest that they may wish to observe any strong emotional reactions they have to the readings and then explore what experiences this reaction might be related to. This assignment brings to the surface the tremendous diversity of life experiences among the students and how these experiences lead to different perspectives and views of themselves and the world.

The weekly narratives are shared electronically among the twenty-five students in a discussion section. Each student also responds electronically with his or her reaction to at least two of the narratives written by the other students in the section.

Out-of-Class Learning Experiences

During four weeks of the semester the students share a written description of an out-of-class learning experience (OOCLE) in lieu of the narratives. The purpose here is to extend the students' learning experience into their everyday environment. One way they can know that they have developed new skills in talking with and listening to people or in exploring multicultural perspectives is by stepping outside their comfort zone of routine activities and actually engaging in such behavior during the semester. How do they know they know? They just did it! This is immediate transfer.

Here are some examples of students' OOCLE activities:

- Interviewing a father with a severe disability from a stroke
- Attending a meeting of a cultural group against which the student was strongly prejudiced
- Attending a "pagan" religious service
- Attending a drag show with gay friends
- Volunteering to befriend a person in the Compeer program for folks with mental disabilities
- Eating at a soup kitchen
- Visiting a shopping mall dressed as a poor person
- Being a weekly conversation partner to an international student
- Interviewing a cousin diagnosed as schizophrenic

Students write a few sentences before doing the OOCLE describing their expectations and what they feel about completing the assignment. They combine this with a description of the actual experience and their perceptions. These reports are shared electronically with the other students in the sections.

I encourage the students to do their OOCLE with another student so that they can compare reactions and observations. I also encourage them to invite other students in the class to visit their own cultural groups, cultural events, or religious services. In this way both host and visitor can learn from the experience.

The writings that the students do in their narratives and OOCLEs are fascinating to read, in part because they are describing their own felt experience. I learn so much about the students from these writings that I hungrily and joyfully read every narrative they share, even as the numbers of students in the course rise.

Transformational Learning in the Lecture Hall

Research on dialogue education often comes from the field of adult education. Fewer examples come from traditional higher education settings. There are many reasons why professors are reluctant to give up the standard lecture format, including peer pressure, reward structures that discourage large expenditures of effort in developing a new pedagogy, and student expectations. I have learned that what you do with the small class you can do with the large class—it just requires more planning and attention to details. This particular course has grown in three years from 35 students to the present enrollment of 410. The transformational character of this course does not appear to have been affected by the very large increase in numbers.

An African-American youth raised in the inner city made this remark: "The most important thing that I learned from this class is that ignorance and hate or racism are not the same thing. Before, if I knew that someone was ignorant, I always assumed that they didn't want to know the truth. Now I see that sometimes they don't know that the truth is out there. Someone or something influenced them from a young age and they never saw a reason to question any of their beliefs. Now I feel that if you can somehow make people see the other side of the coin then you usually have a good chance of changing the way that they feel about something, especially if their feelings have no real substantial foundations."

From a young white woman raised in a middle-class suburb: "I have always considered myself an open-minded person. However, after taking this class I realize now that there is so much I didn't understand about how racism, homophobia, and poverty oppress people and how people such as myself who are not directly affected by these prejudices and forces can unknowingly help to perpetuate them. My eyes have been opened to my responsibility to increase justice for all."

Conclusion

This professor is humbled by the growth and enthusiasm I have seen in these psychology students. Both students and professor acknowledge that the work of dialogue is both demanding and fruitful for all.

References

Allport, G. W. *The Nature of Prejudice*. Cambridge, Mass.: Perseus Publishing, 1958.

Bligh, D. A. *What's the Use of Lectures?* San Francisco: Jossey-Bass, 2000.

Brown, C. R., and Mazza, G. J. *Healing into Action: A Leadership Guide for Creating Diverse Communities*. Washington, D.C.: National Coalition Building Institute, 1998.

Epstein, M. L., Epstein, B. B., and Brosvic, G. M. "Immediate Feedback During Academic Testing." *Psychological Reports*, 2001, 88, 889–894.

McAdams, D. P. *The Stories We Live By*. New York: Guilford Press, 1997.

Michaelsen, L. K. "Team Learning: A Comprehensive Approach for Harnessing the Power of Small Groups in Higher Education." *To Improve the Academy*, 1992, *11*, 107–122.

Vella, J. *Learning to Listen, Learning to Teach: The Power of Dialogue in Educating Adults*. San Francisco: Jossey-Bass, 2002. (Originally published 1994.)

Open Questions for Analysis and Synthesis

1. In terms of the principles and practices, what did you see Jane Connor do that moved students to tell their friends: "You've got to take this course"?

2. How did Dr. Connor use other instruments in a way that showed students they were the subjects of their own learning?

3. Which one part of the process do you see as most revolutionary for an undergraduate psychology course?

4. Notice how Steve Stahl in Chapter Five designs his work with undergraduates. What similarities and differences do you see in these two educators' ways of showing respect?

2

Nutrition Education in an Undergraduate Setting

Elena Carbone

My first day of class! I took my place at the front of the room and looked at the rows of faces. "Here I am about to teach these young people the same material on nutrition that I learned myself almost twenty years ago!" I thought of Parker Palmer's words: "Teaching is a daily exercise in vulnerability. . . . When walking into a new class you can feel the undertow into which you have jumped" (Palmer, 1998, pp. 17, 36).

I felt a very strong undertow. Would I be any good at this? How would I get them to participate? Would I expect too much from them or not enough? Would I have time to cover everything? How would I know if they were learning? At the end of that first semester the students answered those questions for me, and they opened my eyes to the shortcomings of my teaching methods. This chapter illustrates how I subsequently transformed that course—Nutrition in the Life Cycle—using a dialogue-based approach to teaching.

A Required Course

Nutrition in the Life Cycle is a required course in the four-year undergraduate dietetics program at a large public university. I use a practice-oriented approach to teach basic nutrition principles related to the effects of nutrition on growth, development, and health throughout the life cycle. This fourteen-week fall-semester course usually attracts twenty-five to thirty-five upper-level under-graduate students, most of whom are nutrition majors.

I taught the course for the first time during my first year as a university professor. My days were filled with committee meetings, student advising, research proposal deadlines, and the many other duties expected of new faculty members. I had little time to think, let alone get creative about my teaching. So I took comfort in the safety of traditional lecture-style teaching, using dozens of overheads taken directly from the text. At the end of the semester, students used a standard university course evaluation to tell me what they thought:

> "The notes are given too fast and the lectures were very repetitive in the way they were taught."

> "I was very unhappy with the lecture style. Everything was taken right from the book. We could have used classtime learning new things."

> "Break up the lectures by using different teaching tools other than lectures and notes."

> "The guest speakers were always refreshing."

I took these comments to heart and resolved to do better. The content of the course, the textbook, the number of class hours and students, and the instructor remained the same. The only thing I did differently was to implement a dialogue-based approach. Here is what students said at the end of the new course:

> "The professor was creative and made the material interesting. She makes every class a true learning experience."

> "She created an atmosphere of equality . . . so that we all participated in class."

> "I really enjoyed every single class and activity and I feel I have learned more than in any other class I have taken."

> "This is one of the best classes I have taken at the university."

This was not an easy transformation for me to make as a new professor. Initially, I found my traditional content-heavy, teacher-centered course nearly impossible to translate into a dialogue-based, learning-centered format. My first clue about reformation came when I looked hard at the content of the class and discovered that I had far too much information for a semester-long course. I was so concerned about "covering" all the material that I left no time for students to become engaged in the learning process. I was drowning in details and facts. Then I remembered two things I had learned from Jane Vella during her course Learning to Listen, Learning to Teach, which I had taken when I began studying dialogue education. First, less is more. Effective teaching is not about how much information is covered, but about how well the content—knowledge, attitudes, and skills—is understood by learners as demonstrated by their ability to apply, analyze, synthesize, and evaluate it. She had also said, "Don't stay stuck!" So I called Jane and other colleagues, inviting them to help me look at the course from the perspective of dialogue education.

"This is excellent data," Jane said of my lesson on nutritional needs of women during pregnancy. "But it is not learning as it stands, is it? Make it a learning task!"

"How about asking the students to come up with an educational program using cognitive, affective, and psychomotor activities?" offered Marianne Reiff. My steps were tentative at first, but as I listened to these experienced educators I grew more confident.

Changing the Design

The first thing I had to change was the class schedule. The traditional Monday-Wednesday-Friday, 50-minute class period would no longer work if I wanted to stimulate ongoing dialogue and have the freedom to create innovative activities that encouraged active learning. I got approval to switch the class to one 150-minute session offered weekly. Although they approved the change, the four other faculty in my department (who have together over seventy-five years of teaching experience) were skeptical. "How are you going to keep the attention of a classroom full of undergraduates for two and a half hours?" a colleague asked. The students were just as wary: "I was concerned about being able to pay attention for a two-and-a-half-hour class," wrote one young man in his class journal. "When I first realized how long the class period was I became worried because I'm horrible at sitting still for long periods of time," wrote another student. As I worked through each week's lessons, a rhythm emerged: start with a warm-up learning task to focus the group, mix in small group work with energizing debates and short lectures, and finish with a closing synthesis task.

Learning Needs and Resource Assessment (LNRA)

Before I could get the students moving to the rhythm, however, I needed to know more about them. My first task was to design a learning needs and resource assessment (LNRA), which invites learners to share information about what they already know about the subject and what they believe they need to know (Vella, Berardinelli, and Burrow, 1998). Now, instead of launching immediately into the course content on the first day of class, we review the course syllabus. I invite students to complete a short survey. This LNRA lets students voice their learning needs, expectations, and concerns. Examples of questions I ask on the LNRA include these:

Name one skill you hope to gain or improve as a result of this class.

What do you feel you need to know about nutrition through the life cycle for your personal and professional growth?

In what ways do you see yourself using what you learn in this class?

We may have time to spend one extra class on a specific issue. If so, which topic would you most like to focus on?

During the second class I share information from the LNRAs and we talk about ways to make the class meet both their needs and the needs of the university. Although the general content of the course is set, findings from the LNRAs directly inform my development of the learning tasks. A needs assessment does not form the course, it informs it.

Learning Tasks

Instead of filling class periods with lectures read from overhead projections, I now create learning tasks for each topic. *Learning tasks* are "open questions put to learners along with the resources they need to respond" (Vella, Berardinelli, and Burrow, 1998, p. 109). The tasks are designed with the learners in mind by responding to the LNRA findings and by providing a mix of cognitive (thinking), affective (feeling), and psychomotor (doing) activities to stimulate critical thinking skills and learning. For example, in response to comments from students about their desire for more applied information about nutritional needs during pregnancy, I developed the following set of learning tasks.

Learning task #1. Warm-up, overview

1A. In pairs, share some of the stories you have heard from your mother, other relatives, or friends related to pregnancy.

1B. Still in those pairs, name one nutrition issue regarding pregnancy that you have heard firsthand from these sources or have read about. Write these on Post-it notes—one thought per note. Post your cards on the front board. We will come back to these.

Learning task #2. Pregnancy stages and changes

2A. In small groups, read the following scenario: You are part of a group of nutritionists who have been asked to teach young pregnant women in the Appalachian area of Kentucky about the different stages of pregnancy and the changes that occur during pregnancy. The fifteen women you will be teaching do not read or write. They have never been to school. You have been asked to provide assistance in explaining a specific topic to these expectant mothers. Each group will select one of four topics, such as changes in body composition, respiration, blood volume, and kidney function.

2B. As a group, choose the handout that offers solid up-to-date content on your topic. Decide one way you can reformat that content to be appropriate for these particular mothers-to-be. We will hear from all groups.

Learning task #3. Nutrient requirements

3A. In groups of three, match the names of the vitamins and minerals with their requirements during pregnancy on the sheet provided.

3B. Review the vitamin and mineral requirements in your text and on the handout materials. Name what surprised you. We'll hear all.

Learning task #4. Postpartum

4A. Listen to a brief review of the postpartum period, and then circle on the handout provided the information that is new to you.

4B. In pairs, reflect on what you circled. We will hear a sample.

Learning task #5. Closing

5A. Refer back to the issues you wrote on your cards and posted on the board in the first learning task.

5B. Remove those cards naming issues that you feel
were addressed during the class session today.

5C. Name the remaining issues and we will respond to
them.

The first time I introduced the fifth learning task, there were so
many good questions left on the board at the end of class that I
invited students to choose one (their own or another student's) to
research and respond to. I reviewed and compiled all responses,
handed out the complete set of questions and answers to the learners, and included a number of these questions on that year's final
exam. This research assignment turned out to be a memorable and
unexpected learning experience that made the course material
highly relevant and interesting for the class.

Well-designed learning tasks answer the question: *How will I
know if the students are learning?* In this case, besides getting feedback from the usual written assignments and exams that quantita-
tively measure learning against a standard, I knew the students
knew how to talk to low-literate women about the complexities of
pregnancy because I saw them do it! Debates, role-plays, case study
questions, and other engaging small group tasks also demonstrate
students' learning. In addition, students are asked to keep two brief
reflective journals. The first year, I invited students to write about
anything related to the class. As a result, the journals lacked focus.
I now invite students to reflect on specific class content in their
course journal. I ask them to write about something that has surprised, inspired, or energized them. They can also include comments
about what they like most and least about the class and suggestions
to make the class a better learning experience.

The second journal is a self-assessment of their current food
habits. This gives them a chance to think about how and why their
eating habits have changed over time. This personal journal also
gives students a chance to reflect on any dietary issues or concerns
they may have. Once students discover there is not a "right" or

"wrong" way to write their journals, they begin to look outside the confines of the academic assignment and give personal meaning to the content by applying it to their own lives. Over the years, I have been privileged to read their many thoughtful comments, unexpected discoveries, and surprising insights. The journals also give me helpful feedback on specific principles and practices I have used to guide the changes I make to the class. The journals are ongoing learning needs and resource assessments.

Learning Domains: Cognitive, Affective, Psychomotor

Kolb (1999) talks about the need to "teach around the learning cycle" in order to appeal to all domains of learning. But how can you do this with thirty-five students when there is so much material to cover? After taking a hard look at the course content, I discovered that the answer was right in front of me. Because we enjoy such a rich variety of experiences throughout our lives, it follows that teaching about nutrition through the life cycle should tap into these diverse experiences. How? By offering different learning tasks that invite dialogue and engagement in the learning process. These stimulate the head (through debates and critical analysis of data), the heart (with reflective journals), and the hands (by using modeling clay to communicate important nutrition information to young children). Designing learning tasks that tap into each of these learning domains also answers the question: *How can I get students to participate?* The success of this approach is evident in their feedback:

> "The idea of teaching and learning through reading, lectures, and active participation . . . helped me gain a better understanding of various nutrition principles."

> "For the amount of information and for the topic of discussions, I couldn't ask for a better way to learn the information. I've always been a hands-on kind of learner, and between the in-class group activities, and the role-plays, I found myself easily learning the material. This was an incredible weight lifted off my shoulders."

"When I come to your class I feel motivated to learn."

"I not only learn a lot, but stay focused by participating in the various class activities."

"I found that the structure of the classes made it not only easy to concentrate, but hard not to pay attention!"

Group Tasks and Environment

I tell students the word "team" stands for "*together each achieves more*." This at once captures the importance of group work and the environment needed to foster it. In contrast to the traditional rows of chairs I accepted during my first year of teaching, students who now enter my classroom find desks arranged in one large circle. I watch their faces and hear them murmur: "Where are the rows? Where is my seat? Where does the teacher sit?" Although it may feel odd, and even uncomfortable at first, students soon learn that by the end of the semester everyone will sit in virtually every seat and work with every member of the class. Moving chairs from the large circle into clusters of five or six facilitates small group work. Making these simple changes to the classroom environment helps start the dialogue process from the first day and encourage co-learning. My students have made that clear:

> "Group work really helped me feel comfortable with being one of two men in the class. I got to know the women in the class, and with the relaxed atmosphere of the class, I found gender to be of no issue. This was pretty important to me because at first I was overwhelmed, and now I don't even think about it."

> "The group activities are very helpful, and I think that it helps make the information clearer when you are discussing it with other people rather than reading it on your own. It also gives us a chance to talk to our classmates, and makes the classroom environment friendlier."

> "I was skeptical that I could obtain nutrition knowledge from my peers. I was wrong! We did learn from each other."

Transfer and Impact

Students in this dietetics program take several courses with me and I hear from many of them after graduation. I therefore see evidence of how they transfer their learning, not only from class to class but beyond the university into their world of work. I celebrate when I hear students asking open questions and reflecting deeply about some topic we discussed in class. I also celebrate when students actively apply their knowledge and skills. As these students put it:

> "You told us we would be surprised at how much we know. You were right. Your class has given me an understanding of my knowledge suitable not only for an exam but also for a career."

> "My understanding follows me outside of the classroom, too. I am able to answer so many questions that people ask me about nutrition. I get excited when people ask me for advice."

Next Steps

My use of a dialogue-based, learning-centered approach has transformed me from a lecturer into an active educator. In his book *The University in Ruins*, Bill Readings (1996) invites us to think about knowledge as a conversation among a community rather than a simple accumulation of facts. This statement highlights a key point: that students are part of our learning community. Knowledge and critical thinking skills will be gained only if we actively encourage students to engage in dialogue-based conversations that explore, analyze, and question the facts as they make their way toward real meaning.

Conclusions

I have learned to educate by trusting the process and navigating the ebb and flow of the classroom dialogue as it unfolds, rather than forcing it into a neat format. By relinquishing control over every aspect of the learning process, I have found what Jyl Felman (2001) refers to as my *authentic voice*, and in the process I have gained a sense of self (Palmer, 1998). I feel grounded and more confident as an educator and enjoy teaching more than ever. Adopting a dialogue-based education approach has been an evolutionary process for me. The transition has been tremendously rewarding. As I move from using this approach in the classroom environment to developing formal conference presentations and research proposals, I no longer ask, "Will I be any good at this? How will I know if they are learning?" Now the questions are these: "How will I creatively engage my audience when I have only ten minutes to present at this professional meeting?" and "How will I craft my next dialogue-based research proposal so that it is understood and appreciated by funders?" Dialogue education can be useful at many levels.

References

Felman, J. L. *Never a Dull Moment: Teaching and the Art of Performance.* New York: Routledge, 2001.

Kolb, D. A. *Learning-Style Inventory (Version 3).* Boston: McBer & Co., 1999.

Palmer, P. J. *The Courage to Teach.* San Francisco: Jossey-Bass, 1998.

Readings, B. *The University in Ruins.* Cambridge, Mass.: Harvard University Press, 1996.

Vella, J., Berardinelli, P., and Burrow, J. *How Do They Know They Know? Evaluating Adult Learning.* San Francisco: Jossey-Bass, 1998.

Open Questions for Analysis and Synthesis

1. What one thing did you see Elena Carbone do to use dialogue education's principles and practices in her redesign of the undergraduate course?

2. Chapters Three, Eleven, Fourteen, and Seventeen all offer stories of dialogue education at work on nutrition issues. What similarities do you see between these cases?

3. Name one thing that Dr. Carbone did in terms of the principles and practices that made her course particularly useful to the young undergraduates.

3

Creating a Culture for Dialogue in a Nutrition Education Program

Meredith Pearson

The Expanded Food and Nutrition Education Program (EFNEP), a federally funded program, has benefited low-income families throughout the United States since 1969. This case study describes my experience in finding the right approach to make dialogue learning the foundation of a new EFNEP curriculum.

In the earliest days of this program, the USDA Cooperative Extension Service, which is an integral part of land-grant universities, hired paraprofessional educators based on their ability to relate to their clients. These paraprofessionals brought nutrition education into the homes of low-income learners. Over time, however, the one-on-one model became financially unsustainable and was supplanted by group lessons. Group lessons were based on a telling-demonstration model where the paraprofessionals served as experts and the learners were the recipients of information. This model has not changed in decades.

Throughout my career as EFNEP director at Kansas State University and later at the University of Massachusetts, I have believed that there is untapped potential for reaching all EFNEP learners and effecting greater improvement in dietary behavior. My vision for EFNEP has always been of a program in which all learners have a voice, a program in which all learners are excited about learning, take responsibility for learning, and improve their diets as a result of that learning. Unfortunately, my initial efforts to implement this vision did not meet with success. I attempted to make dialogue education the foundation of the EFNEP model through staff workshops. However, I learned that workshops were insufficient to effect the organizational change needed to sustain such a radical departure from business as usual. Finally, my golden opportunity presented itself in the form of a staff decision to design a new EFNEP curriculum at the University of Massachusetts.

The Seven Design Steps

We used the framework of the Seven Design Steps as follows.

Who: The Learners and Leaders

The curriculum design team, consisting of the state EFNEP director (myself), an administrative assistant, a curriculum writer, a graphic designer, and consultant Joye Norris (Learning by Dialogue, Inc.), organized the project and facilitated the learning. The learners in this project included the six county EFNEP supervisors and their twenty-six paraprofessional educators. When I accepted a new position at the University of Maryland about midway in the project, we decided to use the opportunity to include the EFNEP staff in Maryland (and later Pennsylvania) in the pilot study of the new curriculum to test the efficacy of innovation transfer.

As already noted, EFNEP has been a program of USDA's Cooperative Extension Service since 1969. It is now one of the largest federally funded nutrition education programs in the country, providing nutrition education to low-income families, especially families with young children. Its primary focus is to help the learner make healthy food choices, manage the food dollar, and handle food safely. The educators in EFNEP are community-based paraprofessionals, usually from socioeconomic backgrounds similar to the EFNEP learners. They are trained and supervised by county extension agents who are university-based.

The need to revise the curriculum was prompted by recent shifts in the racial and ethnic characteristics of Massachusetts citizens; the alarming drop in EFNEP participation, in large part as a result of welfare reform; and the equally alarming increase in obesity and related chronic diseases, especially in low-income populations. The most compelling reason for the change, however, was staff awareness of the need to revise current teaching methodology to improve program effectiveness in helping learners improve their diets.

My vision was to create a dramatically different EFNEP curriculum in which the paraprofessional educators moved from a telling-demonstration model to a demonstration-dialogue model. I was well aware of the challenges I would face in this project. EFNEP paraprofessionals had great pride in what they considered to be the participatory nature of EFNEP and the growth they had witnessed in many of the participants. My challenge was to develop support for a dialogue-based curriculum while honoring the paraprofessionals' considerable accomplishments.

What, When, Where: Content, Time Frame, and Site

We began the project in Massachusetts in spring 2000, and for the next two years developed both the dialogue-based curriculum and dialogue-based processes to effect organizational change to support the new model. In Chapter Fourteen Dr. Jean Anliker, a Massachusetts colleague, describes paraprofessional training for the curriculum Choices: Steps Toward Health.

What For: Achievement-Based Objectives

By the end of the two-year period, we intended to have accomplished the following:

- Conducted a needs assessment to determine the learning needs of EFNEP staff, collaborators, and participants

- Listed the content of the new EFNEP curriculum

- Reflected on the nine articles of the learning by
  dialogue tutorial, and on their applicability to EFNEP

- Practiced the seven facilitation skills

- Designed a learning by dialogue training for
  paraprofessionals

- Coached the paraprofessional staff in using the Choices
  curriculum

- Evaluated the effectiveness of the Choices curriculum

How: Learning Tasks and Materials

The first step in the project was to carry out a learning needs and resource assessment (LNRA), using focus groups made up of EFNEP paraprofessionals, collaborators, and participants. We enlisted the assistance of the supervisors and paraprofessionals in developing the focus group questions and recruiting the focus group participants. This served to reassure the staff that they were an integral part of the curriculum project from the beginning.

We learned from the focus group data that EFNEP staff and participants held similar views. They wanted programming that addressed what the learner wanted to know, not just what EFNEP wanted to teach. This is what Paulo Freire (1972) described as *thematic analysis*, identifying the needs of the group. They also wanted a safe learning environment, respect from the teacher and their peers, and opportunities for active participation in the learning. The results of the needs assessment reassured the design team that dialogue education was a reasonable alternative to consider in designing the curriculum.

Our first challenge arose from the need to shift from our current teacher-content focus to a learner-process focus. Staff resistance to this challenge can be seen in these comments made at one of our early curriculum design meetings:

"The dialogue approach certainly involves the participants, but our experience shows that our clientele also want information beyond the basics that a curriculum with limited content allows."

"Our clients have so little information about nutrition and food preparation. There isn't enough time at our classes to give them all the information they need and help them apply it."

"Our paraprofessionals are well-trained in nutrition. We should focus on giving participants research-based information rather than having participants give each other information that in many instances is wrong."

I was not surprised by this resistance. Extension has a long tradition of providing research-based information to the learner. Remember, EFNEP staff are university-based. I expected that moving to a focus on application would be a gradual process.

In July 2001, we involved the supervisors in a learning task using the format of a summer tutorial including nine readings on basic theories of brain-based learning. Study questions accompanying each article were designed to connect the information with the supervisors' prior learning and experience in EFNEP and to prepare them for designing paraprofessional training. For example, in our study of an excerpt from Palmer Parker's *The Courage to Teach* (1998), we asked: "From your own EFNEP experience, describe how paraprofessionals are functioning as both experts and connectors." And in reading *Designing Brain-Compatible Learning* by Parry and Gregory (1998), we asked, "What are your suggestions for a more brain-compatible paraprofessional training model?"

Throughout the summer, dialogue was conducted by e-mail. Supervisors discussed their reactions to the articles and answers to the study questions. The response to this learning task was mixed. Some staff members said, "We learned all this in our adult education classes!" But several of them were very interested and e-mailed in-depth analyses of the articles. One said, "I loved reading the articles. It gave me a more academic understanding of dialogue and brain-based learning."

By fall 2001, the first draft of the Choices curriculum was completed. Our next step was to design a special event to "roll out" the curriculum draft, celebrate its progress, and test the lessons in their current form. We held a three-day retreat for the state design team and the EFNEP supervisors from Massachusetts, Maryland, and Pennsylvania in Craigsville, Massachusetts, on Cape Cod. The retreat agenda was structured according to the principles of dialogue education. On the first day of the retreat, we focused on seven skills used in facilitating dialogue: inviting, asking, waiting, affirming, weaving, energizing, and embracing. The first learning task was to form three-member teams and find objects in nature to represent each of these seven skills. This is an example of a learning task that Jane Vella describes as "respecting the experience of the participants and their ability to respond at the symbolic level" (Vella, 2000, p. 2). It was an effective way to model dialogue education and provide an opportunity to experience our beautiful surroundings. This was followed by a series of learning tasks providing practice in the facilitation skills, using auditory, visual, and kinesthetic ways of knowing. The room was filled with the voices, laughter, and dialogue I had envisioned for EFNEP.

The agenda for the second day of the retreat involved the first piloting of the lessons, providing the supervisors with an opportunity to use the materials. It also marked the beginning of the supervisors' transition from their role as learners to their additional role as trainers-facilitators. They were demonstrating the lessons to the new learners from Maryland and Pennsylvania, who were seeing the materials and the methodology for the first time. At the end of the day, we provided an opportunity for facilitators to reflect on their experience by considering the following feedback questions:

- What did you like about your teaching and facilitation? (facilitators)

- What did you like about their teaching and facilitation? (participants)

- What would you do differently? (facilitators)

- What are your suggestions for change? (participants)

- What comes to mind when you think about training-supporting paraprofessionals? (all)

This is an example of *praxis*, the process of experiencing, reflecting, and making decisions about future behavior. With continued revision and extensive graphic design efforts, the Choices curriculum was ready for piloting in spring 2002. A conference for the participants from all three states was held in Massachusetts to train the EFNEP paraprofessionals and to demonstrate four of the seven Choices curriculum lessons. EFNEP staff took home materials to begin the pilot study.

Why: Evidence of Learning, Transfer, and Impact

The entire first year of the project was devoted to gaining staff support for dialogue. When I decided to accept my new position in Maryland, I was concerned. However, my fears were unfounded. The project progressed in the second year with my having only a peripheral role, and the design team continues its commitment to dialogue.

Principles and Practices

A number of principles were particularly pivotal to the success of this project. *Respect* was a cornerstone of Massachusetts EFNEP and continued to be in this project. We showed respect by devoting almost a full year to meeting monthly to discuss focus group data, select curriculum topics, and consider alternative lesson activities. This gave supervisors an opportunity to express their thoughts—and perhaps hold on to the old model a little longer! It was important to honor their need to do that.

We endeavored to create a *safe learning environment* by sequencing the supervisors' participation in the curriculum development process from simple to complex. Starting with *group discussion and interaction*, we moved to individual study in the tutorial and subsequent dialogue on the Internet, and then involved the supervisors in the more complex tasks of designing and facilitating the paraprofessionals' training.

At the Cape Cod retreat, we practiced the principle of *praxis* by providing a time for reflection and feedback at the end of lesson demonstrations. On the last day of the retreat, the design team received a delightful surprise from the staff, who presented an original song and dance to represent the seven facilitation skills. Further evidence of *transfer* could be seen with the Pennsylvania staff, who designed their paraprofessional training plan on the long ride back home from the retreat. They designed a paraprofessional training program on facilitation skills, posted facilitation skills banners in their offices, and provided staff with a wallet-size card listing the dialogue facilitation skills. This staff development process is ongoing now in EFNEP.

Issues in the Use of Dialogue

One of our biggest obstacles in this project was the need to move our focus in EFNEP from transfer of information to applied learning. We spent months reaching consensus on what we were going to teach, or perhaps more importantly, what we were *not* going to teach. Initially, the university EFNEP staff had strong feelings of responsibility for giving learners the most information possible. However, the dialogue education model involves both process and content. Intellectually the staff knew that behavior change was the goal of our program, but in practice it was difficult for them to justify spending as much time as we were proposing to help learners create personal meaning that would result in behavior change. Current evaluation studies will present evidence to EFNEP on the effectiveness of this curriculum (results not yet in at this time).

A parallel issue that will continue to require our attention is the transition from the educational model of our childhood—that of the teacher as the giver of knowledge and learner as receiver—to the dialogue education model in which educator and learners are co-learners. This is a particularly sensitive issue for paraprofessionals. The paraprofessionals usually begin their careers in EFNEP with a high school education. EFNEP provides training, mentoring, and released work time for taking college courses. Many of the staff, after many years of part-time schooling, have earned their bachelor's degrees. They serve on local boards and committees in the community, and they are very proud of their accomplishments. Relinquishing their role in the classroom as experts and becoming co-learners require a willingness to share the spotlight. It will be important to provide opportunities for the staff to express their feelings about this issue.

The third issue is one of innovation transfer. How can this dialogue education curriculum be transferred from the base at the University of Massachusetts to other EFNEP sites? This is an important action research agenda.

Conclusions

This curriculum and staff development project has required me to place the highest priority on the process of learning rather than on the content of learning alone. As a result, I have made an important transition to learner-centered curriculum design.

The experience has required a willingness to devote an extraordinary amount of time and effort not only to designing the staff development program required to support the curriculum project but also to structuring all staff interactions intentionally as dialogue to effect a basic change in the organizational culture. I had not anticipated how challenging or time-consuming this project would be, and how tenaciously educators would retain their hold on familiar content-centered curriculum. I found that a key element in this process is my own attitude. It was essential that the design team communicate their confidence in the effectiveness of this new system. In effecting the transition to dialogue education at a university-based EFNEP program, we found that attitude is everything!

References

Freire, P. *Pedagogy of the Oppressed*. New York: Herder & Herder, 1972.

Palmer, P. *The Courage to Teach*. San Francisco: Jossey-Bass, 1998.

Parry, T., and Gregory, G. *Designing Brain-Compatible Learning*. Arlington Heights, Ill.: SkyLight Professional Development, 1998.

Vella, J. *Taking Learning to Task: Creative Strategies for Teaching Adults*. San Francisco: Jossey-Bass, 2000.

Open Questions for Analysis and Synthesis

1. In what ways did you see the Seven Design Steps were helpful to Dr. Pearson as she designed this training program?

2. Which of the principles and practices helped her deal with the issue of paraprofessionals who needed to be seen as instructors?

3. What struck you about her realization that the focus needed to move from sharing information to applied learning?

4. How did the feedback questions used in this program implement many of the principles and practices?

Dialogue Education at a Weekend College
An Accelerated Master's Degree in Education

Marianne Reiff

Ionce used dialogue education to solve a serious management problem. As the administrator who helped develop an innovative master of adult education degree program at a southern college, I stepped in to respond when a class of adult students splintered off from their instructor. They were well on their way to disbanding and leaving the program altogether. It was clear that the explosive events of the previous few weeks were taking up most of their energy. I heard that the class wanted to stay together and finish the degree program, but expressed serious doubts about it. The text for the next course in this cohort's sequence was Jane Vella's *Learning to Listen, Learning to Teach* (2002). I had read the book earlier and was excited and impressed by it. I also knew there was no opportunity in the class as it currently existed for much new learning. So I set the group a uniquely challenging task: to use their negative experience as a case study to check out the principles of adult learning presented by Vella in her book.

What evolved was a course in which they examined what had happened to them in relation to adult learning theory and twelve selected principles of dialogue education. This learning task led to their constructing a theory about learning. For me this experience was a real-world testing ground for dialogue education, and it stood the test. The group survived and prospered to the end of the program, and I wanted more. After the course I wrote to Dr. Vella, who responded to begin an ongoing learning exchange grounded in mutual respect. Dialogue education, to which I was introduced through a crisis, now provides a rock-solid theoretical foundation for all my teaching.

This chapter looks at a similar class in an accelerated master of education program. After offering an overview of what a Seven Step design looks like for the entire course, which is entitled Dimensions of Learning and Teaching, I will use snapshots from my experience teaching it to show how selected principles and practices of dialogue education work at the university level.

The Seven Design Steps

The Seven Design Steps were applied in this case as follows.

Who: Participants

Working teachers in the public schools who want to complete a specialized master's degree are the students in this accelerated program. This particular cohort included twenty-one teachers from a two-state radius. They ranged from first-year teachers to teachers nearing retirement.

Why: Situation

The course, Dimensions of Learning and Teaching, is the first in a sequence of courses in a master of education program at a progressive New England university with both traditional and accelerated adult programs. Students begin their graduate work with this course. The learning cohorts formed here remain together throughout the graduate program.

When: Time Frame

Classes meet one weekend a month for a three-day intensive schedule. Two such intensive twenty-one-hour sessions make up the core classtime. In addition, students communicate with each other and with the teacher during the month between classes.

Where: Site

The site for this cohort was a high school. The students moved between a classroom and a full computer lab. The classroom was equipped with media support and had tables and chairs rather than desks. This master's program is designed to be geographically central to as many students as possible. This particular group included students who lived ten minutes away and others who drove in from neighboring states.

What: Content—Skills, Knowledge, Attitudes

I often refer to this course as a "Frankencourse" because of the wide range of content prescribed by the university. Classes in the program include Cultural Contexts of Education; Teaching and Learning Styles and Motivation to Learn; Cooperative Education and Small Group Dynamics; Research, Reading, Speaking, and Writing Skills; and Computer Technology for Educators. The overarching goal for the course is effective socialization into graduate study.

What For: Achievement-Based Objectives

The complete design lists multiple objectives for each content area. Here is a sample:

By the end of this course, all will have:

> *Identified the barriers to positive diversity in schools today*
>
> *Examined the historical background shaping individual teaching*
>
> *Compared learning style and teaching style*
>
> *Distinguished between cooperative and teacher-directed learning*
>
> *Practiced using APA format in writing a research paper*

How: Learning Tasks

Learning tasks are the nuts and bolts of the course. In *Taking Learning to Task,* Vella defines a learning task as "an open question put to a small group who have all the resources they need to respond" (2000, p. 137). She provides a comprehensive exploration of creating and using learning tasks. It is important to note that this is the point where, previously, I would have begun planning a course. I would have used the texts, my knowledge base, and my assumptions to construct presentations that would work for students. Course planning has radically changed. Using the Seven Design Steps guarantees that I do a significant amount of intentional work before I even get to the classroom. I have always thought carefully about what to include in a course but rarely progressed beyond listing the course objectives. For example, one of the content areas I know I will include in this first graduate course is research writing skills. My first step is to name the specific skills, knowledge, or attitudes I will teach. If I include the skill of writing in APA format, I systematically identify the achievement-based objectives specific to that particular skill, and for every objective I construct at least one sequenced learning task. Figure 4.1 shows an example of this planning process; one piece of course content flows into a specific achievement-based objective supported by a series of learning tasks.

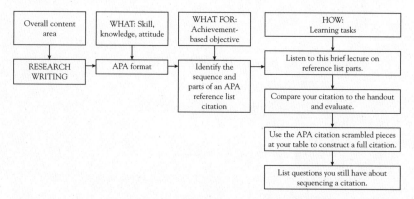

Figure 4.1   Connection Between Design Steps: What, What For, and How

Planning and teaching in this way provides a flexible blueprint. I know what I am doing and why I am doing it. I no longer have to defend or second-guess my practice. I trust the design and can feel confident changing it. And in the end, I will be able to answer if, and to what extent, learning has happened.

Safe Enough to Meet the Challenge of Learning

On a Friday at 5 P.M. after a full workweek, schoolteachers came together with people they did not know previously, in a place they had never been, to do something they had never done before. As Vella put it: "People have shown that they are not only willing but also ready and eager to learn when they feel safe in the learning environment" (Vella, 2000, p. 6). In this course, planning for safety began with the learning needs resource assessment (LNRA), which I sent out prior to the course, and my follow-up phone calls to some class members. Before they began the course, students had been given time to peruse the complete course overview and provide input to inform the course design. Still, they had questions: *Who am I in this group context? Who are you? What am I to do?* These men and women had the courage to show up when a sense of safety in the course was still developing. I knew they needed to feel safe enough to continue.

A Physical Environment for Learning

Attending to the physical environment may seem an unlikely place to address an educational principle such as safety. However, I have found it to be one of the most productive and most overlooked. The classroom environment is of special interest to new graduate students coming into the space for the first time. Getting to the class site in time to "claim" the environment is crucial to developing safe entry for learners. I make it a point to meet and consult with the custodial staff. To a person I have found them very interested in whether adult learners learn, and they have helped me time and again to arrange the space, adjust room temperature, and set up equipment. I meet with site and lab coordinators and make sure all the equipment works. Before learners arrive I set out and organize all materials. I can then meet the learners when they arrive with calm attention and full interest. Throughout the weekend, an accepting physical environment complements rather than impedes the grouping, regrouping, and moving that are inherent in dialogue education.

Whenever possible I opt for a structure that is familiar, dependable, and visible. I have also found that adult learners can do amazing things if they can visibly see what they are to do. The classroom space, walls, the halls are all used. Every session starts on time with a review of the posted learning agenda. We review it again as we close. We have definite opening and closing rituals each day. The learning tasks are posted in plain sight and reinforced. I initially resisted posting the task I had just given verbally; I thought it was unnecessary. But experience has shown me that people really do retain only about 20 percent of what they hear (Knowles, 1980). In fact, the percentage may be even lower for retention of verbal instructions. I used to find myself spending excessive amounts of time and frustrated energy restating and clarifying tasks and responding to group confusion. Now the learning tasks are posted for all to see.

Roles and Group Norms

I deal with roles and group norms in the classroom as follows.

Establish Clear Roles

Who are you? Who am I? Who am I in relation to you? One of the main reasons to define clear roles early in this course is that such roles for learners and teachers at the university level already exist for adult learners. These traditional roles are very strong. They create expectations about who does what with whom. Public schools have similar institutionalized roles too, so the Dimensions of Learning and Teaching course is further complicated by the fact that the learners who are here on weekends turn back into teachers come

Monday morning. Their work roles differ greatly from the roles they are expected to play in dialogue education.

By being explicit and clear about my role, I can model it for learners. Learners want to know that I have credentials, that I am competent and experienced. They must then claim and reframe the role of autonomous learners for themselves. As I model my new role in the dialogue, they begin to reshape theirs. Once begun it is a surprisingly rapid metamorphosis!

Getting clear about roles is a first step toward building sound relationships, which is another key principle of dialogue education. Adult learners demand a complex relationship with someone they respect. They want interpersonal dialogue. They do not want a dictator and are not looking for a "pal" (Carbone, 2002; Reiff, 1993). The best way I have found to start a discussion about roles is to use the distinction Vella (2002) draws between the consultative voice (suggestions) and the deliberative voice (decisions). Here is a story that shows the importance of clear roles.

At the end of the first weekend of this particular course session, a challenging cooperative learning task was set in motion. Learners were assigned to content areas and placed in heterogeneous groups. During the month between the two weekend classes, they were to plan as individuals, then come into the assigned group the second weekend to blend individual work into an extensive formal group presentation. I could feel the anxiety level soar as I introduced the learning task. However, there was enough of a feeling of safety that they could absorb the initial shock waves, and the voltage leveled off as, together, we identified the relevance and feasibility of this complex task. Clarifying questions were raised and answered. This happened because it was expected to happen as part of the normal process. We had practiced such behavior throughout the course.

Clarity, however, does not always mean agreement. Even after realizing this project would allow cooperative learning, there was still lobbying for same-school or homogeneous groups for convenience and simplicity. And even after a fine group discussion of how heterogeneous groupings would promote reflection and analysis, several learners changed the names around on the task sheet during break. The need for familiar ground was that strong! I had to act. Clear role definition and respect between learners and teacher supported me. Although I acknowledged their anxiety and creativity, I did not make excuses for or pretend this was a simple task; nor did I apologize for the difficulty. I reinforced the intent of the learning task and answered questions for clarity. Learners always have the right to resist. I had the right to project my confidence that they could do this difficult and complex task involving content and process, and then I restated the task in my deliberative voice as professor. I had presented my part of the learning exchange. The learners, feeling courageous now rather than victimized, made their choice. They felt safe enough to try the learning task as assigned. Together we put the original names back under the original topic headings and met in small groups to start the planning. I felt the positive energy level rise once again as they got to work.

My response to this situation honored the principle of respect for learners as subjects of their own learning: "Adults as subjects of their own learning need to know that insofar as possible, they themselves decide what occurs in the learning event" (Vella, 2002, p. 12). Respect for the learners means respect for their capacity to do difficult learning tasks together. Meeting a challenge such as this actually built safety in the class. The clear roles established early on worked for us.

Make Norms Explicit

All groups have norms, defined most commonly as the acceptable standards of behavior that are shared by members of a group. In every group, in every class, norms emerge. During the first weekend of this course I always focus on establishing norms to ensure that those that do emerge support the learning process. It is critical to make the implicit explicit so the group can move forward to the challenges of learning and not stay stuck in process. Richard and Patricia Schmuck (1975, p. 168) were among those to examine this sequential aspect of class development: "Indeed, if the members of a class never develop a foundation of basic interpersonal trust and closeness, they will have a hard time proceeding to more advanced stages of group interdependence."

When there is explicit discussion of acceptable standards for a learning-centered classroom it extends the process of establishing clear roles by establishing how the class will be conducted. The learners connect the principles guiding the course to their own work in the course. For example, they learn up front that they will be working in small groups (teamwork) and responding to learning tasks designed to incorporate ideas, feelings, and actions. They learn that they are expected to be active participants, and the term *active* is clearly defined and framed as *praxis*—action with reflection.

This explicit norming does not take long, but it must be intentional and accompanied by setting the technical product outcome expectations of the course. This is directly related to grading. I do not begrudge learners the grade discussion. It is relevant to them and to me; it is an important part of the evaluation system. Being explicit, detailed, and clear about course product outcomes is important. In fact, if product expectation is not clear, the ambiguity gets in the way of learning.

Confluent Education

The principle of learning with ideas, feelings, and actions (Vella, 1995, 2002) is based on Bloom's taxonomy of educational objectives, and it leads the teacher to design learning tasks that include aspects of each element for optimum learning possibilities. The power behind the idea of getting the whole person engaged in learning is supported by my graduate work in confluent education. This has at its core the premise that effective learning results from the integration or flowing together of the affective and cognitive elements in individual and group work (Brown, 1990). Continued work in management and group dynamics theory indicates that the most productive work groups balance the needs of individuals, group maintenance, and task maintenance (Coover, Deacon, Esser, and Moore, 1985). Graduate work in an accelerated program that includes two twenty-one-hour sessions is not in any way abridged. Students need all the power and efficiency they can get. We hit the ground running. As one student put it: "When you said 'hit the ground running' I felt like I'd be hitting the ground all right, after jumping off a cliff. I can't believe I survived!"

So even on the first Friday night, significant content learning tasks, intentionally sequenced from simple to complex, are explained and begun. This is a way to make visible the complete picture of the learning exchange—an active exchange between teachers and learners from a foundation of trust to create and use new knowledge. For example, on the first night learners will have anxiety, needs, and questions, even after having completed the LNRA. New causes for anxiety and new questions emerge as they form into a group. That does not stop them from doing serious content work. A critical component in feeling safe is doing significant work. We create an environment that is safe enough to meet the challenge of learning.

Individual questioning, small group formation, and significant content work for learning all happen simultaneously, by design. In this intensive weekend course for educators, I include feedback skills and class synthesis notes. These are examples of ways to build and support a framework to bring order amid the creative chaos of the learning challenge. These are ways to implement the axiom: "Be highly structured in order to invite spontaneity" (Vella, 2002).

Feedback Skills

During each class I include a series of learning tasks aimed at introducing and practicing the skills of giving and receiving feedback. Most adult learners are afraid of feedback. They do not have the words to use and are afraid of offending, and they are afraid of being attacked themselves when their turn comes. In Dimensions of Learning and Teaching, learners learn and then practice specific elements of *giving* effective feedback—such as "feedback that is directed toward behavior which the receiver can do something about" and feedback that "is specific and descriptive rather than general and judgmental" (Vella, 1995, pp. 48–49). They also learn and practice effectively *receiving* it. More important, these feedback skills are themselves used, critiqued, and refined as an integral part of the course. They inform our emerging communication system and become our language of safety.

Effective feedback skills prove both practical and productive as students design, write, and rewrite research papers. In this particular class, through peer interviews and editing sessions, learners benefited from both giving and receiving professional critiques. They became confident in their skills and thrilled with the power of this type of dialogue—gaining solid information on strengths and suggestions for change from individuals they trusted and respected. The bottom line is this: learning is facilitated by effective feedback, whether positive or negative. Time spent in learning tasks around feedback is an investment in safety that produces immediate and ongoing rewards.

Class Synthesis Notes

At the end of each weekend the walls of our classroom are papered with charts showing the students' vibrant and detailed work. I take all this and synthesize it into class synthesis notes, which I send out to all of them. These notes speak of the active doing that formed the class. Synthesis notes reinforce and document that learning. The experiential learning shown on the walls of this exciting classroom and captured in the synthesis acknowledge the amount and significance of the work done by the learners.

I agree with Vella (2002) that it is the instructor's role to structure the learning, set tasks without ambiguity, provide resources, and then get out of the way so the significant work of learning can happen! Class notes offer me the opportunity to link concepts generated in class to theory or other key points, and suggest further readings.

Meeting a Live Problem

In this particular course session, there was a noticeable undercurrent of tension between some class members during the second weekend together. Anxiety over possible conflict was palpable from table to table and clearly was getting in the way of learning. I addressed this live issue by inserting a new learning task into the day's agenda. I made the discontent explicit and framed it as part of the usual developmental process. I described a normal group formation process using Tuckman's (1965) four-part forming, storming, norming, and performing model. I invited the class to look at their own group formation process. They were able to identify and resolve the source of the conflict and plan for problem solving if it happened again. The learners were able to do this because they had the tools. They knew how to give and receive feedback. They were comfortable working on difficult learning tasks in groups. They were coming from a base of mutual respect, and they wanted success in this course for themselves and for the group.

The learners' experience with the practice of dialogue education allowed them to take on this new task and resolve their conflicts in about forty-five minutes, rather than stewing in them for the whole weekend and possibly carrying them on to their next course. The structure held in the face of this challenge. Teaching through dialogue education does not mean letting go of control, but rather holding it differently.

Conclusions

Planning a university course based on the principles and practices of dialogue education (Vella, 1995, 2002; see also the appendix to this volume) is a huge investment of time and energy. I do it for the reward of knowing exactly what I am doing and why I am doing it. I do it because I learn along with the graduate students. I do it for the joy of working with learners who, having been drawn into learning by these principles, are transformed themselves into teachers who can use dialogue too.

References

Brown, G. *Human Teaching for Human Learning: An Introduction to Confluent Education*. New York: Penguin Books, 1990.

Carbone, E. *An Innovative Approach to Nutrition Education Informed by Key Principles and Practices of Adult Education*. Unpublished manuscript, University of Massachusetts at Amherst, 2002.

Coover, V., Deacon, E., Esser, C., and Moore, C. (eds.). *Resource Manual for a Living Revolution*. New York: New Society Publications, 1985.

Knowles, M. *The Modern Practice of Adult Education*. New York: Cambridge Books, 1980.

Reiff, M. *Adults in Graduate School: A Qualitative Study of How Experience Differs for Persisting and Nonpersisting Students*. (Doctoral dissertation, University of California at Santa Barbara, 1992.) *Dissertation Abstracts International*, Mar. 1993, *DA1-A53-09*, 3084.

Schmuck, R. A., and Schmuck, P. A. *Group Processes in the Classroom*. Dubuque, Iowa: Brown Company, 1975.

Tuckman, B. W. "Developmental Sequence in Small Groups." *Psychological Bulletin*, 1965, *63*, 384–399.

Vella, J. *Training Through Dialogue: Promoting Effective Learning and Change with Adults*. San Francisco: Jossey-Bass, 1995.

Vella, J. *Taking Learning to Task: Creative Strategies for Teaching Adults*. San Francisco: Jossey Bass, 2000.

Vella, J. *Learning to Listen, Learning to Teach: The Power of Dialogue in Educating Adults*. San Francisco: Jossey-Bass, 2002. (Originally published 1994.)

Open Questions for Analysis and Synthesis

1. Examine the model shown in Figure 4.1. What does it tell you of the focus of dialogue education in this case?

2. How did the Seven Design Steps work for Dr. Reiff as she prepared for this forty-two-hour course? How was this process different from usual modes of preparation?

3. Dr. Reiff makes much of the small group interaction and learning tasks done together. Which of the principles and practices came into play to make this work well for all learners?

5

Dialogue Education in a Videoconferencing Classroom

An Undergraduate-Level Early Childhood Certificate Program

Steven I. Stahl

V ermont is a small state, studded with mountains, rivers, and valleys, with a population of about six hundred thousand people. The mountains and valleys create serious impediments to travel, especially during the long and sometimes severe winters. To provide in-depth training to child care providers across the state, the Family Center of Washington County (the Family Center) in Montpelier, in collaboration with Community College of Vermont (CCV), established a training program using a statewide network of videoconferencing facilities. In this chapter, I offer a general description of the program—the Child Development Associate (CDA) Training Program—and details of one of its sessions, to demonstrate how this course was developed and implemented using the principles and practices of dialogue education. Here is an example of dialogue education in a community college undergraduate course.

The Seven Design Steps

This program was shaped as dialogue education through the use of the Seven Design Steps.

Who: Participants and Leaders

There were between twenty-eight and thirty-four actively employed child care providers and Head Start home visitors enrolled annually in this undergraduate course sequence. They worked with children, infants to five years of age, in center-based, family child care or home visitor settings. There was never more than one man enrolled in any given year. Participants' caregiving experience ranged widely from as little as six months to more than twenty years. Some participants had never taken a college course, whereas a few had college degrees in other fields. Participants were screened to ensure adequate writing skills to succeed in an undergraduate-level program. Use of the Internet for this program was not feasible. Among sixty program candidates enrolled during the first two years (1995 and 1996), only one had Internet access. Many students did not even have regular access to a computer for word processing. In 2002, convenient Internet access was still lacking for about half of the participants. I was the instructor for all classes during the first three years. I was employed by the Family Center and met the instructor requirements for the Community College of Vermont. All learners were assigned an early childhood professional as mentor as part of a practicum at their work site.

Why: Situation

The goal of this program was to increase the number of community child care providers competent to serve children with disabilities in a typical child care setting. In 2002, there were over forty-one thousand children under the age of five living in Vermont, and over 8 percent of them had a disability. Because the percentage of the population living in a rural area is higher in Vermont than in any other state, family isolation and lack of public transportation are two natural problems.

At the time this program was started in 1994, fewer than .02 percent of family child care providers had a degree in early childhood education. Most cited "raising my own children" or "babysitting" as their primary source of knowledge about children's needs. In center-based preschools, fewer than half the child care providers had a degree in early childhood education. A further indication of the need for training was the number of child care providers who had the nationally and state recognized CDA credential, highly valued as an indicator of quality care by the state of Vermont. In 1994, only ninety-two providers had this credential out of twenty-five hundred regulated facilities. This program was the only statewide program offering a college-based preparation track for the CDA credential.

When: Time Frame

Classes took place once a week for three hours per class, usually from 5:00 to 8:00 P.M., following the academic calendar. This was integrated with a four-credit field experience during which an early childhood professional conducted six formal observations and feedback with the course participant at his or her place of work. The total number of college class hours was eighty-four for two semesters, plus the four-credit practicum.

Where: Site

Each year, five of the twelve interactive television studios in Vermont were selected around the state. Each studio allowed for students to see, hear, and speak with participants at the other four sites through multiple television monitors and cameras. Each site had between three and fourteen participants. An exceptional feature of the facilities was that each site had a technician to aim and zoom cameras and adjust sound. Aside from the instructor (myself), who rotated through the sites, there were no other course facilitators.

Occasional private communications between sites were conducted using dedicated telephone lines.

Two of the twenty-eight classes were held face-to-face. Learners came to Montpelier for the first face-to-face class during the third or fourth class, after having had an opportunity to meet one another over the TV. The last class of the program was also face-to-face, and it was used for closure.

What: Content

There were two general content areas for this program. The first-semester course focused on supporting physical, cognitive, and emotional growth of all children. The second-semester course, Introduction to Early Intervention, built on the first course and focused on supporting children with disabilities and their families.

This chapter describes the fifth class of the second course. The success of this particular session, Family-Centered Practice, depended on the sense of community, respect, and trust established, as well as the skills, knowledge, and attitudes (SKAs) that had been developed from all prior sessions and the learners' reflection on and application of these SKAs in their workplace.

This session and one that followed were very powerful learning opportunities. They provided an occasion for participants to get a glimpse into the lives of parents of children with disabilities and to recognize the incredible struggles they go through. It was a time when participants could ask parents questions in a safe environment. These two sessions often provided decisive motivation for child care providers to overcome long-held reservations about serving a child with disabilities. The remaining class sessions developed the SKAs that were needed for many providers to take that leap.

What and What For: Content- and Achievement-Based Objectives

Table 5.1 provides the session content, and the corresponding achievement-based objectives for Course 2, Class 5, Family-Centered Practice: Part 1.

Table 5.1   Connections Between Content and Objectives

What: Specific Content	What For: Achievement-Based Objectives
	By the end of this class learners will have:
Concerns about caring for a child with disabilities	Identified and shared personal concerns about inclusion of a child with disabilities in the regular child care setting
Parental perceptions of inclusion issues	Dialogued with parents about their perceptions of issues surrounding inclusion of children with disabilities in the child care setting
Conflicts involving other professionals	Examined and solved a conflict involving another professional
Coping styles and strengths of families	Compared family coping styles and strengths
Circle of friends and professionals	Compared the circle of friends of a typical child and a child with disabilities
Conflicting priorities between providers and families	Examined conflicting priorities between parents and providers

Needs Assessment Procedures

All participants received a three-page learning needs resource assessment (LNRA). These were collected and analyzed prior to the first class. The curriculum was informed significantly by the first year's LNRA results. Results of the LNRA were shared orally, though in retrospect, I believe that providing a written copy would have been more respectful and provided more opportunity for examination and comparison with the students' own needs. At the end of the course sequence, individual LNRA forms were returned to students for reflection on their goals and actual learning. A common response was that they had not realized how much they did not know. Exhibit 5.1 provides a compact version of the LNRA.

Exhibit 5.1   Learning Needs/Resource Assessment Survey

By completing this needs assessment, you will be giving your input into the training program in which you will be participating. Your input will be very important to the development of specific course content. This course of study will be designed to address your needs. At the end of the program this form will be returned to you to allow you to compare how well the program content met your needs. Following are the objectives of this program:

- To learn "best practices" for *all* children birth to five years old

- To develop positive attitudes toward integrating infants, toddlers, and preschoolers with disabilities in regular child care settings

- To gain a broad knowledge base about specific disabilities, chronic health conditions, and accommodations for them in regular child care settings

- To identify the availability of professional resources, including health care providers and special education personnel

- To be well-prepared for assessment for the CDA credential

These goals will be addressed using the framework of the CDA competency areas. Considering the overall goals of the program, please complete the sentences in each area listed on the following pages. Do not be overly concerned with writing your input in the appropriate section. All input will be valued.

For each of the six competency goals of the CDA credential below complete the following two sentences:

I would like to learn more about . . .

A situation that a family or that I myself encountered that I would like ideas about is . . .

1. To establish and maintain a safe, healthy learning environment

2. To advance physical and intellectual competence (including physical and cognitive development, communication skills, and creativity)

3. To support social and emotional development and provide positive guidance

4. To establish positive and productive relationships with families

5. To ensure a well-run, purposeful program responsive to participant needs (program management)

6. To maintain a commitment to professionalism

Two or three parents of children with disabilities co-presented at each of the family-centered practice sessions. Even if some class participants were parents of children with disabilities themselves, it was important for us to hire external co-presenters to provide an unbiased perspective. This provided safety for students who might not feel comfortable discussing such personal information. These parents were asked to share a history from prebirth, describing the support they received, conflicts with others they encountered, personal struggles, and both positive and negative experiences with child care. Parents were prepared for dialogue and were encouraged to bring personal photographs to give the class a better sense of their child.

The Learning Tasks

I provided numerous resources to the learners in a large packet mailed at the beginning of the semester. The participants also used two textbooks that included discussion of family-centered practice issues.

Learning task #1. Your concerns

1a. In small groups generate a list of all concerns you have about caring for a child with a disability in your child care setting. Write your list on a chart so all in your group can see it.

1b. In the large group, address those concerns. As new concerns are raised by other groups, add them to your own group's list.

This learning task resulted in a list of the issues that still concerned the participants at this point in the course. Sharing these lists demonstrated respect for participants' concerns and provided co-presenters insight into the group.

In a videoconferencing environment, group activities have some limitations and some opportunities that would not be present in a face-to-face environment. In this task, for example, participants put their chart on camera so it could be seen at all remote sites while it was being presented. The site technician was able to split the screen so that the face of the presenter was seen simultaneously. Small group activities were no different from in a face-to-face situation. Out of respect, and to maintain a safe learning environment, I never listened in on small group discussions without the participants' knowledge of my presence even though it was possible to do so.

Learning task #2. Parents' stories

2a. Listen to these stories from our guests who are parents of children with disabilities.

2b. What are your questions for our guests?

By this point in the course, the videoconferencing technology had become transparent for most students. An incident illustrates this: one student laughed when she realized she was addressing her comments to my image on the monitors, although I was in the same room with her! Dialogue flowed quite naturally across the state from site to site, although comfort with the technology was not universal. Little courtesies were developed, such as waiting a few seconds before speaking in order not to interrupt someone from a distant site, and stating one's name to identify oneself first when speaking.

Learning task #3. Coping styles

3a. Choose a family you know well. List some coping styles and strengths of this family. Share with your site group. Write these on a chart so they can be shared with the larger group across the state.

The biggest surprise here was learning how differently we all cope with stress, and the realization that we cannot expect others to cope in the same way we do. The stories were rich, but were all in the context of the parents who were present and whose strength and apparent success in coping was compelling. Notice that this task is entirely inductive: they all have had a great deal of experience with families!

Learning task #4. Our values and theirs

4a. In your small group, describe one time in your work with families when you saw that your values and theirs differed. Share your responses with the statewide group.

4b. Ask the copresenter parents present how their response might differ from yours. We'll hear their response.

I noticed how parents and other learners shared perspectives not previously considered. There were sometimes what appeared to be irreconcilable differences among these perspectives, but through dialogue, new understandings were gained, even if issues were not fully resolved.

Learning task #5. Circle of friends

5a. View the section of the video in "With a Little Help from My Friends" that describes the circle of friends and professionals in a child's life. Name in your small group what is different for a child placed in a special classroom, compared with a typical child in a regular classroom or in your child care setting.

5b. Share the differences you have identified with the large group.

This use of a video in a telecommunications course was successful because of the learning task done in the small group. The different perspectives were shared and documented. The video was not seen as prescriptive but as evocative of theory appropriate for their context.

Principles and Practices

Using dialogue education in a distance education environment relies on the same principles and practices as those used in a course taught face-to-face. The following are a sample of the principles and practices we relied on in the design and implementation of this undergraduate college course. In fact, all of the named principles and practices of dialogue education were operative during this course.

Learning Needs Resource Assessment

Though this step is important in any program, a distance environment is enhanced greatly by such communication between students and teacher prior to the course.

Immediacy

Materials and concepts were designed for use in the classroom as well as in the work setting, often resulting in immediate *transfer* of learning occurring during the program.

Praxis

One student mentioned how important it was to be able to apply ideas the next day in her work setting. She knew that her doing so would be followed by class discussion the next week. This was the single most valuable aspect of the program for her. Another student reported, "Every other person in the class has had an impact on what I now do in my program." She was including everyone, not just those present at her site.

Learning Tasks Done by Students

Having students carry out learning tasks was particularly important in maintaining engagement in this videoconferencing environment. College courses taught via videoconferencing are often lectures using a talking head; the dialogue education design prevented this.

Respect and Affirmation

According to Bruner, "Any subject can be respectfully taught at any level" (cited in Kolb, 1984). Vella (1995) stresses the importance of lavish affirmation; "What is encouraged here is the learning, not the product" (Vella, 2002, p. 152). One child care teacher recognized the parallel between the program's instructional methodology, family-centered practice, and child-centered practice. She wrote in a reflection assignment:

> What surprised me was the correlation in our work with children using a child-directed approach: your teaching style in class, in which you guide the format yet leave it up to us to find out the answers on our own, and the framework behind the IFSP (Individualized Family Service Plan). All of these philosophies rely on mutual respect for everyone involved. The use of positive reinforcement and important communication skills such as listening and feedback is so very important if we are to understand another person's world.

Learners as Decision Makers

Upholding this principle is what contributed most to the learning and increased self-confidence of the participants of this course. One administrator in the state's child care services division commented, "People from the CDA course seem to be popping up as leaders all over the state."

Adult Growth and Development: Learning That Goes Beyond Content

The principles and practices described by Vella (1995) and the activities described in this chapter supported several developmental intentions identified by Taylor, Marienau, and Fiddler (2001) that enhanced the personal growth of participants beyond the focused content of the course. These examples illustrate that dialogue education, even at a distance, can go beyond simple inquiry-based or constructivist learning approaches. The personal growth of participants that occurred during this program was an unexpected but most welcome outcome. Increased self-esteem developed as a result of numerous aspects of the program, including the following:

- *Knowing as a dialogic process*. Participants learned to associate knowledge not with static fact but with contexts and relationships.

- A *dialogic relationship to oneself*. Learners found ways to address fears of losing what was familiar and safe to reach new understandings about the world and their relationship with it.

- *Connection with others*. Class members became adept at addressing the affective dimension of their work, while respectfully confronting differences in perspectives (Stahl, 2001).

Strategies Used to Enhance the Effectiveness of Videoconferencing

Here are some of the strategies we used in the course to make the most of videoconferencing. These are all simple courtesies and attentions. In this setting they worked well for excellent teaching and effective learning.

Trusting That Learning Is Really Happening

Initially, the most disconcerting feeling for me, as an interactive television (ITV) instructor, was the uncertainty about how participants were responding to the lessons. A good deal of trust was necessary to let the students work independently, particularly when those at remote sites were neither seen nor heard during small group activities. I had students complete reflection assignments weekly. These were both revealing and comforting to me as instructor. In addition, I used occasional simple feedback surveys with all the students and found them very helpful.

Using a Laptop Computer

I used a laptop computer linked to the ITV system to delineate tasks and for creation of class-generated lists. We used word processing software and PowerPoint presentation software regularly. Using a word processor in a videoconferencing situation is similar to using a flip chart in a traditional classroom. What I wrote could be seen and read easily at all sites simultaneously. It also had the advantage of being printable for later distribution to students.

Quick Pacing

When a learning task was assigned, a relatively short time was allowed for response. This period was extended when participants indicated that they needed more time to complete the task. The pace was always quick. Keeping students on-task is more difficult in a videoconferencing environment because the instructor may not know when the group is distracted. I felt, however, that some off-task behavior was actually desirable to promote personal connections between learners. These connections might extend beyond the life of the program.

Emphasizing Small Group Interaction

Small group learning tasks created a safe place for students to share ideas without feeling uncomfortable about "being on TV" or presenting to a large group. Many students commented that most of their learning occurred in their small group work. Without small group work, opportunities for all individuals to engage and dialogue would have been compromised.

Promoting Peer-to-Peer Interaction Through Camera Work

The instructor is usually the center of attention in an ITV environment. In order to foster peer-to-peer interaction, I encouraged the technician at my site to put camera shots on the group rather than on me. When I was speaking, the image was sometimes split so students in the class could be seen. It was critical that when students at another site were speaking they could feel that they were in dialogue with other students, not only with the instructor.

Sending Copies of the Class Design to All Sites

Hard copies of the class designs were mailed to sites for students to access before every class session. This was necessary, because on-screen text often did not remain on the monitors of distant sites long enough for students to read and reread instructions. We still posted the instructions on the monitor. This gave the students clear visual messages about what they were supposed to be doing and when. At times when I failed to use this visual aid, the class tended to get lost.

Returning Homework Quickly

Students appreciated rapid return of their homework. Homework was collected at each class session and mailed to me by a student. I reviewed and sent it by return mail to the studio for the next class session. This provided important feedback so students could make improvements and maintain momentum for future assignments.

Development of Theory: Dialogue Education in Distance Teaching

The child care provider program described in this chapter was a launching point for me into the field of distance education. I have for several years now also been adapting the principles and practices to Web-based instruction. I have developed manufacturing courses for business, curricula for universities, and train-the-trainer courses for teachers who want to teach on the Web at the university level. Whereas the old paradigm for distance education was independent study, new technologies have allowed the development of community and dialogue without regard to time or place. However, thoughtful design is essential to support these capabilities.

Conclusions

Designing for new modes of learning puts new meaning on several of the Seven Design Steps. For example, "where" now often refers to someone's home or office and to the specific tools and technologies learners can access. "When" no longer refers only to a specific time frame but also to how much time to allow between tasks. And "who" now needs to consider whether the learners can work well independently and if they have the necessary computer skills. The "why" and the "what" seem to be the only steps that have not changed. The "what for" remains central: achievement-based objectives that lead to learning tasks. *How* one creates the interaction with the content, with other students, and with the instructor may vary dramatically. For example, addressing auditory and kinesthetic learning styles can be extremely challenging, and in most cases requires off-line assignments. The exciting part is that the process and principles all work to demonstrate that the fundamentals of learning have not changed. New technology enhances epistemology.

References

Kolb, D. *Experiential Learning*. Englewood Cliffs, N.J.: Prentice-Hall, 1984.

Taylor, K., Marienau, C., and Fiddler, M. (eds.). *Developing Adult Learners: Strategies for Teachers and Trainers*. San Francisco: Jossey-Bass, 2001.

Stahl, S. "Working with Parents as 'Expert' Co-presenters." In K. Taylor, C. Marienau, and M. Fiddler (eds.), *Developing Adult Learners: Strategies for Teachers and Trainers*. San Francisco: Jossey-Bass, 2001.

Vella, J. *Training Through Dialogue: Promoting Effective Learning and Change with Adults*. San Francisco: Jossey-Bass, 1995.

Vella, J. *Learning to Listen, Learning to Teach: The Power of Dialogue in Educating Adults*. San Francisco: Jossey-Bass, 2002. (Originally published 1994.)

Open Questions for Analysis and Synthesis

1. What did you see Dr. Stahl do to use the principles and practices to ensure learning for all involved in this undergraduate videoconferenced course?

2. How did the Seven Design Steps seem to work for him?

3. What one thing did you see him do that struck you as most effective for building the confidence of these child care providers?

6

Dialogue Education at a Student Union
College Students as Adult Partners

Jay Ekleberry, Mary Hoddy, Tara Cordes

This chapter describes how dialogue education became the
modus operandi for the diverse program offerings at the Student Union of the University of Wisconsin.

The Wisconsin Union

After listening to the dialogue at an impromptu meeting of the current
student officers of the Wisconsin Union, the program director does
not feel the need to add much. The officers are sharing ideas about
how they plan to conduct a transition meeting with the incoming student program board. At the center of the discussion is how to create
a safe environment for the new board and ensure respect for the
knowledge and experience that these new leaders will bring to the
meeting. The program director is pleased with the meeting planning
that is being done and quietly affirms the direction of the student
leaders.

The Wisconsin Union is officially known as the Division of
Social Education of the University of Wisconsin-Madison. Since
1997, efforts have been under way at the Wisconsin Union to bring
more dialogue education to the training of both the student leadership and the part-time staff. Using peer-to-peer learning with
dialogue is at the core of these efforts. A willingness to stay engaged

in the established dialogue leads to new ideas that were unknown before the dialogue began. The key to creating a dialogic organization is keeping the core principles of training in dialogue (Vella, 2002) at the forefront while encouraging both practice and praxis. Five years of efforts to instill dialogic adult learning principles while offering opportunities to use and reflect on those principles have planted the seeds of a dialogic learning organization.

The Wisconsin Union is one of the busiest and most active student unions in the world. Over twenty thousand people pass through its doors daily. Approximately 1,000 part-time employees and a permanent staff of 160 provide programs, services, and facilities seven days a week.

The union serves as the unifying force on the large and decentralized University of Wisconsin campus, which is a community of forty-five thousand students with a staff of approximately fourteen thousand. In addition to offering a wide variety of basic services from food to recreational opportunities, the union's student program board and approximately three hundred volunteers offer close to a thousand programs annually. These are attended by over three hundred thousand people.

The Wisconsin Union has a long history of student management of both the program and its day-to-day operation since its inception in 1928. The union is governed by the Union Council, which is a board of fifteen with nine student members. The three officers of the student program board are also the officers of Union Council. The council and its committees, with student majorities, deal with all aspects of the union's operation and program, except staff personnel issues. In day-to-day operations the union makes liberal use of student manager positions in all sectors. Student building managers are on duty most open hours of operation. The daily decisions of the union, whether determining overall policy or granting a customer a refund, are made by students. These decision makers are the targets of the union's efforts at training in dialogue.

Dialogue as Part of the Leadership Model

The student committee director sits behind the closed door of the program director's office, contemplating the question of whether she will continue to be a member of the student program board or simplify her life immensely and resign. The program director asks her to consider what kinds of things she would hope to learn and accomplish should she decide to stay on. The student director easily generates a list of significant personal learning and program goals to aid in this important decision.

There are some fifty-five student leaders of the union's programs, including three officers, ten committee directors, and a variety of area coordinators. Their leadership training enables them to lead the approximately three hundred student volunteers who make the thousand program offerings happen each year. This training covers everything from the union's history to volunteer management to how to conduct effective meetings. The expectation is that these student leaders will then take these skills and train the student volunteers with whom they work.

The staff of the Wisconsin Union who advise these student leaders use dialogue education and the Seven Design Steps (Vella, 2002) to coordinate the overall training and in the individual training sessions at leadership retreats. The goal is to establish a true partnership in meeting the mission of the union.

Student Advisers: Union Staff Mentor Student Leaders

In their role as educators, student advisers in the student-staff partnership help ensure that the student leaders are the subject of their own learning (Freire, 1972) during their time at the union. This means the learning is centered on the student leaders, what they bring to the partnership, and what they would like to take away from the experience. The students are not perceived as instruments for the implementation of the union's agenda. Rather, they are seen as partners advancing an agenda that they helped design. Full respect is given to the experience and know-how that students bring to the relationship.

"In the long run it is this mutual sharing of experience and aspirations, this friendly give-and-take among the older and younger members of the community, that has made the union a thriving, exciting, and rewarding institution" (Butts, 1970, p. 50).

Another role played by the student advisers is as questioners. There are certainly times when they offer direct answers, options, or opinions. But more often they help the student leaders put another frame around an issue by asking powerful questions. This also helps push the dialogue further in directions that are important to the individual student. The participants achieve fuller consideration of the decisions that need to be made as a part of the daily business of the union. This method also aids in the maintenance of the partnership.

Finally, the student advisers serve as models for the student leaders. This modeling goes beyond civility and professionalism. They demonstrate balance between good work, attention to personal needs, and involvement in the community. They champion the power of reflection, praxis (Vella, 2002), and the opportunity to experience true dialogue (Bohm, 1996).

The Power of Peer-to-Peer Learning

The group of student program facilitators is brainstorming ways to bring more engagement and physical motion to the Respect in the Workplace section of the workshop titled Union 101. "We could define respect as a large group." "Why not look at both respect and disrespect on a continuum?" "Sharing stories is more engaging than creating a definition." "How about having participants think of a personal story, stand where they would place their story on a continuum of respect and disrespect within the room, and then share their stories with each other!" These student facilitators are on the road to increasing the level of engagement in the training session and ensuring a greater impact.

Students present all required training sessions to new employees. This peer-to-peer training makes the training more influential and allows the union to set an expectation of dialogue from the very first orientation of its employees. A cadre of student trainers present these workshops on a regular basis in a wide array of topics, from cashiering to food safety to occupational safety. The union's staff education office recruits these student facilitators from the front lines of the union.

All the student facilitators undergo train-the-trainer programs based on dialogue education. Their training is designed to help them model and create an environment of dialogue. They attend bimonthly meetings for continued training and support. Participants regularly engage in team reflection. The skills these student facilitators learn while becoming competent trainers are easily transferred back to their leadership positions in the Wisconsin Union and on campus.

The Seven Design Steps planning model (Vella, 2002) is central to the design, redesign, and evaluation of the learning sessions they present. Student facilitators answer the *who, why, when, where, what, what for,* and *how* questions as a first step to ensuring that they are centering on learning and the learners' needs.

The Challenges of Using Dialogue

The challenges of using dialogue education at the union have been in the learning experiences themselves. One of the biggest challenges is working around the expectations of the learners. They expect lectures on the topic. We teach the way we were taught, unless we learn a better way. Dialogue is seen as that better way and is used both to teach more effectively and to influence the union teaching paradigm.

Another challenge is avoiding alienating the learners by using the language of the methodology. This challenge is addressed by also using dialogue in meetings and workshops. Learning comes in doing and naming—that is, in praxis. A further challenge is that dialogue education takes time! Creating an experience of dialogue education demands adequate preparation. And then there is the philosophical challenge. "Dialogue does not serve those who see human beings as machines in a mechanistic universe" (Vella, 2002, p. 27). A future challenge will occur when we build the dialogue approach into the union's evolving efforts at on-line training.

Advancing and Enhancing the Approach

The effort to incorporate dialogue education over the last five years at the Wisconsin Union has led to an exploration of a variety of related areas. For example, there has been an exploration of the nature of dialogue itself. The works of Senge (1990), Yankelovich (1999), Isaacs (1999), and Bohm (1996) have been studied, wrestled with, and even taught to union staff. This has been done both at the faculty-based University of Wisconsin Teaching Academy and in presentations at professional conferences. This self-directed learning has helped participants understand the importance of creating a "flow of meaning between, through, and among us" (Bohm, 1996, p. 6).

Because it is based in dialogue and the belief that every system has positive aspects, appreciative inquiry (Cooperrider and Srivastva, 1999) has become a corollary area of study and a broadly used tool. *Appreciative inquiry* is a research approach that focuses on the affirmative and positive elements in a project. It has been used for strategic thinking, annual performance evaluations, and student leader exit interviews. The union also hosts a campuswide appreciative inquiry group that meets monthly to advance the knowledge and use of this philosophy. The approach has been identified as a key tool to help with efforts in improving campus climate. It works hand in hand with dialogue education. (Darlene Goetzman writes of this process in Chapter Twelve.)

This in turn has led to new efforts at better understanding and teaching the art of listening and coaching. Identifying *empathic listening* (Yankelovich, 1999) as one of the core elements of dialogue has forced the authors of this chapter to challenge our own levels of listening. We have also studied co-active coaching to help others advance the art of listening. Co-active coaches see others as "naturally creative, resourceful, and whole" (Whitworth, Kimsey-House, and Sandahl, 1998, p. 3). The students help set the agenda and the students and staff design an alliance to deepen the learning and forward the action. This has led to efforts to create "appreciative listening"—listening with assumptions suspended (Bohm, 1996) while in an appreciative frame of mind.

Given the learning-centered nature of this approach to training in dialogue, time has been spent studying and incorporating the wealth of brain-based learning research (Rose and Nicholl, 1997) that has recently emerged. This has refocused and refined the attention paid to the cognitive, affective, and psychomotor aspects of learning (Vella, 2002) and the personal learning styles of the students.

A Paradox for Students and Staff

Providing dialogue education to the students at the Wisconsin Union has created an expectation of this approach in all their learning. Their experience has shown them the kind of learning that occurs through this kind of engagement. By learning about the approach and successfully practicing it themselves in their own training efforts, they know that this methodology takes learning to a higher level. They know firsthand how creating learning in a dialogue environment can be effective in advancing a group of learners and in generating new knowledge.

The paradox develops when these students take this personal philosophy back to their primary reason for being at the university: getting academic credentials. The high degree on which their formal education still depends on a monologue-lecture approach leaves the students questioning its efficacy and quality. This same paradox confronts staff at the union who find themselves often disappointed in the professional development workshops or professional conference sessions they attend that are based on the traditional monologue model. The question that we confront daily at the union is how to move the University of Wisconsin to comprehensive dialogue on learning.

Conclusions

The student president of the Wisconsin Union is making his final remarks to the assembly of approximately three hundred volunteers at the end-of-the-year recognition banquet before passing the gavel to the incoming president. As he reflects on the year these student leaders have just experienced, he shares his feeling that the strength of the student program board lies in its learner-centered nature.

The Wisconsin Union strives to be one of the leading builders of community and community leaders on the University of Wisconsin-Madison campus. It has identified learning in dialogue and the creation of a dialogic institution as one of the keys to meeting this mission. Because of its successes in training both student leaders and part-time employees, the union is seeking methods to extend this dialogic philosophy to all the professional staff at the Wisconsin Union. Practice and praxis with dialogue education over the last five years have allowed the authors of this chapter to recognize quality trainers on the campus and in professional organizations. The union continues to seek new opportunities to influence the campus community while maintaining a commitment to present work at the union. We trust that refining this dialogue on learning will help the union extend this concept to the greater campus community.

References

Bohm, D. *On Dialogue*. New York: Routledge, 1996.

Butts, P. *The College Union Idea*. Bloomington, Wis.: Association of College Unions International, 1970.

Cooperrider, D., and Srivastva, S. *Appreciative Management and Leadership*. Euclid, Ohio: Williams Custom Publishing, 1999.

Freire, P. *Pedagogy of the Oppressed*. New York: Herder & Herder, 1972.

Isaacs, W. *Dialogue and the Art of Thinking Together*. New York: Currency/Doubleday, 1999.

Rose, C., and Nicholl, M. *Accelerated Learning in the 21st Century*. New York: Delacorte Press, 1997.

Senge, P. M. *The Fifth Discipline—The Art and Practice of the Learning Organization*. New York: Doubleday/Currency, 1990.

Vella, J. *Learning to Listen, Learning to Teach: The Power of Dialogue in Educating Adults*. San Francisco: Jossey-Bass, 2002. (Originally published 1994.)

Whitworth, L., Kimsey-House, L., and Sandahl, P. *Co-Active Coaching*. Palo Alto: Davis-Black, 1998.

Yankelovich, D. *The Magic of Dialogue: Transforming Conflict into Cooperation*. New York: Simon & Schuster, 1999.

Open Questions for Analysis and Synthesis

1. Examine a similar case of role transformation in the story of Chilean physicians in Chapter Twenty-Two. What are some ways you saw the team at the Wisconsin Union invite staff and faculty to change their roles?

2. How did you see the team incorporate parallel theories on learning and on evaluation into their new program?

3. If you were a student about to take a course at the Wisconsin Union and you faced a dialogue education design, how do you think you might feel? What did you see the team do to deal with issues of safety in this case?

7

Transformative Learning in Faculty Development
A Case Study from South Africa

Sarah Gravett

How can higher education teachers best be guided to adopt a teaching approach that deviates considerably from their existing practice? This is the challenge I faced when I received a request from the curriculum committee of a group of higher education institutions in the greater Johannesburg area. I was invited to assist them in designing and implementing an improved teaching methodology for the new curriculum they were in the process of developing. The teaching approach at these institutions could generally be termed teacher-centered. I aimed to help them adopt a teaching approach that would engage learners and teacher in mutual inquiry and exploration—learning-centered dialogic teaching (Gravett, 2001), informed by a social constructivist epistemology (Cobb, 1994; Driver and Scott, 1995). This chapter gives an account of that teaching development process.

The Development of Teaching: A Transformative Learning Perspective

Apps maintains that transformation cannot be imposed, because people are reluctant to change set patterns of thinking and behavior if they are not convinced that it is essential to do so. True transformation presupposes transformative learning by individuals. It involves an "enhancement of personal reality, as well as conversion of reality" (Apps, 1994, p. 211).

This implies that the fostering of transformative learning (Mezirow, 1998) is fundamental to development processes that aim to effect substantial revision of existing ways of thinking and doing. I argue that teaching development that focuses only on the improvement of technique or skill usually culminates in cosmetic changes. The teaching development process was consequently grounded in the notion that an intentional focus on fostering transformative learning about teaching practice would strengthen the likelihood of enduring and consistent change in teaching (Cranton, 1996).

Transformative learning occurs when a person faced with a disorienting dilemma modifies old assumptions or develops new assumptions or views of the world. The triggering event—the disorienting dilemma—leads through a process of critical reflection to an awareness of inconsistency among an individual's thoughts, feelings, and actions, or a realization that previous views and approaches do not seem adequate any longer. This kind of learning also includes an assessment of alternative views, a decision to negate an old view in favor of a new one or to make a synthesis of old and new, resulting in more dependable knowledge and justified beliefs to guide action (Wiessner and Mezirow, 2000).

In the terms developed here, this implies that teaching development activities should take as the starting point the faculty's points of view on being a higher education teacher—in other words, their informal (personal) theories of teaching (Fox, 1983). These tacit beliefs should then be brought into critical awareness through reflection on content, process, and premise (Mezirow, 1998). Content reflection refers to the *what* of beliefs, in this instance teachers' conceptions of the teaching process, and the meaning of both knowledge and learning. Process reflection alludes to *how* they came to the views they hold; premise reflection is on the *why* of beliefs—

why they perceive, think, feel, or act as they do during teaching. Teaching development activities then build on this reflection. This will assist teachers in consciously constructing an *informed* personal theory of teaching, which includes offering an explicit view of knowledge and learning and making clear how they perceive the role of students in relation to their teaching task. I firmly believe that teachers' conceptions of learning and knowledge have a direct bearing on their practice and the quality of student learning. For example, if teachers view knowledge as a body of fixed stable facts to be acquired by students they will teach to transfer these facts. Then, these teachers' assessment procedures most likely will require students to reproduce these facts. As students' perception of the assessment procedures in a course is generally the single most important influence on their learning (Biggs, 2000), students will focus their learning on complying with the assessment requirements they anticipate. They will reproduce the facts offered.

The Process of the Consultation

The process began with a workshop in which faculty were guided to voice and examine their assumptions, expectations, and feelings about teaching, knowledge, and learning. I hoped that this reflection and discussion would enable them to become aware of and clarify their beliefs and feelings and to identify gaps, flaws, and discrepancies in the belief system that informed their teaching, thereby opening it to revision. Thereafter, participants were guided in exploring and assessing the epistemology underlying dialogic teaching and the fundamentals of this approach (Gravett, 2001). Throughout the workshops participants did learning tasks (Vella, 2000) in learning teams.

I approached my role as that of mediator between the participants' existing personal theories of teaching and the dialogic theory of practice that I hoped we would co-construct. During this process I deliberately avoided advancing a specific version of dialogic teaching. I intentionally modeled a dialogic approach, hoping that I was conveying to the participants a way of being and doing. I also attempted to create a space conducive to participants' constructing their own versions of dialogic teaching, through not prescribing to participants but involving them in learning tasks designed for this purpose. Here is an example of such a learning task:

Learning task #3. The implications of a social constructivist perspective on learning for teaching

3.1. Listen to a short lecture on a social constructivist perspective on learning.

3.2. Having listened to the lecture, individually write down what you view as the core ideas of this perspective. Share these with your learning team. We will share a sample.

3.3. Examine the handout on a social constructivist perspective on learning. Underline what you find significant. What are your questions? We will share a sample.

3.4. In your learning teams describe four ways in which your knowledge of the learning process as gleaned from the lecture and handout will inform your teaching. We will share a sample.

I believed that a deep understanding of the fundamentals of and the epistemology underlying a dialogic approach, coupled with their encountering dialogic teaching in action, would enable faculty to construct a version of dialogic teaching that would fit their dispositions and contexts.

This phase of the teaching development process was conducted over a period of six months and consisted of twenty-four hours of face-to-face interaction spread over four workshops, involving approximately sixty faculty from all three colleges. Although participation in the workshops was voluntary, it was highly recommended in the colleges.

The participants were invited to keep a journal in which they recorded their feelings, their needs, and their problems with their implementation of dialogic teaching. These were supposed to be shared regularly with other participants at a meeting chaired by one of the participants (a coordinator selected by the faculty) at each institution. I hoped that this would allow the teachers to take ownership of the process. The coordinators monitored the implementation of the dialogic teaching approach and met with me twice during the first six months of implementation to facilitate feedback. Thereafter, I was available as consultant but the onus rested on the teachers to contact me for assistance via the coordinators.

Investigation and Findings

The purpose of the investigation was to understand the process involved in the construction and adoption of a new teaching approach that requires considerable revision of teaching practice. I employed qualitative data-generating methods. I kept a research journal in which I charted the progress of the teaching development process. Open-ended questionnaires were administered to gauge the participants' experiences of the workshops, and the feedback sessions with coordinators were tape-recorded. I further inquired into the teachers' experiences of implementing dialogic teaching through in-depth interviews after approximately ten months of implementation. The data generated were analyzed continuously and inductively by seeking recurring themes that would shed light on the purpose of the investigation (Merriam, 1998).

It was evident during the first workshop that the majority of participants had never intentionally reflected on their teaching practice and that many teachers lacked self-knowledge about it. This was confirmed by the participants' responses to the questionnaire that was administered after the workshop. Many mentioned that although they were very familiar with concepts like teaching, learning, and knowledge, they realized that they "did not quite understand" what these concepts imply. Their responses contained many contradictions. Notwithstanding that some participants described teaching as a "two-way process in a very complex issue," they saw themselves as teachers in the roles of "transmitters of knowledge, information, and wisdom." I believe this to be indicative of an inconsistent personal theory of teaching, which is usually the result of previous training focusing nonreflectively on techniques and skills without challenging prospective teachers intentionally to construct an informed theory of practice based on an explicit epistemology.

After analyzing the feedback of the first workshop my assumption that teaching development should commence with teachers critically reflecting on and articulating their existing informal theories of practice was reconfirmed. The data seemed to suggest that the critical reflection, induced through dialogue and reciprocal inquiry during the workshops, created a cognitive disequilibrium in the participants. Wlodkowski (1998, p. 107) explains cognitive disequilibrium as "the tension people feel when they experience something that does not fit what they already know. This tension causes them to involve themselves with the new experience until they can understand or fit it into what they know or can do." I believe that the disequilibrium induced by their critical reflection made the participants more responsive to the new teaching approach. Furthermore, the teachers' reflection gave me valuable insights into their existing views on teaching, learning, and knowledge, which I could then use as a base for the dialogue in the workshops that followed.

The main themes that emerged from the open-ended questionnaire and interviews were that all the participants regarded the workshops they attended as valuable and felt that the experience had been "positive and stimulating" in that it made them "actually think about what they were doing." Many also indicated that the workshops provided an opportunity for transformed perceptions about and meanings for teaching, learning, and knowledge, resulting in a general acknowledgment of dialogic teaching as a viable approach.

However, the feedback sessions with the coordinators and the interviews that were conducted with a sample of participants revealed that many struggled with implementation, although there were differences in the experience of faculty at the three participating institutions. Faculty at one institution (College A) voiced enthusiasm even though they expressed some difficulties. The data revealed that the majority endorsed dialogic teaching at College B, but that many struggled with implementation. It appeared that the majority at College C reverted to teacher-centered teaching, and some expressed serious misconceptions about dialogic teaching.

The faculty of College A indicated that they found dialogic teaching demanding, but that they and their students were generally flourishing. Typical comments included expressions of surprise at "what students can actually achieve if one involves them actively and trusts them as people who are able to think for themselves." Some mentioned that they valued the insights they had attained into the conceptions that students bring to the educational situation and how these influence students' learning: "Giving them time to discuss these things [issues they are about to study] helps me tremendously. I can try to slot into their thinking." Faculty at this institution attributed their relative success to the positive attitude and continual support of the management team and to collaboration and mutual assistance among staff. These teachers upheld the support system we initially set up at the institutions in that they held regular informal meetings to discuss problems, share successes, and support each other.

At the other two institutions this system ceased to exist after the initial six months, even though there was still a definite commitment to teaching development from the management of College B. The important role that support and collaboration play in sustaining changes in an organization, as reported by the faculty of College A, seems to be consistent with research reported by Yorks and Marsick (2000) on transformative learning in an organizational context. The interviews conducted with participants involved in a critical reflection program suggested that "sustaining changes in points of view in terms of behavior was most likely to occur with the continuous support of others. Participants who were isolated from other participants upon completion of the program were less likely to exhibit changes in behavior." In College C the support system not only dissolved, but it seemed that the member of the management team responsible for the management of teaching was not committed to the adoption of dialogic teaching in the institution. She expressed pessimism about the feasibility of implementing this approach because of a "lack of resources" and "student resistance." Her pessimism seemed to reverberate with many others at this institution.

Faculty from all three institutions expressed concerns about the issue of control. They admitted that they had felt safer and more in control with their old way of teaching. One of the teachers voiced her feelings of vulnerability: "I believe that dialogic teaching is the best way to go. But I feel very unsure of myself. With my old teaching I knew what to do. Now I ask myself all the time if I am doing the right thing. What if students don't do the work when they are working in groups?"

Another participant said: "I must confess. The teaching went well . . . well, most of the time. I enjoyed the interaction with the students and I think most of them also felt that the classes were stimulating. But then, just before the examinations, I started to panic. What if the students fail? And then I gave a lot of detailed lectures."

The feelings of insecurity were aggravated by the negative reaction of some students who resisted an approach that required active participation, probably because they were accustomed to a "banking" approach to education (Freire, 1972) in which they are the recipients of education from a know-all teacher: "Some students complain. They want you to do everything for them. If you don't lecture all the time and give them notes, they say that you are not doing your work." Faced with such adversity many of the teachers confessed that they often felt discouraged and wanted to revert back to their old way of teaching, which they felt at least provided them with the illusion of being in control.

A reservation expressed by many participants revolved around their ability to be "skillful dialogic teachers" without "more training in dialogic teaching methods." Participants insisted that they understood the fundamentals of dialogic teaching and that they were convinced of the benefits of implementing this approach, but that they needed tangible guidance in the "how" of dialogic teaching. This resulted in more workshops for College A and College B, in which a specific model for implementing dialogic teaching based on the Seven Design Steps (Vella, 2002; Gravett, 2001) was explored.

Conclusions

What insights have I attained from this teaching development process designed to facilitate transformative learning with the aim of enabling participants to become dialogic teachers? It was sobering to realize that responsiveness to an alternative approach, evidence of transformative learning in a teaching development process, and participants' positive experience of the process do not necessarily mean that a transformation of teaching practice will follow. Continual supportive relationships and a supportive environment seem to be vital when people are trying out new roles (Taylor, 1998; Mezirow, 2000) so that problems encountered may be addressed and successes celebrated, thereby reinforcing new perspectives and building competence and self-confidence in new roles.

I am still convinced that development aimed at facilitating fundamental change in teaching practice calls for the fostering of transformative learning involving critical reflection on and dialogue about assumptions on teaching, knowledge, and learning. However, I have come to realize that critical reflection and dialogic engagement do not necessarily enable teachers to use the epistemological knowledge that they construct as a basis for designing a personal teaching methodology consistent with the epistemology. Thus, contrary to my earlier belief that prescriptive "teaching recipes" should be avoided during teaching development, I am now moving toward the position that a teaching model for teachers to emulate could provide essential security, in turn allowing confident experimentation with a new way of teaching. A model could play a crucial role in building self-confidence and competence by granting faculty the opportunity first to follow the model, then to experiment with the model, and then to use it as a base for gradually constructing a personalized and contextualized teaching methodology. The model becomes a safety net. I am, however, still struggling with the question of when such a model should be introduced during a teaching development process. Should one, after having explored the fundamentals and rationale of an approach, invite teachers first to experiment freely with the approach without the restraints that a specific model inevitably provides? This could be advantageous to the development process. Introducing the model after some experimentation means that the teachers would have some experiential knowledge to draw on, and the model would then probably be more meaningful to them, because it could address their felt needs. However, as gleaned from the teachers' experience in this action research study, not introducing a specific model reasonably early in the process seems to lead to feelings of doubt and insecurity that can result in teachers resorting to the approach that is familiar, and thus comfortable, to them.

Therefore, when involved with similar teaching development processes in the future, I will most likely introduce the model explicitly as part of the initial development process. Thereafter, I will invite the teachers to experiment with the model, which will then be followed up by a feedback session (another workshop) in which questions, problems, and successes will be examined, discussed, and celebrated. Such praxis might make all the difference.

References

Apps, J. W. *Leadership for the Emerging Age: Transforming Practice in Adult and Continuing Education*. San Francisco: Jossey-Bass, 1994.

Biggs, J. *Teaching for Quality Learning at University*. Buckingham, U.K.: Society for Research and Open University Press, 2000.

Cobb, P. "Where Is the Mind? Constructivist and Sociocultural Perspectives on Mathematical Development." *Educational Researcher,* 1994, *23*(7), 13–20.

Cranton, P. *Professional Development as Transformative Learning: New Perspectives for Teachers of Adults*. San Francisco: Jossey-Bass, 1996.

Driver, R., and Scott, P. "Mind in Communication: A Response to Erick Smith." *Educational Researcher,* 1995, *24*(6), 27–28.

Fox, D. "Personal Theories of Teaching." *Studies in Higher Education,* 1983, *8,* 141–163.

Freire, P. *Pedagogy of the Oppressed*. New York: Herder & Herder, 1972.

Gravett, S. *Adult Learning. Designing and Implementing Learning Events. A Dialogic Approach*. Pretoria, South Africa: Van Schaik, 2001.

Merriam, S. B. *Qualitative Research and Case Study Applications in Education: Revised and Expanded from Case Study Research in Education*. San Francisco: Jossey-Bass, 1998.

Mezirow, J. *Transformative Dimensions of Adult Learning*. San Francisco: Jossey-Bass, 1998.

Mezirow, J. "Learning to Think Like an Adult: Core Concepts of Transformation Theory." In J. Mezirow and Associates (eds.), *Learning as Transformation: Critical Perspectives on a Theory in Progress* (pp. 3–34). San Francisco: Jossey-Bass, 2000.

Taylor, E. W. *The Theory and Practice of Transformative Learning: A Critical Review*. Information series no. 374. Columbus, Ohio: ERIC Clearinghouse on Adult, Career, and Vocational Education, 1998.

Vella, J. *Taking Learning to Task: Creative Strategies for Teaching Adults*. San Francisco: Jossey-Bass, 2000.

Vella, J. *Learning to Listen, Learning to Teach: The Power of Dialogue in Educating Adults*. San Francisco: Jossey-Bass, 2002. (Originally published 1994.)

Wiessner, C. A., and Mezirow, J. "Theory Building and the Search for Common Ground." In J. Mezirow and Associates (eds.), *Learning as Transformation: Critical Perspectives on a Theory in Progress* (pp. 329–356). San Francisco: Jossey-Bass, 2000.

Wlodkowski, R. J. *Enhancing Adult Motivation to Learn: A Comprehensive Guide for Teaching All Adults*. San Francisco: Jossey-Bass, 1998.

Yorks, L., and Marsick, V. J. "Organizational Learning and Transformation." In J. Mezirow and Associates (eds.), *Learning as Transformation: Critical Perspectives on a Theory in Progress* (pp. 253–284). San Francisco: Jossey-Bass, 2000.

Open Questions for Analysis and Synthesis

1. Have you ever felt the "disequilibrium" that Dr. Gravett describes? When? In what way do you see it as a necessary aspect of valid, significant learning?

2. What do you see as the decisive difference between the three cases described here? What do you believe Dr. Gravett could have done differently to deal with the opposition and the apathy met in two colleges?

3. A significant issue here is the use of a structured model for practice before learners can make their own theory and construct their own appropriate practice. What is your view on this: Use a disciplined, structured model or not?

Part II

The Public Sector and Not-for-Profit Organizations

In the public and not-for-profit sectors, the use of dialogue is welcomed by a democratic and populist tradition that claims to celebrate inclusion and dialogue. The principles and practices of dialogue education seem to fit these sectors, as well as challenge the distance that often exists between their stated policy and daily practice.

When dialogue education took over the design and practice of volunteer training in the well-known national Court-Appointed Special Advocate, or CASA, program (Chapter Eight), men and women who are passionate about what happens to children caught up in the court system found themselves learning what they needed to know to do their difficult and demanding job. Cynthia Bizzell shows how a curriculum and support materials offering a model can be effective in training tens of thousands of volunteers to quality performance. Her description is a useful segue from Sarah Gravett's realization that a strong guiding hand is necessary in teaching.

A team of designers and educators (Chapter Nine) show how a program of dialogue education can prepare teachers to work with a population perceived difficult to teach. Valerie Uccellani, Jyaphia Christos-Rodgers, and Mack Slan show the challenges of that program, and some initial indicators of impact. The New Orleans Jobs Initiative is funded by the Annie E. Casey Foundation. Its research focuses on discovering and documenting working models for safe communities. When the late Darryl Burrows (to whose memory we have dedicated this book) called me two years into the NOJI program, he confessed that he was confused. "Who are these kids?" he asked. "When I go to the classes, they greet me with courtesy and respect, engage me with open questions, and challenge me with alternatives, asking, 'Mr. Burrows, how about . . . ?' Jane, did *they* take the course in dialogue education or did their teachers?" As you see from this chapter, dialogue education creates an environment that is contagious.

The Mountain Microenterprise Fund (Chapter Ten) is another training program to prepare people for successful work—as entrepreneurs. Greg Walker-Wilson and his dialogue consultant, Joye Norris, show how they worked through significant obstacles to redesign training in business skills from a "banking" model to dialogue. Barbara Gassner (Chapter Eleven) also developed a group of entrepreneurs through a dialogue education program with welfare mothers. Her faith in their capacity to learn and to earn proved well-founded.

Working with the board of a county literacy program, Darlene Goetzman (Chapter Twelve), of Literacy Volunteers of America, demonstrated how appreciative inquiry, a process of evaluation and planning, can be enhanced by dialogue education. Attempting to change national policy is the agenda of NETWORK, a social justice lobby located in Washington, D.C. Michael Culliton (Chapter Thirteen) shows how dialogue education informed the formidable task of teaching NETWORK members across the country ways to influence Congress to deal equitably with welfare-to-work legislation. Jean Anliker (Chapter Fourteen) shows how materials in a nutrition curriculum were changed based on dialogue education. A state model is now available to the national Extended Food and Nutrition Education Program. Statewide efforts at enhancing the skills and knowledge of math and science teachers in Vermont through dialogue education have created a model that is being examined by other federally funded state math and science teacher institutes. The VISMT program is described by a team of instructors (Chapter Fifteen).

Karen Ridout shows how dialogue education informs strategic planning practices with not-for-profit board members (Chapter Sixteen) and Valerie Uccellani (Chapter Seventeen) demonstrates the development of a dialogue education training model in California's WIC program, the federally funded program for women, infants, and children that is in every state of the union.

Each of these cases can be seen as model-building. What occurs in California WIC is being examined in Wisconsin and Florida. What VISMT does successfully can be shared by math and science teacher institutes in all states. The North Carolina GAL volunteer training program is now being used by CASA nationally. Both public sector and not-for-profit sector programs are being touched by the accountable magic of dialogue.

8

Dialogue Education Goes to Court

The National Court-Appointed Special Advocate Association Prepares Volunteers Through Dialogue Education

Cynthia Bizzell

In the twenty-five years since the founding of the National Court-Appointed Special Advocate Association (CASA), over one million abused and neglected children have been helped by this program's volunteers. Community volunteers of CASA come from all walks of life, represent diverse cultures, and have varied educational backgrounds and experience. The characteristic common to them all is that they want to speak up for abused and neglected children whose cases are before our nation's family court judges. Today, there are sixty-thousand volunteer advocates serving in over nine hundred CASA (known in some states as Guardian ad Litem [GAL]) programs operating in all fifty states and the U.S. Virgin Islands. These volunteers participate in a thirty-hour training program in preparation for their role.

In June 2000, the National CASA Association published its revised *CASA/GAL Volunteer Training Curriculum*. The acknowledgments begin as follows:

> This revision of the National CASA Association *CASA/GAL Volunteer Training Curriculum* owes a debt of gratitude to Jane Vella, whose work on adult training through dialogue formed the basis for the training

approach, and to Cindy Bizzell, curriculum developer/ editor of the North Carolina Volunteer Training Program, whose application of the principles of adult learning to the North Carolina curriculum was the model for this revision of the NCASAA volunteer training program. Cindy served as a consultant to the committee, spending countless hours reading every piece of this manual and making gentle, positive suggestions that have kept it true to the learning principles on which it is based.

This chapter presents the steps we took in developing that curriculum, using dialogue throughout the process and showing it in the product.

The Curriculum Story

The North Carolina Guardian ad Litem (GAL) program was established in 1983 and is the statewide advocacy program that recruits, screens, trains, and supervises citizen volunteers who serve as advocates for abused and neglected children whose cases are before the state's courts. The North Carolina GAL program is a member of the National CASA Association network.

As staff were hired in North Carolina to launch the local programs, they were given a slim volume: *Legal Proceedings Involving Children: Abuse and Neglect Cases* (1997). This was a handbook for both attorneys and volunteer guardians ad litem representing children in abuse and neglect cases. It included eighty pages of text plus court forms and worksheets. This was the program's initial volunteer training course.

In the GAL program's first dozen years, as advocacy practice evolved and experience deepened, staff expanded the content of the training they provided to volunteers. Resources and materials that could supplement training were shared from program to program. By 1990, the training programs in local field offices were highly individualized and delivered training content mostly through staff lectures and guest speaker presentations. The volunteer trainees did few activities during training to apply the content to which they were being exposed. Local program training requirements ranged from twelve to twenty classroom hours.

North Carolina GAL volunteers completed their required training program with excessive theory and little experience applying that theory. They would finish their training, be sworn in by a judge, and then ask, "Now what do I do?" When new volunteers were assigned to cases, they were mentored one-on-one by program staff. However, as caseloads continued to climb staff had less time for individual work with volunteers.

In 1995 the program's budget was reduced by the state legislature. Lawmakers commented on the lack of uniformity and standardization across the state in GAL volunteer training and practice. Some programs were very strong and had a good reputation in their communities; others did not.

The budget reduction carried a decrease in the program's attorney fees. This resulted in staff taking on more of the nonlegal tasks that their attorneys had previously provided, resulting in even less staff time for volunteer mentoring and supervision than before. In addition, the program was understaffed even prior to the cut.

GAL had a training committee made up of local and state staff who were working on training issues, including attempting to revise the state's training manual, which by 1995 was largely a collection of information for volunteers. The budget cut prompted the state GAL office to move ahead with its plans to standardize its volunteer training curriculum. As assistant administrator of the program, I agreed to coordinate our efforts. I contacted Jane Vella on the advice of a colleague who knew her work. I took our training manual to her. She agreed to review it and offer suggestions for how she might help in the revision of our curriculum. I returned to see Jane a week or so later. She asked me, "Do you have a match?" I got the subtle suggestion that the training program needed a complete overhaul.

Jane suggested that I attend the Learning to Listen, Learning to Teach course of Global Learning Partners, Inc., and then lead the GAL curriculum creation project. She agreed to contract with our program as an adviser. I participated in the course and saw how teaching and learning designs based on principles for accountable adult learning resonated with the mission and philosophy of the GAL organization.

As I began the project, I proposed the following five guiding principles to senior staff:

- Training design strategically includes and excludes content based on its *relevance* to ensuring that the goals are achieved.

- Training is *accountable* to equip the learners to do the job they will be asked to do.

- Learners *practice* all components of their role during training.

- The approach of training design shifts the focus from *what the trainer is to cover* to *what the learner needs to learn*.

- Staff supervision of volunteers will focus on *strategic case issues* rather than process issues.

Guided by the Seven Design Steps, I worked with the senior staff to define *who* (the participants) for the training. We wrote broadly to invite participation from a diverse volunteer pool. We decided that *when* (the time frame) would increase to twenty-five hours and *where* (the site) would continue to be local program sites across the state. The *why* (the situation) reads as follows:

> These participants are coming together to be trained as guardians ad litem. They need knowledge, skills, and practice to be able to

1. Approach each case with the single goal of advocating for interventions and services designed to ensure as soon as possible that the child-client is in a safe, stable, and permanent home, and that court intervention is no longer necessary.
2. Work within the parameters of federal and state laws governing child abuse, neglect, and dependency cases.
3. Under the guidance of Guardian ad Litem staff they need to

> Independently gather facts and do continuing research about their individual cases to ascertain the needs of the child-client

> Collaborate with the child-client (when possible), the child's family, the department of social services, and other service providers to identify the appropriate resources for meeting the needs of the child-client and to determine where those resources are available

> Consistently design and present to the court fact-based recommendations that appropriate resources be ordered to meet the needs of the child-client

We drafted the *what* (content) and *what for* (achievement-based objectives) for review by the training committee, attorneys, judges, volunteers, and staff. In our collaboration, we named no fewer than thirty-three content areas and fifty accompanying achievement-based objectives.

I worked with local staff to create four training cases that were included in the curriculum along with juvenile statutes and court forms relevant to the volunteers' work. By the end of January 1997, I had written learning tasks for eight of the thirty-three units, using Vella's Four I's as a model (Vella, 2002): each unit had an anchoring task (*inductive work*), a learning task to present content material (*input*), a learning task in which participants applied the content just as they would be required to in their volunteer role (*implementation*), and a learning task that invited their creative use of the information (*integration*).

Jane Vella redesigned her Learning to Listen, Learning to Teach course, creating the course Training for Trainers of Volunteers to introduce GAL staff to dialogue education. This gave them an opportunity to try out this new approach by teaching a single unit from the GAL training. Eighty-three GAL staff attended one of six Training for Trainers of Volunteers classes in January through March 1997. During these sessions, they offered ideas for the learning tasks for many of the remaining units. Many of their suggestions are currently part of the curriculum. By May 1997, the curriculum was complete and ready to be tested in training sessions across the state.

Staff were invited to try out the new curriculum during the rest of the year and give feedback and suggestions for improvement. In January 1998, the North Carolina Guardian ad Litem program adopted its new curriculum. Here is one volunteer's feedback in a letter to a staff member:

> The GAL training I received was invaluable and "right on the money."
>
> Ongoing support and patience with my inexperience from staff is excellent and very much appreciated. Just

enough support to keep me headed in the right direction and just enough leeway to allow me to develop my own appropriate skills. Thank you.

In April 1999 the North Carolina GAL program hired a training administrator with funding from the National CASA Association. Mary Gratch, who had served as a local program director, brought a practitioner's touch to the curriculum. She worked collaboratively with staff to continue to revise and improve the curriculum, ensuring it maintained its dialogue approach and was accountable to its learners.

The Bridge from North Carolina to National CASA

As the North Carolina GAL curriculum was being developed, the program was sharing its experience with other states through the national CASA network. In October 1996, I gave an overview of the training program to state CASA/GAL directors. I was then invited to design and present a workshop—Introducing Dialogue into Your Volunteer Training Program—at the organization's conferences in 1998 and 1999. This workshop introduced participants to dialogue education and invited them to experience it for themselves. In 1999, the workshop time was increased from ninety minutes to three hours. During this longer session, participants used dialogue education to design training sessions with content I provided on a recent juvenile law change. In 1998, I was invited to be a member of the National CASA Curriculum Advisory Committee.

The National CASA Volunteer Training Curriculum Story

In 1998, the National CASA Association began the process to revise its 1990 comprehensive volunteer training curriculum by convening a curriculum advisory committee composed of representatives from a diverse group of state and local programs in the network. At the initial committee meeting in November 1998, members were given a copy of Jane Vella's *Training Through Dialogue* (1995). At this meeting, I gave an overview of dialogue-based training and shared North Carolina GAL's volunteer curriculum design experience with the group.

National CASA asked its member programs to complete a comprehensive survey to ensure that the curriculum revision would address the training needs of the CASA/GAL network. The curriculum advisory committee used the survey information to update the list of skills, knowledge, and attitudes required of volunteers. They determined the goal of the training to be to develop volunteers who are competent, reasonably autonomous, able to exercise good judgment, and focused on the best interests of the child in their role as CASA/GAL volunteers. The committee set a course for development of a skill-based, interactive, case-based, and practical curriculum to meet this goal (*Curriculum Advisory Committee Report*, 2000).

Paralleling the Seven Design Steps, the committee named new content (*what*) as it updated the skills, knowledge, and attitudes required of volunteers. It named the situation (*why*) in stating its goal for the training. The achievement-based objectives (*what for*) were delineated in the committee's decision to develop a skill-based, interactive, case-based, and practical curriculum. The participants (*who*) would remain broadly defined to invite a diverse volunteer pool. The site (*where*) would continue to be the local program training sites, and the time frame (*when*) would be no more than the forty hours required in the 1990 curriculum. By late 1999, we were ready to proceed to design the learning tasks (*how*) and contract with a curriculum writer.

Mary Gratch was hired to write the national CASA curriculum. She was already serving as a resource to the committee because of her work continuing to update and improve the North Carolina GAL curriculum. In June 2000 she completed the draft of the national curriculum, which paralleled the North Carolina GAL curriculum in its firm grounding in the dialogue approach.

A subcommittee of the curriculum advisory committee convened in March 2000 to design the training of facilitators course for the national CASA curriculum. The chapter "How Adults Learn" features fourteen of Jane Vella's principles of adult learning. The chapter "The Design of the Volunteer Training Curriculum" delineates her Four I's with new labels: Inductive learning tasks are labeled *anchors*, input is called *content*, implementation is named *application*, and integration is *future use*. The learning activities in the volunteer curriculum are coded in the facilitator notes as anchor, content, application, or future use activities.

In August 2000, a group of representatives from eight diverse programs was invited to participate in the national CASA training of facilitators course and then to pilot the new volunteer curriculum in their CASA/GAL programs. The curriculum advisory committee and National CASA Association program staff met in November 2000 and determined the revisions that needed to be made to the curriculum based on the pilot group's feedback. Mary Gratch then incorporated the feedback and completed the national curriculum in time for its scheduled release date.

Conclusions

The training session evaluations that have been shared with National CASA are positive. CASA network programs are enthusiastically using parts of the new curriculum in their training programs. The curriculum advisory committee is currently working with National CASA staff to develop an evaluation tool to determine the effectiveness of the new curriculum over time, in particular after volunteers have served on their first case. We have examined learning and transfer; now it is time to study indicators of impact (Vella, Berardinelli, and Burrow, 1998). This case shows how important it is to review and redo materials that are not effective, and how vital it is to get input from every level. This is a story of a praxis experience that will continue.

References

Curriculum Advisory Committee Report, 2000. Seattle: National Court-Appointed Special Advocate Association, 2000.

Legal Proceedings Involving Children: Abuse and Neglect Cases (3rd ed.). Raleigh: Administrative Office of the Courts of the State of North Carolina, Apr. 1997.

National CASA Association. *CASA/GAL Volunteer Training Curriculum* (rev. ed.). Seattle: National CASA Association, June 2000.

Vella, J. *Training Through Dialogue: Promoting Effective Learning and Change with Adults.* San Francisco: Jossey-Bass, 1995.

Vella, J. *Learning to Listen, Learning to Teach: The Power of Dialogue in Educating Adults.* San Francisco: Jossey-Bass, 2002. (Originally published 1994.)

Vella, J., Berardinelli, P., and Burrow, J. *How Do They Know They Know? Evaluating Adult Learning.* San Francisco: Jossey-Bass, 1998.

Open Questions for Analysis and Synthesis

1. What do you see the match as a symbol for when Bizzell was asked, "Have you got a match?"

2. Bizzell refers to selected principles and practices in this chapter. What *other* dialogue education principles and practices do you see her using in this situation?

3. What one thing did Bizzell and her team do that you see you can do in your work?

4. What do you think Bizzell means in the last paragraph of this chapter when she writes, "This is a story of a praxis experience"?

9

Changing the Self, Changing the System

A Workplace Success Program Succeeds with a Dialogue Approach

Valerie Uccellani, Jyaphia Christos-Rodgers, Mack Slan

O urs is a world of great inequities and lost potential. Fortunately, many powerful efforts are in place to change that. This chapter describes a program of the New Orleans Jobs Initiative (NOJI), which is part of a five-site national effort to build the possibility that low-income adults find and keep jobs with family-sustaining wages, benefits, and career paths.

Dialogue Education Arrives and Takes Root

NOJI's commitment to dialogue education began far away from New Orleans, in the city of Cleveland, in 1996. In that year, Dr. Jane Vella entrusted two of her Jubilee fellows to teach the course Learning to Listen, Learning to Teach. One of the participants in that course, Darryl Burrows, was so taken with the principles of dialogue education that he began to apply them, with rigor, to the urban African-American communities where he worked. Burrows became inspired by the reaction he observed among colleagues and learners. So in 1998, when he became the executive director of NOJI, he brought with him a strong commitment to apply these principles. For over four years, all NOJI staff and the staff of collaborating organizations have studied and worked with dialogue education principles in many different ways on a daily basis. Dialogue has not been a step in NOJI's journey, it has been the ground we walk on.

NOJI's most visible use of the dialogue approach has been through a twenty-one-day course entitled Twenty-First-Century Success Principles (a copyrighted name), which recognizes social connections, personal coping skills, and knowledge of predominant workplace culture as key factors to workplace success. The course content is deep, drawing on national research and local perspectives (Wilson, 1997; de Jesus, 1998). Staying faithful to principles of dialogue education, NOJI first developed a twenty-one-day topical outline, then a coursebook of structured learning tasks for teachers and a day-by-day workbook for the learners. To date, nearly seven hundred New Orleans residents have completed this demanding course.

NOJI's Design for Course Leader Preparation

Like other change efforts, NOJI aims to be more than a learning opportunity for individuals; it also works to reform the system, broadening labor opportunities and social realities. In the spirit of Paulo Freire, dialogue education is viewed as a tool of the people for transforming their world. Twenty-First-Century Success Principles course leaders are a critical layer in NOJI's overall scheme to bring about personal and systemic change. They influence the program participants directly through their teaching, and they influence the system broadly by spreading and voicing what they learn as instructors. This chapter focuses on NOJI's preparation of course leaders as channels of change.

Who

NOJI looks for course leaders who have a specific set of qualities and experiences. We have found that effective course leaders already know what they are going to teach: they have successfully found and kept jobs with family-sustaining wages. They may have little or no formal teaching experience, but they show that they can listen well, and patiently. Many are active in faith-based ministries and bring a spiritual perspective to their work. All course leaders to date have been African American and are longtime residents of New Orleans. Many have come through a struggle to survive and be successful. Their actions and bearing in the community still convey that they have not forgotten "where they came from."

Two GLP-certified instructors teach the course leader training sessions. Over time, several NOJI staff and consultants have become certified by Global Learning Partners (GLP) so that at least one GLP instructor has personal experience as a NOJI course leader.

Why

Most NOJI participants have held jobs but have not been able to keep a job with family-sustaining wages. Therefore, NOJI course leaders need to understand the underlying issues of unemployment and underemployment. Course leaders also need a framework for melding their own personal experience with the content of the course. They need to understand why the Twenty-First-Century Success Principles coursebook is structured as it is, so that they can adapt it and enhance it without destroying the intention of the learning tasks. Finally, they need guidelines for modeling the dialogue approach, and the keys to workplace success, so that all participants learn by watching their course leaders.

When and Where

There are three phases to course leader training: dialogue education (thirty learning hours, five days), individual field observations and study (three to four weeks), and workshop and practice teaching (thirty-five learning hours over three weeks). The best locations for this training have proved to be the same community centers where course leaders, in turn, teach NOJI's participants.

What and What For

The content of the course leaders' extensive preparation process intentionally builds at each phase. Phase one matches the standard content of the GLP introductory course: Learning to Listen, Learning to Teach. Here, NOJI emphasizes what is most critical in order to *use* (rather than design) a dialogue-based curriculum effectively. Learning tasks use examples from the field of workplace development but focus entirely on adult learning theory. After guided field observations, course leaders begin to study, in depth, three keys and eight habits for workplace success. Fundamental content includes code switching, self-affirmation, self-efficacy, coping with racism in the workplace, we're *all* difficult people, and can-do consciousness. In this final phase, course leaders practice how to teach Twenty-First-Century Success Principles effectively using principles of dialogue education. Achievement-based objectives are named throughout as a basis for self-assessment. These are also used for NOJI's assessment of course leader readiness.

How

NOJI designed this course leader preparation process with evaluation in mind. In phase one, course leaders' practice teachings demonstrate such key skills as the use of dialogue (not monologue) in sharing information and the effective exchange of feedback. In the final phase, practice teachings demonstrate such skills as completing the learning cycle when leading a task, avoiding getting "hooked" into parent or child mind-sets with co-teachers or participants, and carefully balancing safety with challenge across learning tasks.

After all three phases are completed, new course leaders are selected and paired with experienced ones to teach Twenty-First-Century Success Principles. NOJI does structured observations; course leaders also self-assess weekly on their strengths and areas for improvement. The focus is on transfer of the dialogue approach as a means to teach workforce success. Through course leaders' consistent modeling, we have found that participants learn principles and practices of dialogue education along with those of workplace success. Imagine, if you will, a room full of "brothers," African-American men—some out of school for many years, others newer to adulthood—working their way through this intensive twenty-one-day preemployment program. After a short lecture on some complex concept such as code switching, these learners themselves suggest a move to the circle to talk together better. There, they begin to ask open questions to probe and challenge one another's thinking. They offer one another—and the course leaders—suggestions in the form of "How about . . . ?" Clearly, the course leaders' transfer of dialogue principles has enhanced the participants' own use of dialogue for growth and self-expression.

Course Impact

How has the course leaders' use of a dialogue approach affected participants in the Twenty-First-Century Success Principles course?

Impact 1

NOJI participants have completed this demanding, monthlong course at a high rate of 83 percent over the last four years. Some 70 percent of program graduates have successfully transitioned into GED programs, technical training, or paid work. To date, 67 percent of NOJI graduates have stayed employed at least six months, a dramatic difference for many. But the most convincing evidence of an impact is, perhaps, what we hear and see from participants directly. Outwardly shy or angry adults on day one of the course find their voices. Over fifty videotaped graduation ceremonies are marked with self-affirming words, and thanks, from individuals who often say they have never felt so proud, so confident, so "ready" as they feel on that day. "I have had many jobs. I said, 'No way do I need this course. Twenty-one days? Are you crazy? I need a job now.' But I learned so much—not only about getting a job and keeping a job—but knowing myself and staying true to myself. I learned that

I can talk and that I have something to say." Participants who have retained their jobs report that their experience of Twenty-First-Century Success Principles (and in particular their relationships with their course leaders) has helped them make wise decisions. "I saved that workbook, you know—the green one we used in the course—and when I feel like I'm going to lose it—myself or my job—I go back to my notes and the stuff we talked about." We ask: Are changes in participants a result of NOJI's focus on workplace principles, or on principles of dialogue? The answer is *both*. They are now inseparable.

Impact 2

How has the approach affected the course leaders and the organizations of which they are a part? NOJI has witnessed much growth in course leaders as professionals and as educators: three NOJI course leaders are in the process of being certified as GLP instructors. Three have also become full-time NOJI staff. Many have grown their own businesses or ministries since their work with NOJI and they make many applications of dialogue education to their work. One entrepreneur recently shared a story of how the approach had transformed his business with budding musicians in New Orleans: "I suddenly saw what had been missing—I had to give them learning tasks—they needed to be accountable to themselves and follow a stepwise process for learning the skills they needed. It worked *great!*" Many NOJI course leaders are now sought after as consultants and workforce development specialists. They use dialogue education to shape new programs and advocate in arenas of the workforce development system. They advocate at national conferences to practitioners, policymakers, and funding organizations. They design for the Ford Motor Company, the New Orleans Neighborhood Development Collaborative, and the City of New Orleans. Their use of dialogue principles is influencing systems beyond NOJI as an organization.

The Principles: How They Work for Us

Although we have certainly fallen short at times, dialogue principles have guided all of NOJI's work with course leaders.

Safety and Respect

Safety and respect are established at the initial interviews when several different NOJI staff ensure that no applicant is being turned away based on the personality or culture of the interviewer. Mutual expectations, time commitments, and learning objectives are laid out in writing. Each phase of course leader training begins by invitation; no promise is made of a job at the end. We aim to honor course leader applicants' desire to explore all aspects of the job up front by arranging for veteran course leaders to respond to questions and share perspectives that neither NOJI staff nor GLP staff could share. Written feedback is offered in the context of a private conversation between the observer and the course leader, at a time convenient to the course leader. If there is a mismatch between a course leader's self-assessment and NOJI's expectations, we examine how NOJI might change to offer more support. NOJI participants are very vulnerable, requiring excellence in course leaders. Course leaders are not invited back to teach if they are not modeling the principles of workplace success or dialogue education. Their work should feel safe, but not secure.

Sequence and Reinforcement

Sequence and reinforcement have proven fundamental to course leader success. It has been tempting to take shortcuts—to abbreviate preparation or throw the leaders into a full twenty-one-day teaching experience without practice and feedback sessions. But we have seen value in the sequence and in learning over time. At first, course leaders are asked to stay quite faithful to the learning tasks as written. Co-teachers are rotated into pairs that mix and broaden their unique approaches. As they observe the innovations of more experienced co-teachers, they get ideas. As a result, course leaders have added important dimensions to the course, such as diversity in the workplace, the history and meaning of being African American, strategies for mindful budgeting and savings, and vocabulary building. They weave in song and inspirational visitors.

Development of Theory

NOJI has always been committed to assisting the people who have had the most difficulty accessing family-supporting jobs, and in this community they are overwhelmingly African American. From the beginning of this program, this commitment has meant attending to the relationship that individual job seekers have to societal systems and to historical racial oppression. Much of the work is intentionally antiracist and related to a larger movement: organizing to bring about equity in society. NOJI has received leadership and mentoring from the People's Institute for Survival and Beyond, a national collective of antiracist community organizers and educators. All course leaders and staff participate in the basic two-and-a-half-day workshop titled Undoing Racism, which focuses on history, culture, and power as tools for analyzing how society has been "racialized" and how it can be transformed. These grounded theories have helped to shape NOJI's overall program and the curriculum in many ways, especially in the development of the day titled Coping with Racism in the Workplace. Dialogue education fits well with antiracist principles because it is based on the principle of equity. All who participate are brought to an equal plane in a context of safety and respect as all input is validated. This experience deals directly with the overconfident who might dominate a group and with those whose confidence is shaky. We continually strive to craft learning tasks for participants to consider the realities of workplace racism. As staff, we examine our internal dialogues about race and culture issues, and try to discern wisely how to meet these challenges when they arise in the workplace. We invite course leaders and participants to do the same. The goal is to develop a cadre of course leaders who can facilitate learning and also carry personal insights into their own activities as community leaders and organizers.

It follows that an effective way to approach adult learners is one that resonates with their cultural experience. Among the population that NOJI serves, spirituality (not necessarily religion) is an important focal point that sets the tone for any kind of group work. In addition, an ethic of interdependence, of people looking out for one another, taking care of one another, also pervades the groups that enter these programs: "I feel like I can change my life. It was the group; they made me know I can do this."

NOJI aims to be attentive to these dynamics in designing all program features. The most successful course leaders are those who are aware of these things and make conscious use of them as they facilitate. Over the twenty-one days, each group of learners becomes an extended family, bound by their experience and struggle with the coursework and by a common sense of the importance of faith. At times this has posed some challenges as NOJI has worked to ensure that affirmation of the importance of faith does not feel like the imposition of religion in the learning setting. For example, a moment of silence or centering may turn into a prayer, leaving members of the group feeling left out or offended. This is not an easy balance to manage. NOJI works to have course leaders who are able to bring four sets of values together: (1) the best of the business mind-set; (2) a deep understanding of a learner-centered education; (3) clarity about the challenges that racism poses; and (4) strengths of a culture based on spirituality and interdependence.

NOJI's Present Construct

The use of principles by an organization feeds that organization. At NOJI we have found that respect always meets with respect. Course leaders are expected to be diligent in their course preparation, their attention to the needs of the learners, their flexibility in times of limited resources, their willingness to adjust to organizational changes and oversights. This kind of diligence is a critical part of their teaching because they are modeling diligent work behaviors. Dialogue marks our first encounter with course leader applicants, and we have found that this initial dialogue is invaluable. NOJI invites course leaders to offer feedback on all aspects of their course. This has proven very valuable for the organization. The freedom to give input and direction has, in turn, led many course leaders to engage and invest themselves in NOJI over the long term. The sense of team that has been established among course leaders is not accidental. It was all in the design! Conflict is a good thing. At NOJI we have learned that the greatest learning happens when there is conflict and the principles of dialogue are applied. NOJI has seen this work repeatedly in the Twenty-First-Century Success Principles course, when course leaders use dialogue with participants to nurture relationships in the class. The groups led by these skilled course leaders that have had the most conflict are the ones that speak most about the deep bonds they have developed. We see that that those participants who most internalize the skills of listening and asking open questions are also the ones who have greatest success in the workplace. We are all part of the system. The reliance on antiracism principles remains critical in many ways. For example, many participants have experienced difficulties in previous jobs because they take personally actions and interactions that are not meant to be personal. As they learn to understand racism as a systemic and institutional problem, they become more aware of their own relationship to systems and institutions. This helps them discern what is a personal affront and what is merely the way that business works. They learn to name the aspects of institutional or individual racism that must be addressed. Again, the most skilled course leaders have developed strengths along these lines. They have learned to have "courageous conversations" with the participants they teach that allow them to explore these sensitive and often sticky issues in a safe and respectful and still challenging way.

Conclusions

We have focused here on the use of dialogue education with and through course leaders. When it is enhanced with business, antiracist, and culturally rooted principles, we find that dialogue education has promise for helping individuals get a sense of their power and for improving the way that systems and organizations serve communities. At NOJI we have witnessed many men and women discover their own potential, which has been critical in their journeys to find and keep jobs that sustain their families. There are numerous other ways in which dialogue education has been used at NOJI. We share these new practices at Casey Foundation conferences. We use dialogue in working as a partner with other New Orleans training groups.

Contact us at NOJI for more detail on the Twenty-First-Century Success Principles course, or on the process by which organizations can become certified to use the course in the context of their own work. Our e-mail address is thenoji2000@aol.com.

References

de Jesus, E. *Makin' It*. Gaithersburg, Md.: Youth Development Research Fund (YDRF), 1998. [http://www.teamyouth.com].

Wilson, W. J. *When Work Disappears: The World of the New Urban Poor*. New York: Vintage Books, 1997.

Open Questions for Analysis and Synthesis

1. What do you see of the principle of congruence working in this situation? That is, how did the team's actions described here demonstrate what they were teaching?

2. How did you see the team incorporate new concepts and models into a dialogue education framework?

3. How did you see the Seven Design Steps serve this program?

4. The team reflects on selected principles. What other principles and practices do you see the team using?

10

From Telling to Teaching in Appalachia

The Mountain Microenterprise Fund of North Carolina

Joye Norris, Greg Walker-Wilson

This chapter describes the struggle of an adult education program to find and use successfully resources that could make its vitally important educational work accessible to the people who needed it.

In 1989, the Mountain Microenterprise Fund (MMF), of Asheville, North Carolina, began helping low-income residents of western North Carolina realize their dream of starting their own business and being their own boss. By 1997, in spite of several high-profile success stories, MMF considered closing up shop. Facing a lack of money, the board wondered whether the work of MMF was over. Enrollment in its business-planning course—the springboard for people who wished to get started on their dream by applying for loans—had declined. Of those who did enroll, few were actually completing business plans and taking the next steps.

After a thorough review of the situation, the board and Greg Walker-Wilson, executive director and one of the present authors, set out to reinvent MMF. Supported by a three-year organizational development grant from the Babcock Foundation and by the North Carolina Rural Center, we maintained our original mission but changed the ways in which we met it. Central to that period of change was the training provided to prospective entrepreneurs. If we had any chance to revive the "success story" era, participants had to be better prepared to succeed.

Today we spend much of our energy managing our growth, adding new service areas, and developing a downtown Asheville marketplace for the goods produced by the many entrepreneurs from MMF. We give a lot of the credit for this spirited revival to another decision—made in 1998 after we regained our footing. The business planning curriculum would be redesigned and feature a dialogue approach to learning. This chapter relates the MMF journey from telling to teaching. This journey took much longer than expected, cost more than anticipated, and absorbed more staff time than ever imagined. But it has energized MMF and changed hundreds of lives in western North Carolina.

Our Journey

MMF is a nonprofit organization that provides low-income residents of western North Carolina with business training, loans, and other support so they can start or expand small businesses. Interested people attend an orientation to the program, where they learn about the training, the loan application process, the group support, and membership services. Should they decide that the MMF approach is right for them, they sign up for *Foundations*, a seven-week training program that guides them through creating a business plan.

Upon completion of *Foundations*, they make a presentation of their plan and are certified to apply for a loan. They then join a group of their peers. That peer group decides if the loan should be approved. Group members rely on each other to stay current on payments because delinquency prevents others from receiving loans themselves. For additional support, a new MMF graduate can become a member of MMF, opening the door to more training programs, referrals, discounts, and community support. Currently, MMF counts five hundred businesses that were begun as a result of this program.

Assessing the Current Situation

After conducting interviews with past clients as part of an organizational and programmatic assessment in fall 1998, we saw that many clients were asking us to hold them to greater accountability during the training course. Said one former participant: "I didn't start my business immediately after taking the course because of my family situation. But then when I did start working my business three months later, I had forgotten much of what I had learned in the course. I wish you had made me do a business plan during the course, instead of letting me get by without finishing my assignments and the plan."

Too many participants were working around the edges rather than developing a plan during the course. This meant that fewer people were getting their businesses up and running. Participants were receiving a great deal of information about how to start a business, but they were not practicing skills, sharing knowledge, and consistently applying what they knew to an actual business plan. Their lack of excitement about the course was palpable, and their attendance reflected it.

An assessment of the facilitation of the training at the time revealed a reliance on covering the material by way of lecture. Our trainers were stuck in the "telling" mode. They felt that if they provided the information, participants would turn it into business plans. In the words of one current MMF trainer, folks were "left to their own devices" to interpret information and make it personally useful. The result of the "their own devices" model was clear: completed business plans were not forthcoming.

Resources for a New Model

I had studied the ideas of Paulo Freire and found them compelling. My wife and some friends had taken a course called Learning to Listen, Learning to Teach with Jane Vella, of the Jubilee Popular Education Center. The excitement I heard in their voices when speaking of the experience remained with me. I knew then that when I had the opportunity, I wanted to learn this adult-friendly approach that had captured their imaginations. Rather than tinker with the curriculum in bits and pieces, I suggested that we go back to the drawing board and completely reinvent our program. We would approach it from the exciting conceptual framework of learning through dialogue.

Our dialogue education journey began in earnest in April 1999 when all five MMF staff members and a consultant completed the Learning to Listen, Learning to Teach course, facilitated by Joye Norris. One month later we completed a three-day, customized advanced training design course, using the business planning curriculum as its focal point. In essence, we began designing from scratch a twenty-one-hour business training course that would result in the completion of an actual business plan by each participant.

The essential question we examined was this: What do our participants need to know and know how to do in order to complete that plan? The response to this question would make up the content of the course. More questions were tackled. What would be the most important new information to offer the participants? What could be left out because it would overwhelm them? In what sequence should the information appear? How could learners become engaged with the content so they could make personal meaning of it, practice related skills, reflect on what they learned, and apply it to their business plan?

After the painstaking process of deciding on the content for the seven-week course, we paired up, and each pair assumed responsibility for two sessions. Joye Norris reviewed each lesson, made suggestions, and encouraged the designers. She returned to Asheville and offered two days of facilitation skills training to all staff members. She encouraged us to begin piloting the lessons as they were developed. It was important to find out fairly early how suitable the lessons were for all kinds of learners, for the time allotted, and for the ultimate purpose of developing a business plan. It was also important to reinforce our new training skills, our confidence, and our willingness to leave the "telling" role behind.

A New Curriculum

Full implementation of the completely revised curriculum began in early 2000, nearly a year after we had begun the redesign process. During that same time period, we experienced some staffing changes and quickly brought new staff members into the dialogue approach frame of mind. Since that full implementation, the curriculum has undergone constant review and revision. Although the essentials are in place, we consider the curriculum a work in progress, always subject to change and improvement. The business planning curriculum consists of seven three-hour sessions, titled as follows:

> Welcome, Credit, Personal Budgeting
>
> Planning for Start-Up
>
> Planning for Year One, Financial Planning
>
> Marketing, Part One
>
> Marketing, Part Two
>
> Loan Application Process
>
> Presentation of Business Plans, Group Formation, Certification

The first six weeks of *Foundations* consist of a series of learning tasks laid out sequentially to give participants the skills and resources they need to write a business plan. For example, in one of the two marketing sessions, participants are asked to consider what it is they are selling besides their service or product. This task leads specifically to components of their own business plan.

Learning task # 5. What am I really selling?

5A. In small groups of three, find an interesting advertisement in the magazines provided. As opposed to the actual product or service, what image, quality, sensation, or benefit is being sold to the customer? Write these on Post-its and post them beside your actual product. We'll all see a couple of examples.

5B. Choose one of the businesses in your group. Brainstorm responses to "What are you really selling in that business?" Jot down your responses on a sheet of paper and post it on our "What Are You Selling" wall. Do this for each of the businesses in your group. When you are finished, we will see your results and hear from two or three volunteers who had an interesting discovery!

As with all the segments of the *Foundations* curriculum, participants are asked to complete work on their own business plans both during the class time and also outside of class.

Learning task #6. Products-services and benefits

List the products-services and benefits to the customer for your own business. Examine the products-services-features-benefits section of the marketing plan chapter in your course manual.

Assignments are reviewed at the beginning of the following lesson, or class members may work one-to-one with course instructors outside the classroom. The most significant difference between today's *Foundations* program and our previous training program is the complete shift from a "left to their own devices" framework to a guided, structured process with immediate application to individual business plan development. Course instructors are on-call consultants. Partnering and small group work are key features of all sessions, as is a facilitation style that encourages dialogue and affirms all efforts.

Results of the Curriculum

The motivation to continue to improve *Foundations* has been driven by the new curriculum's dramatic impact on the organization. Demand for the training course has increased sixfold in four years. Most participants are indeed completing business plans and getting ever closer to their dream of owning their own business.

Staff members, some initially skeptical about what seemed to be an overreliance on the soft, process aspects of training, are solidly enthusiastic. One staff member expressed her struggle with the changes and then her delight at the results: "While the design part was very hard, and even intimidating, this is one of the best moves MMF has ever made. I don't know that we would have chosen to do this had we known how difficult it was going to be. But now that we are on the other side I haven't regretted it one bit. It has transformed who we are and how we are seen by our learners."

The notion of having been "transformed" is often reflected in participant reviews. Victoria Lyall, the MMF membership director, noted: "People rave about the class. Some say they were lost but are not anymore. I have seen such an increase in confidence. Most of them know how to plan for a small business. They say they feel more solid, more ready."

When Joye Norris asked me to look back on the entire process of developing Foundations and name what surprised me, I found it easy to respond. I am surprised that we are still working on this curriculum, that it is alive! Everyone has ideas about how it can be improved. Those ideas never stop. We recently added a Spanish version of this course, and that Spanish-speaking teacher has brought even more suggestions. It is an ongoing process—a daily part of our organization and our lives. For MMF, creating a dialogue approach to our teaching has kept us in daily dialogue about how well we meet our clients' needs.

The development of *Foundations* was more than a project and it is more than a curriculum. It is like us—vibrant, always changing, and yet striving to be true to core principles.

Principles and Practices of Dialogue

The curriculum was developed through the collective lens of all of the dynamic principles and practices brought to us through Learning to Listen, Learning to Teach and our ongoing consultation with Joye Norris. Two principles in particular have been the engines that drive Foundations: respect, and adult learners as decision makers.

To say that adults learn best when they feel respected for who they are, what they know, and where they have been is more than a fine sentiment. At MMF, we have seen the principle of respect transform participants from concerned students to confident entrepreneurs. It moves their expressions from vagueness to clarity. Our most important application of respect is at the beginning of the course when we show the participants that all their business ideas are possible and that they, the shapers of the ideas, are capable. Some of us have attended microenterprise conferences where leaders boast of how many people they talked *out* of going into business for themselves. Our curriculum invites participants to come to their own conclusions about the value of their ideas. We demonstrate our belief in them through what we do. We demonstrate the basic premise that anyone can start a business who wants to do so.

Our expectation that learners will draw their own conclusions reflects the second principle—the adult learner as decision maker. At the outset, we wanted to align the *Foundations* experience with the eventual need of our participants to make effective decisions as business owners. We honor their ability to do that by building in constant choice. For example, participants may choose whether or not to speak in front of the whole group. They choose to use—or not use—their business idea as the focal point of a learning task. They choose to ask for additional support, either after class or during the week. The most powerful choice participants make comes at the end of the Foundations curriculum. After they present their plan in any way they choose, they are awarded a certificate of completion. This enables them to take the next steps in the MMF system. According to one MMF teacher, many of the participants accept their certificate, and then, in a private conversation, ask the class leader to hold it for them until they feel more ready. They, not the course leaders, make that choice. This is a celebration of their role as decision makers.

Focus and Tension: Two New Principles

Peter Marks, an MMF program coordinator, noted that people are often hampered by the vagueness of their business ideas. In *Foundations*, they get the time to focus for twenty-one hours on their thoughts, their visions, their plans. Some participants complete plans, some make other decisions. They all get the opportunity to bring their thoughts into focus, examine them, and make their own decisions.

The dialogue-based design with its experiential framework and small group work allows focus on just one thing—a rare privilege in our participants' lives. They practice their thinking and reflective skills and hone in on specifics. Perhaps this opportunity to focus is the most useful outcome of the experience, which they can transfer to other parts of their lives.

To suggest that tension could be a dialogue design principle comes from our experience at MMF, which has taught us to value how tension keeps us honest and engaged and striving for clarity. For example, we always experience a tension between our expectation that our adult learners do the work of the course every week and their ability to manage their own lives. We experience tension between our desire for all of our participants to complete a business plan and the reality that only 75 percent of them do so. We feel strongly about learner safety, so we experience the tension between the need for safety and the need to take risks—which new business owners do by definition. Finally, we experience an ongoing tension between guiding dialogue and just letting it unfold. We see this tension as a motivator, a constant push to focus on what is best for our participants and their development, and not on what is best for us. This is what we mean by learning-centered.

Conclusions

At MMF, we realized early on that the *Foundations* curriculum would never rest easily on a shelf or serve as a one-size-fits-all product that relieved us of worry about the efficacy of our training. We used to tell, but now that we teach we are always tweaking and revising *Foundations* so that it is synchronous with a particular group's energies and dreams.

Dialogue education has given us a language and format within which to improve constantly. What we have not done thus far is focus on the assumptions we made about the outcomes of dialogue education as they compare with outcomes of a lecture approach. This failure is ironic because questioning assumptions is a key marker of dialogue education.

Does participation in a dialogue approach to learning in and of itself give participants transferable group membership skills? Are participants more at ease when speaking in public after experiencing their voice so often in our course? Does the opportunity to function as a decision maker in one's own learning transfer to more ease of decision making in business ownership? Do people become more flexible and open-minded when exposed to seven weeks of dialogue? How do our graduates compare with graduates of similar programs that do not take a dialogue approach? What will we find when we move beyond the anecdotal evidence and ask for quantitative data? This is the current research agenda of MMF. But while we seek answers, we are moving on. Other organizations are asking for *Foundations* as a product they can use. We explain to them that it is much more than a curriculum. It is a way of being, a way of living with focus *and* tension. At the Mountain Microenterprise Fund, the dialogue continues.

Open Questions for Analysis and Synthesis

1. What does the title "From Telling to Teaching" say to you?

2. Notice that the whole MMF team took the courses. What does that tell you about the ensuing success?

3. Why do you think they did not simply "tweak and revise" the old curriculum?

4. The authors name some principles and practices they found useful. What other principles and practices do you see the team using in this story?

11

Welfare to Work via Dialogue Education
The Voices of Bread and Roses

Barbara Gassner

This chapter describes the creation of another set of entrepreneurs—welfare mothers—through a creative dialogue education program. When federal welfare legislation was enacted in 1996, a five-year lifetime limit was placed on a family's access to Temporary Assistance for Needy Families (TANF) in the United States.

I live and work in a rural northern state where lack of transportation, quality child care, and affordable housing plague the efforts of TANF recipients to participate in welfare-to-work programming and to earn adequate income. The same constraints challenge the ability of the state welfare agency to overcome barriers to employment. Most of the state's welfare recipients live in households headed by single women. Slightly more than half of these households have children age six or younger, and about one-third of the recipients have less than twelve years of education. Children make up more than half the recipients of TANF grants.

With the enforcement of stringent time lines on the duration of their grants, adult members of welfare households desperately need to develop skills, knowledge, and attitudes to enhance their ability to earn income. In our rural, mountainous state, jobs are in short supply. This is especially the case for jobs that pay a wage adequate to cover the basic necessities of shelter, food, fuel, transportation, clothing, and utilities. The state welfare agency is committed to meeting the federal work participation rules while also serving families in ways that are respectful and caring and that recognize the mutual responsibility of adult household members and government. To help meet this commitment, the state welfare agency funded a program to provide skills, training, and education to assist welfare recipients with the transition from welfare to work.

Building a Welfare-to-Work Program

On my first day on the job as program coordinator in that welfare-to-work effort, I walked into an office that doubled as a learning center. I was shown a table in the corner of a large room. Under the table sat one box with program files from the previous year. That box was the sole physical evidence in the room that this program existed. I was, in this cavernous room, alone with my thoughts, the box of files, and a copy of the grant agreement between my employer—an adult basic education agency—and the state's welfare department.

My charge was to build on the lessons learned in the previous year of welfare-to-work programming in order to create a curriculum, recruit participants, and design a new program. The lessons on which to build, however, were not to be found anywhere in that room. Where could I go to get the information I needed?

A persistent question echoed loudly in my mind. What do people need to *know*, what do they need to *have* in order to sustain themselves? This was more than a job to me! I drove to my home and gathered a few of the tools of work and creation that I love most: knitting needles, rough wool, skeins of color spun into yarn, and a drop spindle made of beautifully grained wood. I took a detailed drawing I had done of a hand from my wall at home and a quilt square I had made of the ocean tossing under a starry sky. I drove back to my new work site singing the Mary Chapin-Carpenter song "Why Walk When You Can Fly?"

I arranged my supplies in a very large and exquisitely woven reed basket. When I finished the arrangement, I realized that I knew where to find the lessons learned in the previous program: the lessons and the seeds for the future were in the voices of the welfare caseworkers and the voices of the participants themselves. I set to work listening to those voices. Inspired by my love for the work and for making well-crafted, functional pieces of art, I was confident that the program participants and I could build a learning community and make something worthwhile together.

Learning Needs and Resource Assessment

It was clear to me that the barriers to employment in my region were an amalgam of social, geographic, demographic, and economic circumstances. My job was to create a program and a curriculum that would address the needs of these women, and indirectly, the social and economic dynamics that contributed to these needs. I had to hold the focus on my charge: to help welfare mothers address their employability. However, I could also work with the participants to advocate for themselves. I could work with them to develop their voices and to acquire and demonstrate to themselves and others in the community, including potential employers, their ability to work and to bring creativity to their work.

Using the Network

Before I began working in welfare to work, I had designed and implemented a juvenile delinquency prevention effort in the same region. Through this work I had built an extensive network of relationships with both local and regional service agencies and with the families they served. I knew that welfare recipients in the state were accustomed to home visits from their caseworkers.

With the help of their caseworkers, I made calls to referrals and set up a visit schedule. I met the participants as a guest in their homes, over polite offerings of coffee or tea. I told them I was consulting with them to inform my decisions about what they needed to be part of the program. The conversations were casual. When they talked about their junk cars up on blocks in the yard, I shared with them my stories of car troubles. When they talked about their children, I shared that I was a single parent raising a son. Every visit had moments of both laughter and solemnity. I heard their concerns and their hopes for themselves and for their children.

There was no paperwork for them to fill out at the home visits. Intentionally, I waited to fill out the necessary forms until after the learning relationship had been established. I asked them how they got around, how they liked to spend their time (versus what they actually did with it), what they liked about any of the jobs they had held, and what their greatest current challenge was. Once they realized that I took time to listen to what they had to say, they spoke freely. As they relaxed, I asked if they minded if I took notes to use in program preparation. They interpreted this to mean that what they said mattered to me. It did.

The people I met in these visits were by turns embarrassed or defensive about being welfare recipients. They shared their feeling of isolation from the larger community and the feeling that they and their children were perceived as being not as good as everyone else. They opened themselves to naming the things that made them feel most vulnerable. They identified specific needs: transportation, child care, housing stability, a graduate equivalency degree (GED), relief from abuse orders, a job, and the ability to read and write better than they did. They spoke wistfully of things they wanted to learn how to do. They wanted to know how to decorate cakes for their children's birthdays, to sew, to paint, to drive; they wanted to go to secretarial school, to enroll in a licensed nursing assistance program, to open their own daycare so they could be with their children and work at the same time. I was hearing their generative themes.

An Open House

I scheduled an open house at the learning center for potential participants, and I worked with my adult basic educator partners to create an orientation to the emerging program. A significant portion of the orientation was a continuation of the more casual learning needs and resource assessment that I had begun during the home visits. I needed to witness whether these women, often isolated from the community, would risk leaving their homes to be in a group. I needed to know if they would rise to the occasion of joining together as members of a learning program. They rose to the occasion beautifully, if shyly. During their first meeting, participants and their caseworkers, who were also in attendance, wrote the agreements for how we would be together in a group. Our joint authorship of these agreements provided a common understanding of how we would work together not only in learning sessions but during support group sessions as well. The caseworkers stepped out from behind their roles as enforcers of rules and into a new role as resources and partners.

Program Possibilities

In addition to building and maintaining a program structure that modeled safety and respect, I was responsible for teaching skills that are necessary for most types of employment: interpersonal communication skills, time-management and record-keeping skills, computer skills, personal care and hygiene, interviewing skills, basic math and literacy skills. I also had to help participants develop a resume to use in a job search.

In turn, the participants needed to be responsible for their own learning. They had to learn to set their priorities and to keep them. The first weeks of the program were spent in learning simply how to show up. This meant solving transportation and child care problems with the assistance of their caseworkers and learning to use an alarm clock consistently. It often meant asserting to their partners that they were going to come to the program each day, even in the face of criticism.

I made decisions about how to incorporate the participants' interests and needs into the new program curriculum. The dilemma I faced in building a curriculum based on dialogue education was that people cannot engage in dialogue if they perceive they have no voice. The women who came to the program had the voices of victims tinged with the tenacious tones of survivors. They left the program with voices that were more fully infused with a belief in their strengths, and they have gone on to realize many of the goals that they identified for themselves while participating in the program.

In order to write a resume and to practice using their voices to represent themselves, the women needed to have opportunities to name the skills they already possessed, to acquire new skills, and to practice them in a safe environment. In the first year of the program, we made and sold wreaths together. In the second year of the program, we became a bakery and supplied community events with whole-grain breads and fine pastries. The production, delivery, and display of pastries offered practice in skills of both reading and writing. Participants learned planning and time-management skills, budgeting and inventory, and customer services, while they also practiced interpersonal communication skills to develop work plans and troubleshoot. They practiced cleanup and preparation for each day's work, and last but not least, they actually produced a high-quality, healthy food product.

The Seven Design Steps

The program design relied on the Seven Design Steps.

Who and Why

The women who were referred to the program needed to experience safety, and both to experience and to believe in their self-worth in order to take the time and effort to build new skills. They needed to learn to speak confidently and appropriately to express their strengths as well as their needs. It was important for them to develop enough confidence to dare to dream and to state their goals so that the work of pursuing them could begin to take shape in reality. They needed new attitudes about their self-worth.

Their health was noticeably problematic to them. Every participant showed symptoms of disease. Many were diagnosed with one of the following conditions during their participation in the program: obesity, muscular-skeletal conditions, gastrointestinal disorders, asthma and other pulmonary illnesses, such as bronchitis and pneumonia. These conditions were exacerbated by their use of tobacco, alcohol, and other drugs, poor diet, lack of exercise, and lack of the knowledge and skill to create a healthy lifestyle supported by well-informed choices and habits of thought and behavior.

They desired to be healthy, fit, and happy in their lives, but their attitudes expressed fear, resistance, and doubt about their ability to make changes. All showed some symptoms of depression. At the start of the program, they expressed the belief that good health was impossible because there were too many barriers. Soon they were able to acknowledge that their barriers to greater health included their own habits. For their own well-being and that of their children, they desperately needed to develop healthier habits and the skills, knowledge, and attitudes to support these healthy choices.

When: Time Frame

We met twenty hours a week for eighteen months. Some of the participants attended the entire time; others joined us as they were referred by their caseworkers or as their part-time employment schedules allowed. There was a core group of learners, and because we also had variable attendance from a portion of the learners, our agreements to hold safety and respect were shared, practiced, and reviewed each week.

Where: Site

During the first year of the program we moved from the office site to shared space with a local Boys and Girls Club. The location maximized our resources. It also gave the participants an opportunity to share their talents to benefit the Boys and Girls Club. Furthermore, this space included a kitchen. This proved to be an inspiration to the learning design as it evolved.

What: Content

The program content areas included the following:

- Showing up: How to access child care and transportation.

- Time management: Values, priorities, calendars, setting the alarm clock.

- What is power? Our bodies and personal power (we used selections from the audiocassette "Your Body Is Your Subconscious Mind" by Candace Pert, Ph.D.).

- The role of emotions in learning.

- Communication skills: What is a voice? What does it feel like, look like, and sound like to use our voice?

- Breath work and physically supporting our voice.

- Speaking and singing skills: How do we use our voice with respect for ourselves, our children, and other adults in the work or learning place and at home?

- Meditation.

- Planning tools.

- Exercise and nutrition.

- Adult basic education to acquire a GED or ADP or to deepen literacy skills.

- What is community? What gifts do I have to offer community?

- Work simulation: The Bread and Roses Bakery.

What For

The participants' goal was to develop the ability to access their voices and use their voices to represent themselves safely and respectfully. They had to apply their self-knowledge, which would come from accessing and using their voices, to the deeper exploration of meaningful work and to create a product for use in their community. Specific objectives emerged as they found their voices.

How

Early in our learning together we concentrated on expression of personal voice through writing, breath work, and dialogue. With the consent of the group, we explored body image and worked to achieve goals of weight loss and increased stamina through gentle exposure to exercise and play. We used the kitchen to create healthy meals that we shared at midday and swam in the swimming pool at a local college.

The stronger swimmers encouraged the women with fear of the water gradually to allow themselves to trust the buoyancy of the water with the aid of flotation devices. Reducing the risk through the use of safety devices and with the support of the group, each woman developed a growing belief in her ability to learn and do new things. Physical stamina increased, along with self-esteem. The day the last participant came to the deep end of the pool with the guidance of a swimmer companion, we joined in a circle and sang together, bobbing up and down on the buoyancy of our shared accomplishment.

The groundwork we had laid and the careful sequence of learning tasks to build trust was absolutely critical to our success at the pool. Joining other learners bobbing up and down together at the deep end, gently holding each other in buoyant support of our community, arms draped from shoulder to shoulder around the circle, was a high point in the women's experience. And it supplied me with all the evidence I needed of the distance each woman had come from the first day of participation in the program, when the risk to do something so publicly revealing of their attitude of self-worth would have been unthinkable.

Bread and Roses

Prior to becoming a bakery, we studied labor history. At the close of that chapter of our study, we listened to Mimi Farina's song "Bread and Roses," which celebrates the labor movement efforts of women working in the mills in the early 1900s. On the day the song was introduced to the learning group, the benefits of all the breath work, vocalization, exercise, and toning were evident. The women had gone from being unable to sustain a single note with their breathing to singing with one another in harmony. The participants breathed their power into the singing of "Bread and Roses" along with a recording of it by Judy Collins.

The following day we began the practice of being a bakery. From that day on, there were roses on the table, music in the air, and flour, yeast, and water in the kitchen waiting to be turned into bread on two days each week. The other days we planned, wrote recipes, and reviewed what had worked and what we would change about the work plan for the baking production and delivery days we had just completed.

In the first week of baking, we supplied a townwide community planning forum with enough bread for sandwiches to serve almost two hundred people. We supplied an additional six loaves of dessert breads. A few weeks later, we supplied an adult basic education agency with two hundred servings of pastry for their open house. We catered and served that event, giving participants practice in meeting the public with their product.

Impact

As we received orders from other community groups, the participants enthusiastically learned how to bake breads and pastries while identifying the other tasks necessary to a bakery. The women learned to plan their work, do it, reflect on it, and incorporate their learning into the next work plan. They named the skills they were developing and identified those that were transferable to other types of work and expression. They became not only cooks but planners, managers, writers, recorders, inventory controllers, researchers, and caterers. We identified the types of jobs that a small bakery would require and could support and named the businesses with which it would have to interact both for supplies and to market and sell the product. The women had progressed from having little or no experience or understanding of meaningful work and community to being able to map the impact of their work on themselves and on their community. They were moving toward being ready to be successful employees.

When the governor of our state came to our town to speak at a local event, we presented our product to him along with the new brochure about our program and our bakery. The learner with the longest and most consistent participation in the program was chosen by her peers to carry our product, our brochure, and the lyrics of our chosen theme song to the governor. She was so nervous as she tried to speak that she simply handed him the pastry and the brochure. However, earlier in the evening, she had spoken quite freely with members of the community who hosted the event, about the bakery and about our program of learning. Her experiences in the group and with dialogue education had taken her from barely being able to speak audibly in the group in its first months, to sharing her knowledge and experience as a young mother on welfare quite comfortably with other community members, and to facing the state governor. She eventually got a full-time job and has sustained it, working in customer service at a local company.

All the participants in the program achieved observable learning, could name what they had learned, and could represent their skills both in conversation and through use of the written word. All have gone on to practice their skills and knowledge in other settings. Not everyone got a job. Some have been referred to the program for extended participation.

Challenges

Our accountable objective has always been that by the end of their participation, every participant will have gained employment. From a participant and teacher perspective, and even from the perspective of the caseworkers, the time frame mandated for achievement of employment is often not congruent with individual learning needs and with environmental realities, which include job availability, access to transportation, and child care.

Conclusions

The ongoing evolution of dialogue education applied to welfare to work in our state would require a deeper and more informed commitment to this approach. Nationally, we need a concerted and coordinated effort to develop jobs and welfare-to-work programs in which the creation of things of beauty and functional value inspire expressions of healthy community. We need to hear the voices of bread and roses.

Reference

Pert, C. "Your Body Is Your Subconscious Mind" [audiocassette]. Sound True (P.O. Box 8010/BP98, Boulder, CO 80306-8010), 2000.

Open Questions for Analysis and Synthesis

1. What use do you see the Seven Design Steps were to the program?

2. Examine the content of the program. What surprised you about it?

3. What use did you see Barbara Gassner make of the concepts learning, transfer, and impact?

4. How do you think this story of developing entrepreneurial capacity differs from the previous case set in the mountains of Appalachia? How is it similar?

12

Appreciative Inquiry and Dialogue Education Meet in Strategic Planning

Darlene Goetzman

This chapter shows the correlation between appreciative inquiry and dialogue education in describing a planning process undertaken by the local board of Literacy Volunteers of America of Cattaraugus County, New York.

How can planning focus on the positive aspects rather than the problems of a program and therefore develop its generative capacity? An appreciative inquiry (AI) approach to planning calls for looking for what has worked well in the past, seeking to enhance it, and bringing it into the future in order to create viable and energizing strategies for success.

Literacy Volunteers of America of Cattaraugus County, Inc. (LVA-CC) was about to engage in an organization-wide planning process, and the board agreed that we should explore what focusing on positives might lead to. As the person responsible for designing and facilitating the planning process, I also wanted to examine how the principles and practices of dialogue education might be helpful.

Appreciative Inquiry

Appreciative inquiry (Cooperrider, Sorensen, Whitney, and Yaeger, 2000) is a participatory research approach that aims to foster improvement in social, organizational, and personal conditions. Such improvements are the result of cycles of action and reflection coupled with critical consciousness about both (Brooks and Watkins, 1994). A well-crafted design applying the principles and practices of dialogue education creates opportunities for dialogue through meaningful learning tasks in order to draw out these connections.

Traditionally, the five phases of AI are as follows (Cooperrider, Sorensen, Whitney, and Yaeger, 2000; Elliot, 1999; Hammond and Royal, 1998):

- *Spotlighting:* Identifying topics and appropriate questions for focused interviews

- *Discovering:* Interviewing diverse individuals representing multiple perspectives and roles in the organization

- *Dreaming:* Naming which elements of the discovery phase are to be carried into the future as well as imagining possibilities beyond what has already been

- *Designing:* Creating provocative propositions—present-tense statements that depict the change participants want to see as though it already exists

- *Destiny, or delivering:* Developing action plans to actualize the provocative propositions, or sometimes simply a changed attitude that is reflected in practice

In the project at LVA-CC we looked for ways in which these phases of appreciative inquiry and the principles and practices of dialogue education could work together to enhance the planning.

The Program

LVA-CC serves a rural county on the southeastern edge of New York State with an approximate population of eighty-thousand.

LVA-CC is best known for its One-to-One Adult Tutoring Program, which serves adults with limited literacy skills. Other programs include family literacy, available on-site in public housing units, and an incarceration literacy program. In these programs, fifty to sixty trained volunteer tutors provide most of the direct services, with paid staff providing guidance, oversight, recognition, and assessment.

The Process

The planning process would use the participatory research methodology of appreciative inquiry.

Roles

The board's role and my role were clearly delineated. I was responsible for designing and facilitating all phases of the planning process. The LVA-CC board, staff, and other stakeholders were responsible for actively participating in the process. They would produce a document with the named values of the organization and five or six provocative propositions with accompanying action plans. Establishing role clarity is an important principle of dialogue education.

The First Session

I added a new phase to the classic five phases—situation assessment—and placed it first in the sequence. *What is the situation that calls for this planning process?* This question invited responses as part of the learning needs resource assessment (LNRA) used in dialogue education.

In order to begin the LNRA and design a process that was respectful and engaging for the whole LVA-CC organization, we began with a short introductory workshop for the eleven-member board and the director. The following were the achievement-based objectives of that short introductory session. By the end of this one-and-a-half-hour session, participants would have:

- Reviewed differences between "problem solving" and an AI approach

- Listened to a brief overview of what appreciative inquiry means

- Questioned and added to the situational description for this planning process

- Experienced four phases of appreciative inquiry

- Edited the draft of LVA-CC's AI planning process

I had previously interviewed a number of the board members and created this short workshop as an accelerated review of appreciative inquiry so that they could experience the process. This session invited them to name the situation that called for this planning work for LVA-CC as they saw it and to provide input into the process and a time line. Here is one of the learning tasks we engaged in to meet these objectives:

Learning task #3. Design

3a. Review the following description of the situation that calls for this appreciative planning process. Circle any key issues that stand out for you as important for our planning process:

The Present Situation

The timing for this appreciative inquiry–strategic planning process is perfect because the organization is not only not in crisis but flourishing. However, resources (people and finances) are stretched, and the existing office space inadequate for current staff. In terms of programs, it is difficult for the board to choose which opportunities to take advantage of and which to let go of. In addition, as is happening in most government and privately funded organizations, demands for account-ability in every area (program services, fiscal allocations, and so on) are increasing. Although this provides addi-tional opportunity for improvement, it also adds work. Last, the expertise needed to meet these demands is harder and harder to come by.

A vision of and plan for the future that incorporates the organization's values with respect to all of these issues is critical. Appreciative inquiry, in combination with strategic planning, will help to establish a frame of refer-ence grounded in success, celebrating the many remark-able accomplishments already achieved, and allow staff and the board to make more informed choices in their direction setting, fiscal allocations, and operations.

What did you circle? What are your questions? What needs to be added or changed?

The participants' responses to these questions showed what each person saw as important. The group reviewed, modified, and came to agreement about why they were engaging in this planning process. During this introductory event, the decision was made to be as inclusive as possible. Therefore, in the next portion of the learning needs resource assessment we took a sample of other stake-holders' responses to the following survey questions:

Tell us a bit about yourself, both personally and profes-sionally. Please include your length of time and role or roles with LVA-CC, and any other organizational planning you have assisted with. What do you see as the primary strengths and benefits LVA-CC brings to the communities it serves? What do you consider the greatest challenges the organization will face during the next few years?

We enclosed the survey questions with an invitation to the strategic planning retreat. The responses to this survey helped us to know more fully the group we would be working with, and therefore ensured that the process and design were engaging them, honored the group's experience, skills, and diversity, and allowed us to create conditions where participants felt safe to participate meaningfully. We carefully planned the tables to ensure adult learners would be seated with someone they knew and felt comfortable with. We also decided to use tape recorders for documentation so that the pressure of note taking would be limited during the retreat.

The Strategic Planning Retreat

Here is part of the strategic planning retreat design, showing some of the Seven Design Steps.

What For: Achievement-Based Objectives

By the end of this strategic planning retreat, participants would have

- Shared what brought them to this planning meeting
- Listened and added to a brief summary of LVA-CC's recent history
- Named aspects of intentional planning
- Shared stories about their most engaging work with this organization
- Named the values represented in this experience
- Identified critical trends and additional stakeholders
- Offered suggestions for changing interview questions when using these with other stakeholders
- Identified next steps in this planning process

We created this appreciative inquiry as the first learning task of the retreat.

Learning task #1. Your experience with LVA-CC

1A. How did you come to be involved with LVA-CC? What first brought you to LVA-CC? What were your first impressions? What did you hope to accomplish here?

1B. What do you consider to be the two top trends affecting literacy services for adults and families? Why are these important for LVA-CC?

1C. Reflect on your time with this organization. What have been the high points for you? Select one high point, a time where you felt most alive, most happy, a time when you felt you were making a difference and doing creative, useful, meaningful work. What happened? What did you do? Who else was involved? Where did the experience take place? What did the area look like? What did it feel like? What could you hear and see around you? What were your thoughts and feelings? Why was it a good experience? What made the experience possible?

1D. What are your wishes for the future? If you could make three wishes come true for LVA-CC, which would make it an even stronger and more effective organization, what would they be?

The sequence of these questions was important. We were creating a sense of safety, as we first looked closer at our story, building on the past to create a dream for the future. The questions were open, inviting reflection on the individual's experience. Both the director and chair of the board had reviewed and approved the questions. We knew we had done a good job when the room was noisy with dialogue as people began to name what had brought them to LVA-CC, the high points of their involvement, and their dreams for the group's future.

Principles and Practices at Work

Martin Luther King declared, "I have a dream!" He did not say, "I have a strategic plan." The enthusiasm and commitment to involve others evidenced at the retreat were proof of our success in creating engaging and meaningful learning tasks. We saw how focusing on the positive rather than the negative evokes energy to reach out to others and share dreams. This group decided they wanted to involve an even wider constituency. Each person at the retreat agreed to interview three more stakeholders over the next sixteen days and report back. The appreciative inquiry process continued.

A total of thirty-six new interviews were completed and shared at a later board meeting. A number of people told us how difficult it was to stay in the AI mode. However, all felt that the interviewing they had done was valuable. They excitedly analyzed the stories, articulating the themes present in them. The themes were then written on a wall chart for review and eventual consolidating. The awe in the room felt palpable as the group stood silently and reviewed "LVA of Cattaraugus County's Wall of Success." The board president smiled, nodding her head with pride. The ten-foot-by-twenty-foot wall was covered with what thirty-six people had identified as bringing them to and keeping them involved with LVA-CC. Hundreds of note cards lined the other walls as well, naming critical issues, values, and hopes for the future of LVA-CC.

Widening the Circle

The greatest gift and challenge in this process were to honor LVA-CC's call to widen the circle of involvement (Axelrod, 2000). This group knew they wanted to hear even more community voices, and they were willing to do the work of listening and documenting. This increased not only the quality but also the quantity of data we had to work with, and ultimately the length of time needed for the process. Timing the thematic analysis and its conversion into provocative propositions and action plans meant that several more planning meetings would be needed. The likelihood of having the same group of people at every short meeting was slim. This meant that we needed to review the past work each time, so we lost some of the momentum that had been built during early sessions. A solid sequential day and a half for gleaning themes, consolidating, and creating provocative propositions and action plans would have been more energizing.

Ultimately, the LVA-CC planning group created five values statements and five provocative propositions including action steps leading toward their realization. A year later, progress has been made, the funding situation is more stable, and at the same time staff are more aware of the need to diversify. Program expansion is incremental, and space is still inadequate. All agree that the way people work together is well represented by their values statements.

The most noticeable change at LVA-CC is a greater capacity to be reflective and analytical, both individually and collectively. These skills are evidenced by the persistent questions of several people about how any project fits into their mission and values and available resources. Historically, questions were not asked as a framework for decision making. The director put this into perspective when she stated, "We used to just do something that sounded good; now we really consider all the implications of our involvement." In post-retreat interviews, a common theme arose: listening. Several people shared the example of staff members trying and failing to develop a new program that the board had rejected. Staff had learned to accept refusal. Each person who mentioned this situation did so not with derision but with appreciation for the staff's capacity to listen and learn.

"Translating core vision into everything the organization does requires ways of connecting everyone—evoking ownership, commitment, understanding, involvement, and confidence in the vision's promise" (Cooperrider, Sorensen, Whitney, and Yaeger, 2000, p. 138). By completing a learning needs resource assessment, as well as creating a process and retreat designs that were engaging, respectful, and connected to people's view of the situation calling for this work, we built a process for this group to discover their dreams. The principles and practices of dialogue education enhanced and ensured appreciative inquiry.

Dialogue Education and Appreciative Inquiry Meet

Dialogue education emphasizes the use of the present situation as a place of learning: "What is it that made this work?" When we are invited to look deeper into our own immediate experience and create a story of how and why it came to be, we begin to be more responsible for our lives, we see ourselves as active agents. Blaming is what is likely to happen when the focus is on what went wrong, or what is wrong. The capacity to examine indicators of learning, and how *we* might do something differently gets lost in the negativity. In contrast, when we look for what *went right* there is no blaming and therefore no defensiveness. We are able to learn and have a dialogue on a different level by tapping the generative capacity of a situation. A new principle AI adds to dialogue education is to make the positive explicit. We saw this principle in action in LVA-CC's situation when the storytelling insisted on no blaming.

Open questions, energy, and generative themes have long been part of the principles and practices of dialogue education. Appreciative inquiry invites our view of these principles to include not only their capacity for building energy and establishing a clear contextual framework for learning but also to acknowledge by the questions we ask that we are directing the energy. In that energy is change. Change is in the dialogue; the future is envisioned. In other words, action and reflection are in a relationship of mutual causality, they are not separate (Macy, 1991). Therefore, when we direct this energy we must carefully consider what kind of change we want.

If this change is grounded in the best of our past coupled with the greatest future we can imagine, we are creating a new view of the world rather than a preconceived idea of a solution to what has been defined as a problem. We expand our view. "You get what you look for" is a very powerful insight into human behavior and systems. Whether we are speaking of visualization for sports heroes or for obese children who need to see themselves differently, research has clearly documented that our minds have a great influence on what happens in our lives. "It is not so much 'Is my question leading to the right or wrong answers?' but rather 'What impact is my question having on our lives together? . . . Is it helping to generate conversations about the good, the better, the possible? . . . Is it strengthening our relationships?'" (Cooperrider, Sorensen, Whitney, and Yaeger, 2000, p. 18).

LVA-CC's director showed that she had learned these principles when she said, "I knew we had great volunteers, but through the AI process I realized the quality of what they had to offer. Their willingness to help was much greater than I had imagined. Now when someone wants to do something I get out of the way, even if there are gaps. I trust they will figure it out or ask for help."

By creating a shared vision through dialogue, analyzing the past, and creating a dream of the future, LVA-CC has greatly deepened the quality of relationships and therefore the foundation of the organization (Axelrod, 2000; Carver, 1997).

Conclusions

When I was first introduced to dialogue education, I had never heard of Malcolm Knowles, Paulo Freire, or Jane Vella. However, I knew respect, engagement, and enthusiasm when I saw them, and I wanted to know more! Over the years I have found that each principle unfolds itself to me in new ways as I design and teach. I do not always look with appreciative eyes. Yet these insights help me to be more accountable, more responsible, and less judgmental in my work and personal life.

As I continue to explore all that appreciative inquiry has to offer, I know that I am still dealing with a world of problem solving. I can also see that when I label something as a problem I have decided that what is is not as I think it should be. The implication here is that I know how things should be. This can set up a closed system. I also notice that when I am more aware of what in my work and my life is energizing and life-enhancing for others and for me, I spend time and effort with greater equanimity and more joy. As Jane Vella puts it so well, "To re-create is to recreate!" (Vella, 2002, p. 89). When we re-create while focusing on what serves our highest aspirations, as the board of LVA-CC did, our creations can be filled with hope.

References

Axelrod, R. H. *Terms of Engagement: Changing the Way We Change Organizations*. San Francisco: Berrett-Koehler, 2000.

Brooks, A., and Watkins, K. (eds.). *The Emerging Power of Action Learning Technologies*. New Directions for Adult Education and Continuing Education, no. 63. San Francisco: Jossey-Bass, 1994.

Carver, J. *Boards That Make a Difference*. San Francisco: Jossey-Bass, 1997.

Cooperrider, D. L., Sorensen, P. F., Whitney, D., and Yaeger, T. F. (eds.). *Appreciative Inquiry: Rethinking Human Organization Toward a Positive Theory of Change*. Champaign, Ill.: Stipes Publishing, 2000.

Elliott, C. *Locating the Energy for Change: An Introduction to Appreciative Inquiry*. Winnipeg, Manitoba, Canada: International Institute for Sustainable Development, 1999.

Hammond, S. A., and Royal, C. (eds.). *Lessons from the Field: Applying Appreciative Inquiry*. Plano, Tex.: Practical Press, 1998.

Macy, J. *Mutual Causality in Buddhism and General Systems Theory: The Dharma of Natural Systems*. Albany: State University of New York, 1991.

Vella, J. *Learning to Listen, Learning to Teach: The Power of Dialogue in Educating Adults*. San Francisco: Jossey-Bass, 2002. (Originally published 1994.)

Open Questions for Analysis and Synthesis

1. Look at the learning tasks described in this chapter. What difference would it have made in the strategic planning process if learning tasks had not been used?

2. What correlations do you see between appreciative inquiry as described here and dialogue education?

3. Look at Chapter Sixteen, where Karen Ridout shows how dialogue enhanced the strategic planning process in another situation. What similarities and differences do you perceive between that situation and this one?

13

Teaching Communities to Lobby for Social Justice

Michael Culliton

This chapter describes the development and implementation of a national workshop of NETWORK, the social justice lobby, to teach men and women how to work for equitable welfare reform.

The United States Capitol building is in direct view of the offices of NETWORK, a national Catholic social justice lobby. Founded thirty years ago by Catholic nuns who saw the need to work on larger systems that influence poverty, NETWORK has grown from its forty-seven original members to over twelve thousand organizations and individuals. These women and men share a vision of applying social justice to the legislative process.

A national social justice lobby has many challenges. To communicate credibly with Congress, NETWORK must conduct thorough research and detailed policy analysis. To communicate credibly with our members, we must provide accessible educational materials and timely, effective suggestions for action. The same detail and thoroughness that make NETWORK effective with members of Congress has the potential to overwhelm and paralyze members. Dialogue education is necessary in our community efforts.

In the 107th Congress, welfare reform reauthorization was a focus of the lobbying and education efforts of NETWORK. In terms of social justice, NETWORK was troubled by the debate and passage of the 1996 welfare reform law that was, in the words of then

President Clinton and members of Congress, designed to "end welfare as we know it." We were concerned about the effects this reform would have on low-income families.

NETWORK initiated a study to identify some of the impacts of welfare reform. In preparation for the mandated renewal of the law in 2002, NETWORK published and distributed to both Congress and our members two reports: *Poverty Amid Plenty: The Unfinished Business of Welfare Reform* (Cobourn, 1999) and *Welfare Reform: How Do We Define Success?* (Niedringhaus, 2001). We continued to work in a coalition with other groups that shared similar concerns. From our experience, we at NETWORK knew we could influence the debate and outcome of the congressional reauthorization process through education of organized advocates.

NETWORK staff envisioned a national education campaign. This effort included a daylong regional workshop in key congressional districts, a national lobby day in Washington, D.C., and a system for distributing to participants a series of suggestions for timely actions they could take to educate and influence their members of Congress. NETWORK decided to hire a project team: a field organizer to manage the overall effort and an education coordinator who would design the workshop and consult on the creation of follow-up actions.

As the new education coordinator, I came to NETWORK with a history. I had completed a two-year internship program with them in the mid-1990s. In the first year I worked with lobbyists on welfare reform and in my second I designed a voter education curriculum using dialogue education. Later, I served as an educational consultant. From these experiences, I concluded that the deep attraction NETWORK felt to the dialogue approach in theory was accompanied by some suspicion of it in practice.

The project team hosted conversations with key individuals and the full NETWORK staff, asking people to share their expectations, hopes, and dreams for the workshop and the larger campaign, as part of the learning needs and resource assessment (LNRA) (Vella, 2002).

Design of the Campaign Workshop: Making a Noise About the Need

We knew this campaign would be most effective if we could use dialogue education throughout. Therefore, we began our design with the Seven Design Steps (Vella, 2000).

Who: Learners, Hosts, Facilitators

Participants in each workshop were fifty to one hundred NETWORK members and friends. Groups included people from churches, social service agencies, justice organizations, religious congregations, and other individuals concerned about issues of poverty in the United States. These people were interested in lobbying members of Congress about reauthorization of welfare reform and in leading others to take such action. A local host made the site arrangements, promoted the event, and handled workshop registration. A team of three NETWORK staff facilitated each workshop.

Why: Situation

Since 1997, NETWORK had studied the effects of the 1996 welfare reform law on families living in poverty. We knew that millions of people were still struggling to meet the basic needs of their families. The welfare reform law, the Personal Responsibility and Work Opportunity Reconciliation Act of 1996, which established Temporary Assistance to Needy Families (TANF), contained strict provisions designed to get people off welfare, but did little to actually get people out of poverty. Congress was scheduled to reauthorize the law in 2002.

NETWORK, the lobbying group, teamed up with our educational partner, NETWORK Education Program, and with local organizations to provide concerned people with the information and tools they needed to make a difference in the reauthorization process by lobbying their members of Congress and leading others in taking such action.

When: Time Frame

Each workshop was scheduled from 9:00 A.M. to 4:00 P.M. with a one-hour break for lunch and six hours for structured learning tasks.

Where: Sites

NETWORK Education Program conducted twenty-one regional workshops in key congressional districts in sixteen states in one year. Each site provided a large room with tables for small group work.

What: Content

These were the specific skills and knowledge sets participants would learn about:

- Resources for welfare reauthorization

- History and provisions of the Personal Responsibility and Work Opportunity Reconciliation Act (PRWORA)

- Effects of the 1996 legislation

- NETWORK's six message points for reauthorization

- Writing a letter to a member of Congress

- A guide to effective lobbying

- Next steps: an RSVP card addressed to NETWORK

What For: Achievement-Based Objectives

By the end of this six-hour workshop participants would have:

- Identified resources for reauthorization

- Read a history and overview of PRWORA and summarized some of the main provisions

- Examined evidence of some of the effects of the 1996 legislation

- Considered six message points for reauthorization prepared by NETWORK after four years of research

- Selected one of the six message points for in-depth preparation

- Written and mailed a letter to one of their members of Congress on a selected point

- Suggested other message points based on their research and experience

- Examined a NETWORK guide to effective lobbying

- Reviewed possible next steps they could take and completed the RSVP card

How: Learning Needs and Resource Assessment

NETWORK consulted with three workshop hosts. When possible, workshop teams had conversations with local hosts to ensure the design met the needs and interests of the group. Each participant received a folder that included the thirty-five-page workshop design and supporting materials. (These materials are described inside brackets in the learning tasks shown here.) Tables were set with the materials the participants needed for the day.

Each workshop began with a welcome and introduction by the local host. A NETWORK facilitator then offered an introduction to welfare reform and our work on the issue. Visual support for this introduction included a U.S. map and accompanying time line showing the twenty-one workshop sites as well as a map of the workshop region that delineated congressional districts with pictures of the respective members of Congress.

The Learning Tasks

Learning tasks are tasks for the learners, open questions put to the small groups with all the resources they need to respond. We saw that they were the heart of this dialogue education approach.

Learning task #1. All of us as resources for reauthorization

1A. Resources for reauthorization

   In pairs, working with someone you don't know well, design and share your circle of influence. [Circle of influence card.]

   Add a star to your name tag to indicate how you see yourself being a resource to others in this workshop: Green = This is all new to me. I'm bursting with potential. Blue = I have some experience and am still learning. Red = I have experience and can be of help. Gold = I know a lot and can serve as a resource to others.

   Write your name on a label. Place your label next to the picture of your member of Congress on the map of congressional districts.

1B. Introduce yourself to all at your table.

1C. As a table, in one sentence, respond to this question: What do you see that you, as a group, bring to this campaign as resources for reauthorization? We'll hear all.

1D. As you look at the maps and the names on the wall, consider what you just heard: What is one thing you see this entire group brings to your members of Congress as resources for reauthorization? We'll hear a sample in the large group.

Learning task #2. What do we need to know?

2A. Read the description of this NETWORK campaign for reauthorization. Highlight the things that catch your attention. In new pairs, share what you highlighted. We'll hear a sample. [One-page description of the campaign written in question-and-answer format.]

2B. Look and listen to the objectives for this six-hour workshop.

There was a break during which people were asked to form pairs and have one pair stay at the table while others moved to new tables; people were invited to be attentive to the color of the stars on name tags in forming groups, allowing people who were new to welfare legislation to work with people who had experience, thus inviting participants to be teachers as well as learners.

2C. Working individually or in pairs at tables, read a history of the Personal Responsibility and Work Opportunity Reconciliation Act (PRWORA). Highlight what is important to you. If you need clarification while you are reading, ask NET-WORK staff or a resource person at your table.

2D. At your table form two groups and study the provisions of PRWORA. A glossary of related terms is included in your folder as a resource. Group A will study the *six* provisions on pages 9–11. Group B will study the *five* provisions on pages 11–12. Using the form provided, write your summary of the changes. When you need assistance, ask NET-WORK staff or a resource person at your table. Decide how you will present your provisions to the other group at the table.

Provisions of the law were presented in four pages in three-column format: column 1 titled "Provision" (for example, funding, time limits, work requirements), column 2 titled "Under the Old Law," and column 3 titled "Under PRWORA". Columns 2 and 3 offered a one- to three-sentence synthesis of each provision. A worksheet was offered with two columns: column 1 listed the eleven provisions and column 2 was titled "How would you summarize the change?" (History and provisions were used with permission from *Cruel and Unusual Punishment: How Welfare "Reform" Punishes Poor People* [Gordon, 2001].)

2E. Share your summary of the provisions with the other group at your table. After both groups have shared, identify your questions about the general changes in the law.

   In the large group, we'll hear and respond to as many questions as time allows.

2F. The effects of PRWORA

   Take from your folder the sheet with the title "Welfare Reform in (Your State)" and "Welfare Reform in the United States" on the reverse. Study and highlight what is important to you from the two pages. [Data from a report issued by a coalition partner: *How Does Your State Rate?* (2001).]

   Read a sample of what Congress and the public are hearing on page 14. This was an excerpt from a Congressional Research Service report for Congress.

   Select three numbers between one and twenty. Read and highlight the three research items from the NETWORK study and other sources on pages 15–22 that are marked with the corresponding numbers you selected. [Participants had twenty excerpts from research and reporting on welfare reform from studies done by NETWORK, other antipoverty organizations, think tanks, and major newspapers.]

At your tables, share what you highlighted. Add your own experience—that is, what other ways— negative and positive—have you seen PRWORA affect people? Identify, draw, and share an image that summarizes your reaction to what you have studied. We'll hear a sample.

The design continued with further learning tasks designed to meet the achievement-based objectives and to teach the content.

Principles and Practices at Work

Using dialogue education posed several challenges. Among these was attention to a complex *who* (participants) and the dynamic relationship of this group to the *what* (content) in planning and design. It meant a shift from monologue to dialogue in implementation. It presented multiple contexts for evaluation.

As the project team organized the data from staff listening sessions into a Seven Design Steps matrix, two significant patterns emerged. First, in efforts to be inclusive, the *who* was extremely broad. Many different constituencies had been invited to the workshops. Second, in efforts to be thorough, the *what*, or content, for the workshop was more than could be taught in six hours. With the seven steps as a guide, we soon realized that the key to helping select content was a clearer articulation of our *who*.

We looked again at our *why* (the situation): if we were to be successful, Congress needed to hear from a significant number of people, more people than we could gather at twenty-one workshops.

We soon posited that, ideally, after a workshop each participant would lead others in communicating with members of Congress about welfare reform. Further, during the LNRA teleconference with a sample of workshop hosts, people tapped into the creative tension outlined earlier in this chapter; some of the materials we had already distributed about welfare reform contained detailed analysis necessary for Congress but at times overwhelming for our members. Hosts reminded us that people needed concise, accessible materials with clear suggestions on when and what to communicate to elected officials.

As a result, the project team decided that each learning task and the supporting materials must honor what was emerging. Participants needed to leave the workshop with a packet of learning tasks and materials that they in turn could use with others. That would lead this second generation of participants to contact their members of Congress. Further, in the workshop, participants needed to develop the motivation and confidence to do this work. Having made these decisions, we could eliminate content and edit the learning tasks into more concise and accessible language.

Exploration of *who* addressed another design challenge. Staff placed a high value on including in the workshops people who had personally experienced poverty and the welfare system. This raised a number of issues, most notably around the principle of safety (Vella, 2002). For people in poverty, discussion of poverty policy is far more than a cognitive exercise. How could we respectfully invite and elicit the participation of this critical group? After careful consideration, the project team decided that a vital group of participants were social service agencies, meaning both those who offer and receive services. As a result, preworkshop materials, including sample promotional pieces, encouraged hosts to issue special invitations to employees and clients of service agencies.

The design team discovered a dynamic interdependence among the seemingly discrete parts of the Seven Design Steps. In continuing to explore and refine our responses to those simple questions—

who, why, when, where, what, what for, and how—a delicate and profound whole began to emerge. At times, articulating answers to each of the questions seemed tedious and unimportant. However, had we not pursued this rigorous discipline, the resulting design and learning would have been compromised.

From Monologue to Dialogue: Learning to Be a Midwife

It is difficult to find an accurate metaphor for the transition that occurs when we invite others to practice dialogue education. Perhaps an apt image is that of a midwife presiding over a birth: during the difficult stages we offer encouragement and assurance, bearing witness to the pain and struggle, and when the miracle of new life emerges, we celebrate.

Traditionally, the content of NETWORK workshops has been based in the detailed research prepared for Congress. Because an average workshop is two to three hours long, a lecture or monologue approach seemed the most efficient way to deliver the information. Further, because NETWORK membership includes a considerable number of people with graduate degrees and experience in public policy, this format was both familiar and expected.

When staff, who eventually would be facilitating the workshops, reviewed the initial draft, they raised a number of legitimate concerns. Could we ask people to read during a workshop? Why have busy staff fly around the country to facilitate a design that required only a few brief lectures and a lot of hands-on learning? Would our members who were experienced in public policy and lobbying find this design too simple?

Like midwives, we were witnessing the pains of birth. Our job was to listen, coach, and reassure NETWORK staff. We practiced dialogue by listening and incorporating useful suggestions into the design. We respectfully listened to people's real fears and coached them on the principles and practices that shaped the design. We forged ahead, reassuring people that the design would effectively meet the achievement-based objectives and the larger goals we had together set for the campaign.

This process was also evident in the team scheduled to deliver the first workshop in San Antonio, Texas. The team included our senior lobbyist, Catherine Pinkerton, a Sister of St. Joseph who commands the respect and attention of members of Congress. In her eighteen years at NETWORK, she has delivered many workshops throughout the country. She is highly regarded for her in-depth grasp of complex political issues. Although her profound interest in lifelong learning ensured genuine openness to new approaches, her questions and uncharacteristic nervousness hinted at serious reservations about the potential effectiveness of dialogue education with NETWORK members.

Sister Catherine's first learning task in the workshop involved the history and provisions of welfare reform, a topic on which she could easily provide a sound and thorough lecture with minimal prepara-tion. This time, however, always gracious and commanding, she pro-vided a brief and compelling story to introduce the learning task.

People went right to work, two groups per table, studying half the provisions of the welfare law and how it changed in 1996. Next, the two groups taught one another the welfare provisions they had learned. When people were stuck, they asked Sister Catherine or one of the other facilitators for assistance. The energy in the room was palpable as lawyers, case managers, welfare assistance recipients, social justice coordinators from parishes and diocese, community organizers, and retired teachers learned together. They studied the provisions of the laws and how they had changed, many jumping ahead to the effects, saying, "Ah, that's why. . . . "

As group work for this task was coming to a close, Sister Cather-ine approached the table where I was sitting. "It's really working," she whispered, beaming with a combination of wonder and relief. Like the midwife who witnesses the miracle of new life, we knew it was time to celebrate. We were all learning. Our hope was that members of Congress could learn too.

Multiple Contexts for Evaluation: What Is Success?

In dialogue education we look at evaluation in terms of learning, transfer, and impact. (Vella, Berardinelli, and Burrow, 1998). In the Making a Noise About the Need campaign, these were important constructs. Feedback gathered from the twenty-one regional workshops suggested that real learning took place:

"I never fully understood TANF until today. And I never felt like I could really influence Congress until today. I feel like I am part of a larger more influential group."

"An important learning for me was the urgency of educating others about the issues of poverty and the essential items needed in reauthorizing the TANF legislation."

"I found writing a letter to our member of Congress to be useful. It was my first!"

"I think the interactive sections with others helped me to 'say the words' in my own words about the issues. This helped me to take ownership of the issues and the solutions. . . . I knew nothing about lobbying when I came. I now know that I can make a difference."

"The welfare laws have been confusing for me. The workshop has clarified some of the important aspects. I also met some county social workers and will keep connected with them."

"I had felt discouraged in being able to influence anyone on my own. Now I see the numbers (of which I am one part) making a difference. I feel empowered!"

NETWORK also has evidence of transfer. Through our interactive Web site and other communications, we know participants returned to their organization to lead other people in lobbying members of Congress about welfare reauthorization. Still others replicated either one learning task or the entire workshop with their colleagues and friends. Some organized bus trips to the NETWORK lobby day, where 150 people made visits to forty-three senators and forty-five members of the U.S. House of Representatives. More than 90 people made their first contact that day with a member of Congress.

What we still hope for is an impact on Congress. With our coalition partners, we have moved from multiple message points on policy to a simple plea for the Senate to bring the legislation to the floor for a vote. The impact of our work in the chambers of Congress is still to be seen.

This raises questions about the context for evaluation. With projects such as this, how do we truly measure the impact and success of our efforts? In the context of the congressional vote on the issue, we may experience failure this session. But if the context is the hearts and minds of citizens, the indicators are the affective and psychomotor responses of people who know that they know. They recognize that they can *do* basic policy analysis, that they can *do* lobbying, that they can work with others to eventually make a difference. That is success.

Development of Theory: Hologram as Metaphor for Dialogue Education

In *Dialogue and the Art of Thinking Together,* William Isaacs uses the image of the hologram to explore participation and language (1999). This metaphor has rich possibilities for dialogue education.

A hologram is a laser-generated image captured on a special plate. When illuminated by a laser, the plate produces a three-dimensional image. For example, imagine a tulip. If the plate is broken into two pieces, each piece will contain the full image of the tulip. Breaking these two halves will produce yet smaller pieces that continue to display, though less clearly, the full tulip.

An effective dialogue education event embodies the principles and practices of the approach (Vella, 1995), and like a hologram, when broken into smaller *parts* continues to reflect the *whole*. If we as individuals are, as Danah Zohar suggests, "a whole chorus of conversations in harmony" (1997, p. 121), then the dialogue process begins internally, with openness to the creative tensions in my own thinking. Likewise, the principles and practices are evident in the interactions between the two members of a project team, among

staff advising the team, among facilitators and workshop participants, and ultimately, in dialogue between constituents and their
elected leaders.

A Dance with Potential

Given an understandable cynicism toward elected federal officials,
the democratic notion of constituents engaging in dialogue with
Congress may seem naïve. This conclusion is particularly logical if
we are looking to *what is*—the *actuality* of prevailing experience.
Such thinking, however, denies the possibility of *what could be*—
potentiality.

In their primer on new science, *Who's Afraid of Schrodinger's Cat?*
Ian Marshall and Dana Zohar explain that in a quantum world
"potentiality is a second domain of existence, and thus that possibilities are to some extent real entities" (1997, p. 42). If we apply
this to dialogue education and the NETWORK campaign, exciting
potential for dialogue and true democracy emerges.

For NETWORK this is not purely speculative. The campaign
offered evidence that a number of participants engaged in meaningful dialogue with elected officials. Perhaps this suggests that out
of a workshop that elicits from participants newfound potential (to
analyze policy, to speak about laws in their own words, to learn skills
for engaging with political leaders) together we evoke a world where
respectful conversations between officials and citizens is celebrated.

Conclusions

I remember the pain I felt during my weeklong introduction to dialogue education in 1995 in the Learning to Listen, Learning to
Teach course. I realized that my fifteen-year practice of monologue
education had often created an unintended violence, one that
robbed people of the opportunity to engage deeply and wholly with
content, to make both the subject, and by extension, the world,
their own. In my need to be the expert and in control, I also had

robbed myself of two great treasures open to practitioners of dialogue education: learning and joy.

As an experienced practitioner of dialogue education today, I believe that most adult learners are searching for dialogic learning, for settings in which their life experience is honored in the learning of new skills, knowledge, and attitudes. As a person interested in democracy, creating such settings is essential. For how can people ever know that their voices and experiences can count in the halls of Congress if they are not heard and honored in the classroom, training center, community hall, or house of prayer? As Paulo Freire observed, "Democracy, like any dream, is not made with spiritual words, but with reflection and practice" (Freire, 1998, p. 67).

References

Cobourn, H. C. *Poverty Amid Plenty: The Unfinished Business of Welfare Reform.* Washington, D.C.: NETWORK, 1999.

Freire, P. *Teachers as Cultural Workers: Letters to Those Who Dare Teach* (D. Macedo, D. Koike, and A. Oliveira, trans.). Boulder, Colo.: Westview Press, 1998.

Gordon, R. *Cruel and Unusual Punishment: How Welfare "Reform" Punishes Poor People.* Oakland, Calif.: Applied Research Center, 2001.

How Does Your State Rate? Washington, D.C.: RESULTS, 2001.

Isaacs, W. *Dialogue and the Art of Thinking Together.* New York: Doubleday, 1999.

Marshall, I., and Zohar, D. *Who's Afraid of Schrodinger's Cat?* New York: William Morrow, 1997.

Niedringhaus, S. *Welfare Reform: How Do We Define Success?* Washington, D.C.: NETWORK, 2001.

Vella, J. *Training Through Dialogue: Promoting Effective Learning and Change with Adults.* San Francisco: Jossey-Bass, 1995.

Vella, J. *Taking Learning to Task: Creative Strategies for Teaching Adults.* San Francisco: Jossey-Bass, 2000.

Vella, J. *Learning to Listen, Learning to Teach.* San Francisco: Jossey-Bass, 2002. (Originally published 1994.)

Vella, J., Berardinelli, P., and Burrow, J. *How Do They Know They Know? Evaluating Adult Learning.* San Francisco: Jossey-Bass, 1998.

Zohar, D. *Rewiring the Corporate Brain.* San Francisco: Berrett-Koehler, 1997.

Open Questions for Analysis and Synthesis

1. What strikes you about the learning tasks shown in this case?

2. How do you see the Seven Design Steps serving this group as they planned the national workshop?

3. Why do you think Sister Catherine was "courageous" in this situation?

4. What principles and practices do you see evident in this case?

5. In Chapter Ten the Mountain Microenterprise team revised a curriculum as well. And so did the CASA team in Chapter Eight. What similarities do you perceive in each case? What differences do you see?

14

Choices: Steps Toward Health

A Dialogue Education Curriculum of the National Extended Food and Nutrition Program

Jean Anliker

This chapter shows how learning about dialogue education is not enough; teachers and students alike need to create a curriculum and learning materials that are congruent with the principles and practices of dialogue.

I first encountered the Expanded Food and Nutrition Education Program (EFNEP) in 1973, when I was working for the Iowa Maternity and Infant Care Project. I referred new mothers to EFNEP because I knew that the program's paraprofessionals would take the time to go into their families' homes over several months. They would teach mothers how to prepare healthier meals and feed their children using the foods, utensils, equipment, and other resources that the families had available to them. As trained members of the target communities, EFNEP staff taught with sensitivity and understanding, using what I have always called "teaching from the heart." In 1977 I began working with EFNEP, and have either worked with EFNEP or continued to use the EFNEP model in nutrition education for the past twenty-five years.

The Expanded Food and Nutrition Education Program

EFNEP audiences are diverse, including pregnant women, families with children, youth, the homeless, people in shelters and institutions, and others. Throughout the country EFNEP also reaches people of many cultures by recruiting members of those cultural groups and training them to work as paraprofessionals in their own communities.

In establishing EFNEP in 1969, Congress identified the target audiences, the results sought, and the primary mode of delivery. But within this framework, EFNEP has evolved. One-to-one visits once conducted in the homes eventually changed to small group meetings, and then larger groups for greater cost-effectiveness. The educational approach changed as well. Early paraprofessional educators could work side by side with homemakers in their homes, preparing foods and talking about nutrition concerns that the participants expressed. As small groups emerged, however, more standardized curricula were developed to ensure the completeness and accuracy of information provided. One of the most popular national curricula featured a series of flip charts with pictures for the participants to see while the paraprofessionals read a prepared script. Meetings also moved away from homes to community sites, where it was more difficult to assess the homemakers' resources and food preparation was not always feasible.

Eventually larger groups were recruited, often from other agencies such as the Special Supplemental Nutrition Program for Women, Infants, and Children (WIC). The small flip charts were replaced by classroom teaching methods and group facilitation strategies. At the same time, the science of nutrition was advancing and many paraprofessionals sought to provide greater amounts of information to their participants. For many of the low-income EFNEP homemakers, traditional classroom learning had not been a positive experience. Fortunately, most EFNEP supervisors and paraprofessionals were aware of these dynamics and worked to make the sessions practical, interactive, and hands-on. EFNEP has steadily shown positive impacts on the dietary quality, food resource management, and food safety practices of their participants (U.S. Department of Agriculture, 2002). However, there is still room for improvement.

Dialogue Education Calls for a New Curriculum

Dialogue education had the unique capacity to change the EFNEP experience for both the paraprofessional educators and the learners by transforming the entire educational model. Joye Norris, author of *Maximizing Paraprofessional Potential*, had introduced the concept of learning through dialogue to the EFNEP staff in Massachusetts and many other states (Norris and Baker, 1998). In spite of the excitement generated by this approach, however, Massachusetts EFNEP paraprofessionals were having difficulty applying it in their existing curriculum. When the fifth edition of the dietary guidelines for Americans was released (U.S. Department of Agriculture and U.S. Department of Health and Human Services, 2000), it led to a call for the development of a completely new curriculum in Massachusetts (see Chapter Three by Meredith Pearson). Profiting from this opportunity, we chose to develop and test the first dialogue education curriculum for EFNEP in the nation.

Preliminary Planning

A variety of resources informed the development of the new curriculum, including surveys of EFNEP participants; focus groups including EFNEP participants, collaborators, and staff; shifts in Massachusetts demographics and attendance patterns; new dietary recommendations; and the dialogue-based learning model. In February 2001, the Massachusetts EFNEP and Family Nutrition Program (FNP) supervisors met to review the feedback from the formative research and make preliminary decisions about the content and design of the curriculum, and the process for its development.

Curriculum Content

The choice of target messages was the greatest challenge. Advances in the science of nutrition increased the amount and complexity of information available. In addition, EFNEP audiences told us that they wanted to learn more about topics popularized in the media, like weight control, child feeding, and dining out. But in our formative research, participants said they would come to only half the sessions that the previous curriculum had included (six or seven versus twelve). Furthermore, dialogue education demanded more interaction around fewer but more meaningful learning objectives.

It was difficult to let go of traditional nutrition education content. However, one question finally moved the group forward: *What are the key nutrition messages today, compared with thirty years ago?* In answering this question, we were able to focus on seven target issues: physical activity, fruits and vegetables, whole grains, low-fat eating, food safety, food shopping, and eating away from home.

Lesson Design

Considering the formative research and needs of their audiences, the development team and EFNEP staff decided that each lesson should have the following components:

A brief physical exercise

Food tasting or cooking, which could vary in nature from preparing a recipe to simply presenting a platter of fruits and vegetables

At least one principle of food safety, which could be linked to the food preparation or tasting

At least one hands-on learning task

An emphasis on cultural diversity

Time for setting and reviewing personal goals

Application of learned principles for children

Curriculum Design

Once the lesson topics were chosen, the graphic designer worked on the visual identity of the product and packaging design. The first decision was a twist for the topics. Because movement was a new and unique element in the curriculum that would be reinforced in each lesson, it made sense to draw it into the lesson names as well: "Moving to the Mambo" for the movement lesson; "Foods a Go-Go" for eating on the run. Once the pattern began, everyone generated ideas: "Whole Grain Twist," "5-A-Day Salsa," "Low-Fat Limbo," "Kitchen Calypso," "Food Safety 4-Step." The titles gave the lessons energy and a sense of the cultural diversity that characterizes our audience. To further reinforce these elements, we chose music consistent with the title of each lesson. Today, the educators play these pieces as people arrive at the sessions and when they do the physical activities. Some also use the music to mark time for various learning tasks. The lively music adds to the festive atmosphere of each session.

What's in a Name?

What to name the curriculum was an important decision. The team wanted words that would show respect for the learners, honor their roles in the experience, and entice their interest. *Choices* seemed to reflect the process of creating personal meaning for the participants. *Steps Toward Health*, with its double meaning, conveyed both the dance-movement theme and the goal-setting element, where participants are encouraged to make changes one step at a time. And so that became the program title we chose: Choices: Steps Toward Health.

A Picture of Health

The next step was to develop a visual identity. Seven festive colors and simple but bold logos were developed, one of each for each lesson. Although they worked independently to set the focus on the individual topics, they were also integrated to form an overall curriculum logo, showing how a healthy diet can be formed from a collection of healthy choices.

A Box of Resources

The development team chose to print the curriculum on large cards and package these in an attractive box with tabs for each lesson. Three additional tabs marked a welcome section with reference items that could be used throughout the curriculum, a recipe section, and a section for simple physical exercises or stretches that participants might do at home. We printed membership cards to promote a feeling of belonging. Staff found the package innovative, fun, and flexible.

Involvement of EFNEP Staff in Curriculum Development

It is critically important to involve staff in any curriculum they will be teaching (Anliker and others, 1999). The EFNEP supervisors and paraprofessionals know their target audiences and their teaching environments thoroughly. Therefore, staff were involved in the curriculum development process in a variety of ways.

EFNEP supervisors met several times to talk about the dialogue education curriculum, including the scope and sequence, learning tasks, and other considerations. The paraprofessional educators met separately to express their needs and ideas, and as the developer I observed some of them teaching in their communities. Both the supervisors and paraprofessionals submitted favorite activities and recipes.

As I integrated their thoughts with my own, I sought their feedback at several stages. First, I demonstrated a sample lesson to both supervisors and paraprofessionals. Next, I asked supervisors to review and comment on all the draft lesson plans. After these comments were incorporated, we held a three-day retreat for the supervisors to try out the lessons and strengthen their facilitation skills. An advisory group of the paraprofessionals also met to review and comment on all the lessons.

The lessons were revised based on the comments received. Both the supervisors and paraprofessionals were invited to pilot-test the curriculum. The curriculum was officially launched in a three-day training, where the paraprofessionals from each of the Massachusetts pilot offices demonstrated a lesson for the entire pilot group, which also included EFNEP and FNP staff from Maryland and Pennsylvania.

Development Team

The curriculum was developed through a strong three-pronged effort: development and writing, Jean Anliker; graphic design, Lynne Thompson; project management, Cindy Hubbard. Joye Norris provided consultation in dialogue education and reviewed all the lessons. This team worked closely together in all aspects of product development.

Writing

As the author, I came with previous experience in writing an interactive nutrition education curriculum for low-income culturally diverse audiences. I had learned the power of listening to and learning from participants and had applied many dialogue-based principles in previous programs. But as I studied the dialogue education approach with Joye Norris, I acquired a new language and structure that helped the curriculum come alive.

We began with core principles, such as raising all voices, having teachers become co-learners and learners become co-teachers, providing opportunities for personal meaning, and having participants look back and bridge forward to apply what they had learned. We looked at the power of beginnings and endings as key learning opportunities in each session, at language development, and at ways to ensure respect and safety. After exchanging a few drafts, we decided to meet for three days to lay the groundwork for each lesson, and we came away with a strong framework.

The first session, "Moving to the Mambo," introduces participants to the program and its core principles under the heading,

"We're all making choices together." These were designed to stress the importance of the co-teaching, co-learning partnership:

> We'll share in several sessions, and every one of you is important to these sessions!
>
> We'll all teach and learn from each other!
>
> We'll share recipes and foods to taste and want to know what you think!
>
> We'll have a box of materials that you can take home and use.
>
> We'll invite you to participate in our activities but you don't have to say or do anything you're not comfortable with.
>
> We'll set goals together and help each other reach them.

Each lesson is organized around three core questions that participants answer by completing the lesson objectives. The learning objectives of each lesson center on different verbs, so a variety of learning tasks are built into the lesson plans, and the completion of each learning objective can be observed. The specified objectives are met as an integral part of the lesson. Table 14.1 presents an example of the core questions or content and learning objectives for "Moving to the Mambo," put into the dialogue education framework. Then beneath each learning objective, we could list the learning tasks and resources needed to help participants achieve it.

To include food tasting, we added one additional learning objective, "By the end of this session you will have selected a healthy snack you can take with you on a walk."

At the end of "Moving to the Mambo," participants learn how to set simple, measurable, achievable goals for themselves. Then each person is invited to write one goal for increasing physical activity. We also offer three "attachment strategies," or simple things they can do to help them "attach the new information to their brains." We encourage each participant to choose one of the three.

Table 14.1   Core Questions for "Moving to the Mambo"

Questions-Content		Learning Objectives
Question #1:	What is physical activity?	By the end of this session, you will have . . . described what physical activity means to you and done three different physical activities.
Question #2:	Why does physical activity matter?	By the end of this session, you will have . . . decided why physical activity is important to you.
Question #3:	How can you be more physically active?	By the end of this session, you will have . . . advised each other about ways to overcome barriers to physical activity and chosen one or more ways to increase your physical activity in the coming week.

This closure with one personal goal and one attachment strategy, repeated in each of the remaining lessons, enables each person to reflect on what he or she has learned while choosing how to apply that information in the future. Then each subsequent lesson begins with participants sharing in pairs what they did. We also provide charts (a small one for personal use, and a large one for the group), on which people can monitor their progress if they so choose.

Besides the materials used directly for the learning objectives— such as posters, sorting cards, a food safety bingo game, food labels, stickers, and three-dimensional models—we include other materials to reinforce learning. In the welcome section, for example, we include the personal goal chart, a guide for reading labels, and a glossary of food and nutrition terms. In the recipe section, we include a glossary of cooking terms and nearly fifty recipes. Each has icons to show the nutrition principles that may apply: heart-healthy or low- or reduced-fat foods, whole-grain foods, careful handling for food safety, and the inclusion of at least one serving of a fruit or vegetable. In the physical activities section, we include copies of the cards, with adaptations for people with limited physical movement, so participants can do them at home.

Additional Design Elements

Many design elements are included to help guide participants through the curriculum. For example, each card carries a heading marking the lesson in both title and icon. Each of the educator materials, such as the posters and cards, is similarly marked. Icons also are used within each lesson to mark what the learner does: check goals, do a physical activity, talk, listen, watch, taste, do a hands-on activity, and set new goals. The design team felt that these were more important than other types of graphics, since they could serve as signals to both the educators and the learners and reinforce the importance of participation.

Evaluation Plans

The first version of Choices: Steps Toward Health was completed by the end of June 2002, and was introduced at a three-day training session for pilot staff, as already mentioned. During the June training, Massachusetts EFNEP paraprofessional educators demonstrated four of the lessons, and Joye Norris spent a day training staff in the seven core dialogue education facilitation skills: invite, ask, wait, affirm, weave, energize, and embrace. The curriculum was pilot-tested through the fall. Based on what was learned, we will revise the curriculum and release the final version in 2003.

Massachusetts, Maryland, and Pennsylvania began pilot-testing the curriculum in August and September 2002. Each state reached at least one hundred participants. Most were EFNEP participants, but some were participants in the Family Nutrition Program (FNP), another federally funded nutrition education program targeted to food stamp participants. The emphasis of the pilot evaluation, led by Elena Carbone of the University of Massachusetts, is to examine how well the curriculum works at all levels of delivery: for the participants, the paraprofessionals, and the supervisors. Through feedback sheets completed by the participants and paraprofessionals at each session, observation sheets completed by the supervisors, and focus groups of paraprofessionals, we will see what works well and what can be improved. We will also look at participants' stages of change (Prochaska, DiClemente, and Norcross, 1992) and actual dietary practices (assessed through twenty-four-hour recalls and a food behavior checklist) at the beginning and end of the curriculum.

Challenges and Future Plans for Choices: Steps Toward Health

Two of the greatest challenges have been the diversity of EFNEP audiences and the diversity of EFNEP settings. In Massachusetts, EFNEP participants include both men and women, from many cultures, at different life stages, with varying literacy skills and educational backgrounds. These individuals are reached in a variety of settings, including other agency sites, jails, recovery institutions, shelters, and halfway houses. Some participants have little control over the foods that are purchased and served to them; others have a great deal of control. Some facilities allow food preparation and offer enough space for physical movement; others do not. Some settings allow the educators two or more hours to teach; others strictly limit sessions to one hour. These issues create real challenges in making a curriculum meaningful and relevant.

These circumstances are well addressed by dialogue education. Dialogue education invites all participants to work with the topic as it applies to their personal lives, so a richness of views can be exchanged. It also provides a great opportunity for the paraprofessionals to learn more about their learners. Questions can be reworded slightly for different groups. For example, questions about food shopping can be worded in the future tense for people who are in institutions. Furthermore, the openness of dialogue education allows for flexibility in meeting different time frames.

Still, more work is planned to address this diversity. One plan is to establish a Hispanic advisory committee and fully adapt the curriculum for Hispanic audiences. This adaptation will extend not only to language and foods but also to other elements, such as culturally appropriate learning tasks, culturally relevant issues, and even design considerations including graphics and color.

Another possibility will be to expand the number of learning tasks offered in support of each objective so that paraprofessionals can select those most relevant to their audiences. For example, preliminary feedback from a group of men in recovery suggests that men may prefer different types of physical activities.

Conclusions

It has been exciting and rewarding to develop Choices: Steps Toward Health as a dialogue education curriculum and to have the pleasure of working with Joye Norris. But the real excitement has been in learning. It is true: teachers become co-learners and learners become co-teachers in dialogue education. I have learned a great deal in this process from the EFNEP paraprofessionals, supervisors, and all others involved in the curriculum. As we continue to receive feedback from participants we realize that the learning goes on.

References

Anliker, J., Damron, D., Ballesteros, M., Feldman, R., Langenberg, P., and Havas, S. "Using Peer Educators in Nutrition Intervention Research: Lessons Learned from the Maryland WIC 5-A-Day Promotion Program." *Journal of Nutrition Education*, 1999, *31*(6), 347–354.

Norris, J., and Baker, S. *Maximizing Paraprofessional Potential*. Malabar, Fla.: Krieger, 1998.

Prochaska, J. O., DiClemente, C. C., and Norcross, J. C. "In Search of How People Change: Applications to Addictive Behaviors." *American Psychologist*, 1992, *47*(9), 1102–1114.

U.S. Department of Agriculture. *EFNEP FY 2001 Program Impacts*. [http://www.reeusda.gov/f4hn/efnep/efnep01-booklet.pdf]. June 2002.

U.S. Department of Agriculture and U.S. Department of Health and Human Services. *Nutrition and Your Health: Dietary Guidelines for Americans* (5th ed.). Home and Garden Bulletin no. 232. Washington, D.C.: Government Printing Office, 2000.

Open Questions for Analysis and Synthesis

1. What do you see as the most essential element the team used to make certain this curriculum used dialogue education?

2. What principles and practices do you see at work in this case?

3. In Chapter Three, Meredith Pearson writes about dialogue education training for EFNEP staff in a university setting. What connections do you see between these two cases?

15

Vermont Math and Science Teachers Move from Monologue to Dialogue

Kathy Johnson, Peter Perkins, Nicole Saginor

Vermont educators had their work cut out for them when undertaking the mission to "dramatically transform the teaching and learning of science, math, and technology in Vermont." The Vermont Institute for Science, Math and Technology (VISMT) was created in 1992 to fulfill this stated mission as part of the National Science Foundation's Statewide Systemic Initiative grant program. This chapter describes some of that work, and demonstrates how dialogue education contributed to these transformational efforts through one specific aspect of the work of VISMT: the development of a cadre of exceptional teacher leaders, called VISMT Teacher Associates.

The Teacher Associates Program

The VISMT Teacher Associates Program identified outstanding teachers of science, math, and technology in the K–12 grades and also at the college level. They were selected to leave their classrooms for one or two years to provide professional development in high-quality standards-based instruction to other educators in their own school districts or colleges and around the state. In order to make the shift from teaching children to teaching adults, the Teacher Associates received extensive professional development in the content and pedagogy of the national math and science standards and in standards for delivering high-quality professional development. A cornerstone of this preparation was the thirty-hour dialogue education course Learning to Listen, Learning to Teach.

All VISMT projects, including the Teacher Associates Program, address equity. Equity is defined here as increasing the access, retention, and positive outcomes of groups who have not traditionally been known to be successful in science, math, or technology (such as females, people from economically disadvantaged backgrounds, people of diverse racial and ethnic backgrounds, people with disabilities, and others). Dialogue education, based on principles of respect, safety, and inclusion, is a strategy for attaining equity. Developing Teacher Associates who apply dialogue education in their work models equitable teaching that results in sustainable learning.

The Design

Helping teachers to transform their science, math, and technology teaching and learning has taken many shapes in Vermont in the ten years between 1992 and 2002. One frequent approach of the VISMT Teacher Associates is to work with groups of teachers from a specific school over a period of time. The Teacher Associates work with the schools on specific topics, such as selecting new standards-based math programs, or aligning K–12 science curricula with state and national standards. A majority of associates find the Seven Design Steps (Vella, 2002), and the associated principles and practices to be essential in the success of these efforts.

As this chapter title indicates, dialogue education was used in Vermont to move Vermont teachers from monologue to dialogue. This design is one example of how two Teacher Associates used dialogue education (1) to introduce a group of educators to three distinct math programs and (2) to make an informed decision by reaching consensus as a group about which math program the supervisory union would purchase and implement. Typical professional development in the past would have attempted to teach about the three math programs through a series of monologues about the strengths and weaknesses of each.

Dialogue Education

This professional development and consensus-building project took place during the 1998–99 school year in a northern Vermont school system called a supervisory union. This union is one of the largest in the state, comprising thirteen towns, each with its own elementary school and school board. The central administration decided that the entire union would purchase a single standards-based math program to improve the math learning of its students through the middle school grades. VISMT was asked to help educators become familiar with three alternative programs so an informed decision could be made for adoption and implementation in September 1999. The participants in the workshop series included twenty middle-school and ninth-grade educators. The series was led by two VISMT Teacher Associates as lead teachers and two additional Teacher Associates as guest content experts. In designing the learning events, the two VISMT Teacher Associates started with a learning needs and resource assessment (LNRA). They met individually with or telephoned many of the educators who would be involved prior to the sessions. They surveyed their current knowledge about standards-based mathematics and listened to the pulse of the group. After they had completed the assessment, they used the Seven Design Steps to plan the sessions. The activities and learning tasks included the following:

- Exploring current understanding through brainstorming and discussion

- Generating criteria for selection through consensus-building

- Examining and analyzing program materials and supporting documents

- Engaging in math activities from each program

- Debriefing the program elements and the pedagogy of inquiry-based instruction

- Conducting the final analysis of the programs and the process

- Reviewing the conditions and supports needed for successful implementation of new programs

The initial part of the series provided the participants with sufficient understanding of the power of standards-based mathematics and how they relate to the Vermont Framework of Standards and Learning Opportunities. The next sessions focused on the development of criteria for evaluating standards-based programs and applying those criteria to three different programs. Finally, they explored some of the implications of change in the context of the participants' schools.

By the end of the sessions, participants had identified their current understanding of standards-based mathematics, created a list of criteria to be used in decision making, reviewed the philosophy, organization, instructional approach, and resources available in the three math programs, and made a decision to implement one of them. In addition, they had considered different forms of support needed for successful implementation and determined which provided the best fit for the supervisory union. Perhaps most important, the group had grown together through the process to become a true learning community. One of the participants remarked, and many others agreed, how amazing it was that a clear informed consensus was actually reached by a group of twenty educators!

Principles and Practices at Work

The four principles and practices that follow are those most often cited by VISMT Teacher Associates as critical to their success. Each of these principles and practices had an important application in the example described here.

Learning Needs and Resource Assessment

Among the most critical parts of the process used by the Teacher Associates was conducting the LNRA. As one VISMT educator said about doing an LNRA before providing professional development: "It's all about asking first before telling, and being sure to ask in the right way." Another VISMT educator emphasized the "resources" component of the LNRA, although the LNRA often erroneously gets referred to as a "needs assessment" only. Focusing on a group's needs, but not on the resources they bring to the room, is not congruent with what we understand of dialogue education. Gathering information from participants before the sessions takes time and requires advance preparation. VISMT Teacher Associates learned that the time is well worth the effort, because the respect they give their participants always results in a more positive reception and better results overall. More than a few Teacher Associates have lamented, after the fact, that they neglected this piece at great cost. When the LNRA was not completed, Teacher Associates often found themselves surprised by the unexpected. Many of these surprises were great learning experiences for them, but were not necessarily as positive for the participants!

The two Teacher Associates in this example found out before they walked into the room that many of the participants did not have favorable opinions about standards-based math programs. They discovered that not all members of the group wanted the entire district to use one math curriculum, and that not all of these teachers even taught math. In addition, they knew that these teachers had papers to correct and families to attend to, and would not feel respected if the process was not crisp, clear, and in significant ways directly applicable to their work. Here is what one of the group leaders wrote after the first session:

> I just had to let you know how thankful I am for the dialogue education training! My first training was an all-day in-service for the middle school staff. Amy and I worked on it together and tried to plan very carefully in this style. It took a lot of thoughtful work, but we were excited about what we were coming up with. The focus was to be the math program, but we had the entire middle school staff, not just math people, so we were worried about its being relevant to everyone. We decided to present the Vermont Framework of Standards and Learning Opportunities first (based on our needs assessment) and then present the program and tie every component back to the Framework so the idea of "standards-based" would become meaningful. We were a bit nervous for the first few minutes, but then everything pretty much flowed. We had good participation and discussion. People seemed engaged. Good comments were heard and the evaluation forms were very positive. I found it very rewarding to have presented good subject matter in a way that was meaningful and helpful to teachers!

Generative Themes

A second related principle and practice is the use of generative themes to create energy, engage learners, and respond to resistance. The term *generative themes* comes from Paulo Freire's seminal work *Pedagogy of the Oppressed* (1972) and refers to the process of finding what is most meaningful to a group and teaching by drawing on these themes. In this example, one of the facilitators was a Teacher Associate from inside the district who had left her classroom for the year. The other was a teacher leader from outside the district, who was perceived as more neutral. The combination of an "insider," who knew many of the generative themes of the group, and an "outsider," who could offer an objective perspective of how to use the generative themes in a positive manner, helped in the design and implementation.

In one of the initial meetings that preceded the work described earlier, the power of generative themes became very evident. The Teacher Associate was able to marshal potentially negative energy in the group to create a positive dialogue. This session proved to be a starting place for further work:

> I had one day last week where I met a few people who weren't afraid to tell me what they thought. In particular, I addressed a faculty meeting at a local elementary school, about twenty-five teachers. . . . There was some support for the standards-based message but not very much. There were times [when] I felt cornered and almost "attacked." I wanted you to know how much I appreciated dialogue education! I took none of it personally and felt, at the end of an hour, that we [had] had a really good discussion. I was glad that people had a chance to state how they felt. I really believe that is the beginning of change. The good news is that I got invited back! I was originally invited to do a fifteen-minute talk: "Why Standards-Based?" I had prepared a chat but decided I wanted to open it up to their concerns first. I'm glad I did. I wanted you to know how helpful and practical that training was!

Learners as Decision Makers

A third critical principle in this educational effort is the concept of learners as decision makers, or in other terms learners as subjects of their own learning. Many teachers report feelings that professional development is something that is "done to them" rather than something they have any decision-making power over. Often teachers have no say in what the professional development topic will be, when or where it will be, or what their part will be in it. Dialogue education insists that learning tasks be created in which learners have a voice in deciding: What is most significant about the content? What would you add or change? How does it apply in your situation? What part or parts of it has meaning for you?

In the series of workshops described here, a group of educators joined together to learn about and then decide which of three math curricula they wanted to purchase and use for the next several years. The consensus decision-making process was critical in setting the stage for success of the math implementation. One of the lead Teacher Associates said, "For maybe the first time ever, the entire group of teachers felt heard and felt that the curriculum choice was their decision. So often in my work with teachers, they feel they are not the ones making the decisions." The other lead Teacher Associate expanded on this theme by saying, "We really did come to consensus. It was received so well, and people felt the process was really inclusive, that it has become a model for us."

Modeling

Another critical component was the principle and practice of modeling. The teachers joined together to share an experience of learning that modeled the instructional practices they would need to use to implement the new math program successfully. The new standards-based math programs require that math be taught conceptually, with much emphasis on dialogue. Most of the teachers themselves had been taught math in a primarily procedural approach, with little opportunity for dialogue. The new math programs engage students in constructing their own understanding through active learning, communicating their understanding, and thinking through problems with other students. By employing the principles and practices of learners as subjects and modeling, dialogue education provides a learning environment that helps teachers experience their own learning in ways that they can use in their own instructional practice.

Moving Beyond Teaching the Way We Were Taught

Moving beyond teaching the way we were taught requires us not only to understand the difference cognitively but also to feel and personally know the difference between monologue and dialogue.

Professional Learning Communities

The usefulness of professional learning communities has been documented (McLaughlin, 1995). As he put it in his address to the 1995 National Staff Development Council Annual Conference, "Throughout our ten-year study, whenever we found an effective school or an effective department within a school, *without exception* that school or department has been a part of a collaborative professional learning community."

The concept of a professional learning community is carefully laid out by DuFour and Eaker in their book, *Professional Learning Communities at Work: Best Practices for Enhancing Student Achievement* (1998). The book details professional development work that resulted in a dramatic turnaround in an Illinois high school district. According to DuFour and Eaker, one characteristic of a professional learning community is continual professional dialogue and learning. As the example described here shows, we found that by introducing professional development that models dialogue, building collective knowledge, and fostering professional responsibility based on that collective knowledge, we too were more successful in helping teachers create the positive changes they desired in their schools.

Constructed Learning

As schools have attempted to embrace standards-based education and more inquiry-based models of instruction, they have run up against the resistance of some teachers who are unsure of these methods. Often this resistance arises simply because the teachers have never experienced constructed learning in a formal education setting. By *constructed learning* we mean the invitation to learners to make meaning of what they are learning for their own unique context. Many teachers have only had an experience of teaching and learning as giving and receiving facts and information. Schools have long taught as though knowledge originates only outside of the self and must be gathered from experts. This is referred to as *received knowing* and stands in contrast to *constructed knowing* (Belenky, Clinchy, Goldberger, and Tarule, 1986), which is generated through dialogue education. One great challenge of professional development is, therefore, to create a new vision of teaching and learning. All too often the very mention of professional development causes teachers to roll their eyes and recall their experience of the deadly sessions, run by overpaid consultants, that rarely fit their needs and that felt more like something done to them rather than with them. This is because much professional development models *received learning.*

In contrast, *constructed learning* is characterized by real talk or discourse and exploration: talking and listening, questioning, arguing, speculating, and sharing (Belenky, Clinchy, Goldberger, and Tarule, 1986). An awareness of the power of constructed learning is a prerequisite for building a learning community of teaching professionals who become their own experts through their own research, inquiry, and dialogue. Dialogue education embraces a constructed learning mode by insisting on the active participation before, during, and after actual instruction, by honoring prior knowledge of the learner, and by emphasizing not just learning but also transfer and impact (Vella, 2000, 2002; Vella, Berardinelli, and Burrow, 1998).

As we saw in the example of the math teachers described here, when they were offered the opportunity to become their own experts through dialogue, they *owned* their learning and thus were able to transfer it into their practice, creating an important impact in their supervisory union.

Conclusions

The experiences gained by VISMT through dialogue education lay the foundation for a professional learning community with the simple message that teachers have within them either the expertise needed or the ability to generate the expertise through active investigation and dialogue. The experience of dialogue education helps teachers understand that their students as learners can perhaps do the same. The experience of VISMT has been that once teachers get a taste of the exhilaration resulting from the power of their own learning, they are unwilling to return to a model of received learning for themselves or for their students. Although this chapter told the story of a professional development experience in mathematics, there are many similar examples in science and technology education. All the VISMT science materials training is grounded in the principles and practices of dialogue education, as is all the leadership work in training administrators to support standards-based science and math reform and technology integration in their schools. It has become the hallmark of all of VISMT's work, and as such, has come to be expected by the professionals in the field who come to VISMT to learn.

The goal of VISMT to dramatically transform science, math, and technology teaching and learning requires that both VISMT staff and its teacher leaders "walk the talk" of moving from monologue to dialogue in professional development offerings. Change and transformation does not and will not happen by continuing the status quo. As we have seen here, VISMT uses dialogue education as one way of "walking the talk." To meet professional development and equity goals, this group strives to create learning opportunities that allow individuals to shine and develop their full potential within the context of professional learning groups. VISMT has developed new, higher expectations for professional development. Quoting one VISMT Teacher Associate: "Once you've learned about dialogue education, there is no going back."

References

Belenky, M. F., Clinchy, B. M., Goldberger, N. R., and Tarule, J. M. *Women's Ways of Knowing: The Development of Self, Voice, and Mind.* New York: Basic Books, 1986.

DuFour, R., and Eaker, R. *Professional Learning Communities at Work: Best Practices for Enhancing Student Achievement.* Alexandria, Va.: Association for Supervision and Curriculum Development, 1998.

Freire, P. *Pedagogy of the Oppressed.* New York: Herder & Herder, 1972.

McLaughlin, M. "Keynote Address." Presentation at the National Staff Development Council annual conference, Chicago, Dec. 1995.

Vella, J. *Taking Learning to Task: Creative Strategies for Teaching Adults.* San Francisco: Jossey-Bass, 2000.

Vella, J. *Learning to Listen, Learning to Teach: The Power of Dialogue in Educating Adults.* San Francisco: Jossey-Bass, 2002. (Originally published 1994.)

Vella, J., Berardinelli, P., and Burrow, J. *How Do They Know They Know? Evaluating Adult Learning.* San Francisco: Jossey-Bass, 1998.

Open Questions for Analysis and Synthesis

1. What do you think this VISMT program would look like without dialogue education?

2. Which of the principles and practices do you see most operative in the design and implementation of this teacher enhancement program?

3. If you were one of these math or science teachers, what else do you see you would you need from this program to keep these skills and this knowledge working for you?

16

Using Dialogue for Strategic Planning Sessions

Karen G. Ridout

This chapter describes the use of dialogue in the design and implementation of strategic planning programs. At the beginning of each year, many organizations assemble the members of their boards of directors, their committees, and their teams to set their goals for the next several years and to determine their objectives for the coming year. Setting a course and intentionally identifying where they want to be is a primary factor in producing success. They recognize that if they do not know where they want to go or how they want to get there, they allow others to control their course and do not end up with what they want.

As a consultant and facilitator, I am often called in to guide this strategic planning process. The objective of the process, stated by the CEO, manager, or executive director, is basically to determine with the group their goals for the next several years.

For many years I did just that. I set an agenda that included getting input from the stakeholders, identifying strengths, weaknesses, opportunities, and threats (SWOT), brainstorming possibilities and options, setting and prioritizing goals, identifying objectives for each goal, and then writing them up in specific, measurable, achievable, realistic, and time-bound (SMART) terms. I would assign tasks or tactics based on those objectives. We gathered as a group, went through each exercise as a group, and filled many pages of flip charts. It worked, and my clients got what they wanted: a strategic plan.

Often what did not work well for me was dealing with the participants' attitudes before, during, and after the process. As one seasoned board member said prior to the session we were planning, "I believe this planning retreat is essential to do, but I would rather take a beating in the public square than go through it." I have heard many similar words.

Those attitudes changed when I incorporated a learning-centered, dialogue approach in the planning sessions. When I participated in the Learning to Listen, Learning to Teach course, I realized that the efficient approach I was using to facilitate strategic planning sessions could be conducted more effectively. Every person, no matter his or her level of experience or time on the board, has an important contribution to make. The dialogue approach honored every voice being heard. Using dialogue, we transformed the planning retreats into energetic beehives, buzzing with feelings of ownership and enthusiastic commitment and accountability. We still set the goals, do the SWOT analysis, and write the SMART objectives. However, now participants leave with fresh motivation to make a difference in their organization. It happens through collaborative dialogue. Recently a participant said, "I usually am so tired by the end of one of these sessions, but today I'm excited. I can't believe the time passed so quickly and we created so much!"

The Design

How do we provide a fertile environment to promote collaborative dialogue? There are four practices that I experience as key to promoting collaborative dialogue in planning sessions: inductive work, open questions (learning tasks), small group work, and SNOW cards.

Inductive Work

Vella (2002) describes inductive work as *personal meaning-making*. To open a session, I invite all participants to tell their stories—who they are, what strengths they bring, how best to work with them.

This acknowledges each person's value. Doing this conveys the message: "I understand you a little better and you understand me a little better. We can now begin to make this work!" One new board member stated that what she appreciated most about the entire session was this ability to get to know others on the board and their different personalities. These strengthened interpersonal relationships can decide the success or failure of a team.

Questions such as "What strikes you about your organization's mission?" or "What do you see your organization doing to further the mission?" (asked in learning tasks and answered in small groups, then reported to the large group) invite the opportunity for a person to wrestle personally, at the cellular lever, with the meaning of the statement and the actions of the organization. "I feel the mission in my bones, for the first time!" shouted an experienced participant. Accountability and ownership are reinforced.

Open Questions as Learning Tasks

Setting a learning task and having a group do something with it is the catalyst for genuine creativity.

"In groups of four, identify two goals on which you want this organization to focus in the next three years. Tell how the goal will further the mission of the company and why that goal is worthy of organization resources. Write each goal on a SNOW card. As you post your cards on the flip chart, describe your choices to the large group." The dialoguing and debating, the advocating, brainstorming, influencing, and negotiating that happen in the small group provides new ideas for the organization's mission. "An effective strategic plan emerged step-by-step as we built on our mission and vision," concluded one pleased executive director.

Small Groups

Each voice is heard! As a professional facilitator and a personality-type introvert, I have experienced in others and myself the importance of a safe environment. In a small group, a participant can "test" and then reframe the words that often inadequately convey the great ideas and thoughts he wants to impart. He does not have to compete with the extroverts, or with those who may know more about the subject or are in higher positions than he. Such people usually can risk appearing uninformed or not knowledgeable in front of two or three others but would not do so in front of fifteen. As the president of an association said, "The process gave everyone opportunity for input."

Small groups allow people to wrestle with differences in perspectives in a manageable forum. The learning—the idea generation—happens in the small groups. In my experience, when small groups report out, themes and priorities emerge naturally. Rarely is prioritizing a problem. It has already happened. A strategic planning veteran and senior vice president described the experience: "Instantly everyone was engaged, there was equity of input, we didn't have to pull information and comments out of people, and we weren't dominated by the talkers!"

SNOW Cards

A participant who has attended several planning sessions using the dialogue approach says that these colorful notes are addictive: "All we need are blank flip charts, markers, and Post-it notes, and we're ready to go!" It is so simple. Each idea or thought is written, using a felt-tip pen for visibility, on a separate, brightly colored sticky note called a SNOW card—that is, a sticky note on the wall. This is then posted on a flip chart. Several things happen. Each person's actual words are seen by all. There is no paraphrasing by the facilitator or scribe on the flip chart. It is the participant's own words that we read. The participant gets up out of her seat and presents the idea and "sticks" the note on the flip chart (participation). A scribe is unnecessary; the notes are moved around and categorized very easily. A room full of posted flip charts with fluorescent-colored patches evokes a feeling of energy. After one of my sessions, a hotel employee came into the room that was wallpapered with brightly colored flip charts. After briefly perusing the charts, she exclaimed, "I want to be in this class!"

The Difference

What difference does collaborative dialogue make when applied to planning sessions of boards of directors? I see three pivotal results: energy, accountability, and transformation-creation.

Energy

There is energy both during the session and "back at the ranch." As the session progresses, there are clues of emerging energy: enthusiastic, noisy small group work; difficulty in calling participants back to the big group because they are intensely engaged in what they are doing in their small groups; willingness to share insights, ideas, and thoughts. I have never seen a head nod, an eye close, or a person meander away. When these people return to the workplace where plans must be implemented and goals accomplished, they report back to me that the energy they felt during the session continues to fuel action. That energy came from each participant, not from the facilitator or leader, so it continues to exist to serve them.

Accountability

The results of the session—what the group produced—come from the group, with each individual contributing, each person's voice being heard. There is active ownership of the product (the mission statement, goals, operating plan, and so on). "I created it so I must see to it that it is accomplished," said one new board member. Ownership is a great motivator for accountability! A CEO who has experienced the dialogue approach to strategic planning on several very different occasions said this: "The process is the same for any group—no matter how different. The process gets you there—to a singleness of purpose."

In addition, the inductive work that all the individuals do with the mission or vision statements heightens their awareness of the congruence of the organization's actions and its vision, mission, and goals. An executive director concluded, "We now know that we are doing what we are telling everyone we will do." Being authentic requires accountability.

Transformation-Creation

The synthesis of the ideas and insights of engaged participants who are confident in the value and importance of their contributions results in goals and objectives that catapult the organization to a higher level. A new organization emerges—with strengthened vitality and resolve.

Challenges

I have experienced a challenge as I use dialogue. I find I must re-educate clients that the time and the process required will result in a stronger product. We cannot create a new mission statement, list our SWOTs, set our goals, and write the entire operation plan in half a day. One company I worked for focused primarily on the product of the process—the plan. Though much care was given to gathering input from all employees, once we started the goal-setting process with the decision makers, everyone had to put on extroverted armor to be heard. The process was secondary to the product. We efficiently got the planning done. But enthusiasm and commitment waned during the implementation over the next year. What I have experienced since I began using the dialogue approach is that when the process is honored, the product is more viable.

Frequently I am challenged to guide some participants to thinking beyond the day-to-day operations. An integral part of strategic planning is looking at the organization from a wide angle. Clients must go beyond the restraints of limited resources, the pounding competition, the economic challenges to see what is possible. When they broaden the scope of their vision, barriers seem more likely to be torn down. My favorite question is this: "If you had all the resources you needed (money, time, skill, knowledge, workforce, and so on), and you could design your organization, what would it look like?" By setting tasks that progress from the participants' viewpoints to the organization's focus, the group addresses both the long-term goals and the day-to-day operations.

The planning session provides a forum for the participants to express what they want the organization to do. The dialogue approach makes it clear that every voice is important and so every voice should be heard. What is modeled and practiced in the planning sessions—listening to and valuing what each person has to say—is often transferred to the participants' interactions in their organizations. They move beyond "What do we need to do?" to "What are we developing?"

Conclusions

What does success look like? Participants feel their value and worth when they are energized in these sessions to reach deep insights and get in touch with their intuition and so bring forth ideas that, when integrated with the insights and intuition of their colleagues, can transform the organizational vision and mission. Then, because of their deep feeling of ownership of the vision, mission, and organizational journey, they can accountably make it all happen! A dialogue approach facilitates this kind of success in strategic planning.

Reference

Vella, J. *Learning to Listen, Learning to Teach: The Power of Dialogue in Educating Adults*. San Francisco: Jossey-Bass, 2002. (Originally published 1994.)

Open Questions for Analysis and Synthesis

1. If you have ever been a part of a strategic planning session, what was your experience? How does this case relate to your own story?

2. What principles and practices do you see at work in this case?

3. What particular, specific actions do you see in this case that you can use in your work?

17

Dialogue Education in California's Women, Infants, and Children Program

Valerie Uccellani

This chapter asks the questions: How can a very large and well-established organization integrate principles of dialogue education into all aspects of its educational work? How can such an organization incorporate dialogue education practices while honoring differences among learning sites, teachers, and learners? What can these diverse learners and teachers teach *us* about how adults learn? The California Women, Infants, and Children (WIC) Supplemental Nutrition Program, with over eighty local agencies, three thousand staff members, and 1.2 million participants, has begun to provide insights into such fundamental and necessary questions.

Learners, Teachers, and Staff: Diverse in Many Ways

CA/WIC participants include pregnant, breast-feeding, and post-partum women, as well as other caretakers of infants or children under five years of age. Their experience with pregnancy and parenting ranges widely; they may be first-time teen moms, women with many children, grandmothers, single fathers, or foster parents. Most families work at low-wage or seasonal jobs. Roughly 70 percent of California's WIC participants are Hispanic, 15 percent are Caucasian, 8 percent are African American, and 6 percent are Asian. About half of California's WIC participants do not speak English as their first language, and many speak little or no English at all. In fact, WIC participants around the state speak nearly one hundred different languages.

Paraprofessionals make up about two-thirds of agency staff and are the ones who most often interact with the participants. They usually come from the communities they serve—they speak the language and understand the culture of the learners. Paraprofessionals may have little or no formal educational background in nutrition or health when they are hired, but they receive on-the-job training and undergo a lengthy certification process, followed by monthly or semiannual training. They lead most of the group classes at WIC sites and conduct most of the individual education but they are usually not responsible for designing classes.

Other WIC staff include registered dietitians (RDs) and managers. Their role and number vary greatly across sites; most educate participants directly and many also have administrative roles. The RDs are most likely to design participant classes and help train other staff. Local WIC agency managers make sure that core services are provided and monitor the program budget; they exercise authority over nearly all personnel issues and set the vision and goals for their agencies. Managers also have the difficult task of balancing operational expenditures with quality nutrition services. Many California WIC program managers are also RDs; they design and teach largely through staff meetings and staff training sessions.

The Situation: Proven Successes and Common Challenges

WIC has an excellent track record in helping to improve the health of its participants. For example, WIC families tend to have fewer low-birthweight babies, lower incidence of anemia, and better diets than similar families not receiving WIC benefits. Studies also show that WIC helps reduce neonatal health problems. Nonetheless, WIC participants—like the general public—suffer from many nutrition-related chronic health conditions. And although WIC has had success encouraging participants to breast-feed, the rates of initiation and duration of breast-feeding are still lower than in the general population. A top priority of CA/WIC's current strategic plan is to strengthen the educational component of its work in order to improve its families' overall health and nutrition.

At present, the quality of the classes and the one-on-one education depends on the site and the educator's approach. Although many WIC classes are engaging and well received, others rely heavily on lecture and video and do not fully connect the learners to the learning. WIC staff members admit an understandable temptation to "cover a lot of information." As a result, participants may leave without a clear understanding of concepts or of ways they can use new information. Staff members say they want to learn how to sustain learners' interest and to see evidence of learning.

As might be expected, there are some systemic barriers to WIC's educational efforts. For example, like most service organizations, WIC is funded based on number of participants served. This reality creates a daily tension between the quantity of participants served and the quality of services. Time for education is limited—individual sessions usually last from ten to thirty minutes, group sessions from fifteen to forty-five minutes. Because group education is scheduled with food coupon pickup, participants often view the class as a requirement, which may make them less receptive to learning. Finally, participants attend only once every one to three months, and they often see different staff at successive visits, challenging efforts to reinforce learning and develop a clear learner-teacher relationship.

Much of the education and training in CA/WIC is grassroots-based, developed directly by the local agencies themselves for their own participants and staff. This makes it challenging to come to consensus on how to change. But it also allows for many voices to have input and it fosters a tremendous amount of innovation, which are critical factors in the current effort to improve CA/WIC's education.

The Time Frame: Momentum in Year One Builds a Solid Foundation

CA/WIC's current strategic plan began in 2001 and will last through 2006. A decision was made early on (in June 2001) to embrace dialogue education as a central part of this strategic effort. The momentum gained in the first fourteen months has been even greater than what was expected, building a solid foundation for the spread of principles and practices over the next year and beyond.

Learning Sites: Making Adjustments Based on the Principles

California has nearly six hundred WIC sites across the eighty local agencies. Agencies range in size from those with over three hundred thousand participants a month and six hundred employees, to those serving fewer than one hundred participants a month and one part-time staff person. Although the group class space is quite small at some sites, and often filled with children, they show a real creativity and concern on the part of staff: many agencies have embarked on "facelift" campaigns, providing new furniture, freshening paint, and adding artwork.

CA/WIC staff learn in many different venues—monthly training sessions, for example, often unite staff from various sites in a single space of limited size. The setup is often classroom style, but adjustments have begun to allow for more face-to-face interaction and more physical equality among learners and teachers.

The Content of the Learning: For Participants and Staff

Most people associate WIC with coupons for nutritious foods, but it is the educational component that many staff members believe makes WIC particularly valuable for community members. WIC educates participants on numerous topics, such as vitamins and minerals, infant feeding, food safety, and anemia prevention, and also provides basic information on how to use the program and the food coupons. While honoring women's choices by offering infant formula, WIC also actively educates on the benefits of and strategies for breast-feeding. WIC refers participants to a wide variety of community services and also educates directly on such issues as reproductive and dental health, parenting, and child development. In order to serve participants well, staff members are continually educated on the full gamut of health, administrative, educational, management, and communication issues. In brief, the opportunity to apply dialogue education principles in CA/WIC is present on many levels and for many different content areas.

Achievement-Based Objectives: Linked to the Broad Strategic Plan

A comprehensive effort of CA/WIC to enhance learning through the use of dialogue education has been wisely set in the context of broader strategic goals for the organization. These goals are identifying what works in support of nutrition education and building consensus in the California WIC community about responsive, participant-centered approaches to nutrition education. It was decided that dialogue education would be formally integrated into the organization in stages, keeping these long-term goals in mind. The organization would be inclusive (inviting all interested local agencies to join in) but also strategic (working first through managers and RDs, then with paraprofessionals and participants). We planned these objectives for those goals and stated them as achievement-based objectives. By the end of the first year, CA/WIC would have:

- Examined and modeled principles and practices of dialogue education across interested agencies

- Applied principles to the redesign of a sample of WIC classes

- Assessed the learning and transfer of these principles by staff in a sample of sites

- Invited paraprofessionals to study and use the principles in two pilot sites with WIC participants

Implementation: Tough Decisions and Useful Insights

When this work began, CA/WIC staff already actively studied and applied learner-centered principles through their use of such approaches as facilitated group discussion, family-centered education, and stepwise counseling. Therefore, dialogue education was introduced as one more piece of this large, learner-centered puzzle; special attention has been given over the months to name points of overlap between dialogue education and these other valuable learner-centered organizational strategies.

In the first year, over two hundred WIC staff have completed Global Learning Partners' four-day course Learning to Listen, Learning to Teach and many are on waiting lists for scheduled courses this fiscal year. Most staff who have completed the course are program directors, supervisors, and others who design and lead training or meetings, and design WIC classes but do not spend much time directly educating participants. Transfer assessments show that many staff have begun to model principles and practices in a variety of ways. Many say that now they are paying even greater attention to educational practices. They try to understand learners' needs and interests, pay attention to the issues of safety and respect for learners, use visuals and kinesthetic activity as well as small group and pair work, and give learners a chance to do something immediately with what they are learning.

In two pilot agencies, frontline staff have embarked on a formal comprehensive process, developed by and for CA/WIC; this is to be repeated at six to nine additional agencies this coming year. The process is built around a three-day course during which staff study the principles and practices of dialogue education and then apply them by teaching a newly designed WIC class at their sites. The course focuses on respect, relevance, safety, engagement, and learning styles, as well as the use of open questions, pairs and trios, pausing, and affirming. The process also stresses the role of the agencies' leaders, helping them lead and assess more learner-centered classes. Initial results from the two pilot agencies indicate that staff members have embraced the process with enthusiasm. Although a comprehensive study of impact on participants has not yet been done, staff members report that clients are beginning to show a positive response to the use of these principles in WIC classes. Many staff see people enjoying classes more with this approach, and some find that the dialogue provides them, as teachers, with evidence of learning. At one site, staff were inspired by unprecedented applause from clients at the end of a class. The clients said they liked the change in approach and noted: "It's different from the old way of teaching."

Principles and Practices

The CA/WIC program demonstrates several of the principles and practices of dialogue education.

Safety

Safety is a principle that resonates deeply with WIC staff, yet is one of the most challenging to uphold—especially among staff themselves. WIC deals with many potentially sensitive issues—from breast-feeding to weight issues to substance abuse problems and homelessness. Preparing staff to feel comfortable with these issues is a daunting task, often not easily done. Some common practices of dialogue education seem to compound this insecurity. For example, although staff seem to enjoy working in pairs or trios themselves, some feel unsafe asking participants to do so because most WIC participants in a class do not know each other and many have children in their arms. To paraphrase one nutrition assistant: "Participants don't come to WIC to talk to each other." Yet this is exactly what the dialogue design invites them to do! Because staff members usually lead classes alone, they sometimes simply omit parts of the class that do not feel safe to them.

Despite these challenges, local agencies are making strides to increase safety. After having time to experience and practice the new approach, many staff find that their learners in turn feel more comfortable. As one person put it: "The atmosphere is positive. I feel the safety and respect. No one is put on the spot." Another commented: "I work a lot with the safety of the learners. . . . I use more dialogue instead of just talking—asking what they are understanding and what things they think they are learning." A colleague added: "I like what I am doing even more. I am secure and confident about teaching a class."

Open Questions

Open questions have proven to be a useful practice for many staff in their supervisory and teaching roles at WIC. As one supervisor put it: "It's really exciting. In one meeting, staff were making many demands. . . . By my asking open questions they came up with responses that were surprising to them and informative to me, without being confrontational for any of us." But WIC's paraprofessionals may find it uncomfortable asking open questions. Because these staff members usually have little formal education in health and nutrition, it is scary to pose questions that might lead the discussion beyond their range of knowledge. Many of these staff members come from cultures where teachers are greatly respected, even revered. Posing questions (rather than answering them all) can make them feel vulnerable. One of the biggest fears paraprofessionals express about the use of open questions is that it invites "misinformation." This fear may be due in part to the program's traditional attention to facts rather than to process, and in part to designers' lack of understanding of the subtle but powerful axiom: "Don't ask if you know the answer. Tell in dialogue."

Relevance

Relevance is a particularly tough principle to integrate into WIC classes, given the size of the system and the grouping of learners into classes. Although most participants are on the program for a limited time, some return during subsequent pregnancies or with children. One fairly common participant complaint is that they have already "heard" the same class before, which may be absolutely true. But as classes become more learner-driven, they should become more diverse—even classes on the same topic will be as different as the learners who take them! Given their limited time with participants, many staff are embracing the learning to limit, learning to teach attitude.

Other Models That Influence Practice

CA/WIC draws on numerous models and practices to improve family health. Two of these models are also useful in predicting how CA/WIC's educational approaches might change. Developed by Proschaska and DiClemente (1994), stages of change theory suggests that changing habitual behaviors is a process rather than an event. People vary in their readiness to change, change occurs in stages, and education must match the stage of change for it to be helpful. It applies not only to the behavior of WIC participants (that is, the process through which they make health changes) but also to the behavior of WIC teachers; not every educator is equally ready for change and teaching behaviors should not be expected to change immediately.

Another model that has relevance for both health and education behaviors is the diffusion of innovations model, according to which behavior changes in large populations follow an S-shaped curve over time (Rogers, 1995). At first, very few people (the innovators) embrace the change. Change in the general population takes place slowly, until most people (the majority) have changed.

The few remaining (laggards) tend to take a long time to convert. This model identifies many factors that help or hinder change, such as the relative advantage of a new behavior over the old, the levels of risk and uncertainty involved, and the time needed to adopt the change.

Several of WIC's parent-child models posit principles that are notably compatible with dialogue education, such as Ellyn Satter's (1991) model of the family feeding dynamic. For example, according to Satter, children eat as much as they need, children eat inconsistently, and each child's feeding habits are unique. Satter defines a "division of responsibility" between the child and the parent or caregiver that echoes the principle of teacher-learner accountability: parents decide what the child is offered to eat and where and when this takes place; the child decides how much and whether he or she eats.

Touchpoints, developed by renowned pediatrician T. Berry Brazelton (1994), is another model that focuses on the role of parenting in a child's development. *Touchpoints* refers to times just before important stages of physical or emotional growth, although a child's behavior appears to regress or fall apart at this point. The key is to recognize these stages and use them as a point for exploring and learning. Several Touchpoints principles mirror dialogue education: the parent is the expert on his or her child, all parents have strengths, all parents have something critical to share at each developmental stage, passion should be valued where it is found, and practitioners ought to reflect on their contribution to parent-provider interactions.

One well-known theory influencing CA/WIC is that of multiple intelligences, posited by Howard Gardner (1993). This theory expands and redefines the three basic learning styles—visual, auditory, and kinesthetic—outlined in dialogue education. Gardner identifies over seven "intelligences," including musical-rhythmic, logical-mathematical, verbal-linguistic, interpersonal, intrapersonal, kinesthetic, and visual-spatial. Although each individual has his or her preferred learning styles, most benefit from exposure to a variety of styles. This theory has helped WIC staff design more interactive and engaging staff training and participant classes while helping them appeal to the various kinds of learners.

CA/WIC also relies on several public health models, including the spectrum of prevention, which looks beyond the education of individuals to the role of programs and systems (Cohen and Smith, 1999). For example, CA/WIC is participating in community breast-feeding task forces, helping to educate medical providers, and advocating for breast-feeding-friendly policies and legislation to bolster its own breast-feeding education and promotion efforts. Recently, some childhood obesity prevention initiatives also followed this approach.

Conclusions

This chapter opened with some questions. First, how can a very large and well-established organization integrate principles of dialogue education into all aspects of its educational work? As we have seen, the organization can use the principles from the top of the organization, and throughout it, so that staff can experience dialogue education as they begin to use it. In other words, it needs to model the principles if they are to be understood. The organization should go slowly, looking for change first among teachers and then among learners, at various layers of learning in the organization. A common language should be established and when people use a common term, it should be checked for meaning. In this way, apparently simple words like *safety* will continue to stand for complex and powerful concepts. Staff should be kept focused on principles such as respect, immediate usefulness, safety, and engagement, rather than on adopting superficial changes in teaching style, such as the use of sticky notes or music. Drawing on the wise words of tennis legend Arthur Ashe, "Start where you are, use what you've got, do what you can."

How can such an organization be faithful to dialogue education practices while honoring differences among learning sites, teachers, and learners? Organizations can listen to the words and phrases staff use as the approach is implemented—these words and phrases signal which principles and practices are most important and clear in their eyes. They should recognize that some principles and practices may not easily fit with current systems, policies, or routines of an organization. They should celebrate and learn from the way that staff adapt practices to fit the current reality.

What can these diverse learners and teachers teach *us* about how adults learn? Although WIC has only started working with dialogue education, there is a "buzz" of excitement about the new direction. WIC staff members have started to ask that dialogue education be used at statewide meetings and that speakers at statewide conferences follow them. Many staff say that they enjoy their work more now. They find it more interesting and fun. As some have put it: "You know the way we did it before, just teaching—just delivering. This way we make it more exciting, truly interactive. When I teach this way, I learn more."

Although it is still too early to assess most of the anticipated impact of dialogue education, there is a growing commitment to offer meaningful educational experiences that focus on the learning process and the participants' role in that process. This commitment promises to bring WIC closer to its ultimate goal of healthier WIC families while at the same time bringing individual staff and participants closer to each other.

References

Brazelton, T. *Touchpoints: Your Child's Emotional and Behavioral Development.* Reading, Mass.: Addison-Wesley, 1994.

Cohen, L., and Smith, S. "The Spectrum of Prevention: Developing a Comprehensive Approach to Injury Prevention." *Injury Prevention,* 1999, 5, 203–207.

Gardner, H. *Multiple Intelligences: The Theory in Practice.* New York: Basic Books, 1993.

Proschaska, J., and DiClemente, C. *Changing for Good.* New York: Avon, 1994.

Rogers, E. *Diffusion of Innovations* (4th ed.). New York: Free Press, 1995.

Satter, E. *Child of Mine.* Boulder, Colo.: Bull Publishing Company, 1991.

Open Questions for Analysis and Synthesis

1. What one thing did you see the team do in CA/WIC that you want to celebrate?

2. The author mentions some principles and practices. What other principles and practices did you see at work?

3. What other case in this book resembles this one? How so?

Part III

International Education

In the sixties, as developing countries gained independence, their governments sought to help the adults who had never had a chance to go to school to catch up. This was the great laboratory that produced the adult learning theory of Paulo Freire and his peers. In Africa, Asia, and Latin America, adult education, *conscientizao*, nonformal education became a recognized field of study. The Institute of Adult Education at the University of Dar es Salaam, for example, was a prestigious center of research and teaching. Literacy campaigns were mounted in new nation after new nation and theories about adult learning were tested and developed.

Dialogue education was born in the *favellas* of Brazil, the villages of Tanzania, and the streets of Bangkok. It was called many things in many languages, but the central theory was respect for adult learners and their experience and the basic recognition was that the colonial processes of education did not apply. These hierarchical processes and their products—textbooks, curricula, and professors—were accepted and honored in most countries. Students, children and adults alike, wanted and needed a certificate, not necessarily learning. Even today, these students offer the greatest resistance to learning-centered processes that differ from the traditional pattern of lecture and listen.

So the following cases are a tribute not only to the educators but also to courageous students who dared to try a different way of learning. The team from Freedom from Hunger (Chapter Eighteen) has used dialogue education—precisely, the Learning to Listen, Learning to Teach course—to prepare their field workers to teach men and women in developing countries the vital business and life skills they need. Linda Gershuny (Chapter Nineteen) describes a teacher-training program for teachers in primary school in Haiti. Cambodia (Chapter Twenty) is the site of the story told by Gale von Hahmann of a World Education train-the-trainer project using dialogue education. Peter Perkins and Michaela Stickney (Chapter Twenty-One) describe a course in dialogue education they were invited to teach at the Center for Environmental Training in Volgograd, Russia. They taught water engineers and community educators the principles and practices of dialogue so that they, in turn, could design and teach effectively. After ten years of doing the dialogue education training course at the opening of the residency for community medicine at the School of Medicine of the Catholic University of Chile, the very culture of that health care society shows changes. Klaus Püschel (Chapter Twenty-Two) and his colleagues in Santiago are proud of this accomplishment and hope to see the influence of dialogue extend through the medical school.

Peter Noteboom is not only managing director of Global Learning Partners in Toronto, Canada, but also a staff member at the Canadian Council of Churches. His work on racism with churches in Canada is deeply informed by dialogue education. In Chapter Twenty-Three he demonstrates how the principles and practices extend into the earliest stages of preparation for an important learning session with adults.

These international cases are a natural fulfillment of this set of case studies. Dialogue education knows no boundaries.

18

The Double Bottom Line

Dialogue Education in Microfinance Services for the Poor

Robb Davis, Jeanette Treiber, Ellen Vor der Bruegge

When people think of hunger in poor nations, many think of famine. In reality, occurrences of famine are relatively rare. However, occurrences of chronic hunger are not. Currently more than eight hundred million people throughout the world live with chronic hunger.

Poverty is the primary cause of hunger. Poor people do not have the resources—whether land, tools, or money—they need to grow or buy good quality food on a consistent basis. Chronic hunger is a persistent and cyclical condition; its effects spill across generations. To break the cycle, efforts must address root causes, be sustainable, and be implemented by local people. Too many "development" efforts either fail to address root causes or are not sustainable. And despite rhetoric about "local ownership," many still fail to account for what the poor say they really want—the opportunity to earn income and protect themselves against the inevitable physical, economic, and social shocks they must face.

Freedom from Hunger, a development organization, created and implemented its Credit with Education program, a financially sustainable strategy that provides financial and education services to poor rural women, more than a decade ago. Credit with Education is appealing to indigenous organizations seeking a healthy "double bottom line": sustainable financial services that also have an impact on the health and social well-being of the clients they serve.

Credit with Education uses a group-based lending methodology that has been demonstrated to be an effective way to bring credit services to the poor. It begins with women forming self-managed credit groups. The women in each credit group jointly guarantee each other's loans and accumulate savings. These borrowers invest small loans in microbusinesses, such as food production and trading in local markets.

However, experience shows that credit alone is not enough to reduce chronic hunger and ease poverty. Therefore, in Credit with Education, when the groups meet to repay their loans, the women participate in informal dialogue education sessions during which they discuss health, nutrition, family-planning practices, and sound business strategies. Learning sessions last no more than thirty minutes to respect the members' busy schedules. Though individual sessions are brief, topics are treated in depth over several meetings. Trained credit agents facilitate the sessions. Clients (that is, participants in the program) analyze recommended practices, compare and contrast them with local practices, and plan actions to make changes in their households and community. The term *credit agent* is used throughout this chapter. Microfinance institutions deliver credit services and also facilitate and teach education sessions. Though this chapter refers only to credit agents, in other contexts the learning sessions described are taught by facilitators outside credit programs.

Session designs favor learning tasks that require physical movement and tap into clients' feelings about the content. Though Credit with Education provides an integrated credit and health and business education service to clients, this chapter focuses on the role of credit agents as both teachers and learners in the process. It describes their training, the materials they use to facilitate education sessions, and how they interact with credit groups. It will be important to distinguish two levels of education and training: the training credit agents receive to prepare them to deliver the education sessions and the community education sessions they teach to clients. This chapter focuses largely on the former.

The Seven Design Steps

We studied the principles and practices of dialogue education before designing this new program. An operative practice is the use of the Seven Design Steps: who, why, when, where, what, what for, and how.

Who: Participants

The credit agents who facilitate the education sessions are usually young men and women with secondary school education. They are usually employed by local nongovernmental organizations (NGOs), credit unions, or rural banks. They often work in distant rural areas with a poor infrastructure, traveling as much as three to four hours each day to provide services to clients in village banks, visiting as many as fifteen to twenty village banks each week. Credit agents usually have no experience in the health and business topics they teach. Most want to increase their knowledge and skills.

Credit agents are often the first to understand the value of health and business education for the clients they serve. One group of credit agents in West Africa welcomed the introduction of Credit with Education, noting that their clients routinely requested them to stay after meetings to discuss their businesses or the health of their families. Though it adds to their workload, most field agents welcome the opportunity to build their own knowledge and skills base. In addition, facilitating education sessions has other rewards. In Haiti, a group of clients praised a credit agent for teaching them what they needed to know to care for their children better.

Why: The Situation

Despite the commitment of Freedom from Hunger to Credit with Education, the program would not succeed if local organizations were not interested in a value-added loan product responding to the demands of clients who want more than just loans.

To make this education happen, credit agents need to learn about the latest recommended practices on the various topics they teach. In addition, they must learn how to use teaching guides. And they need timely training to prepare them to teach the next health or business topic in the sequence.

When and Where: Time Frame and Site

Quality delivery of village banking services requires credit agents to pay diligent attention to clients. Allocating time to train credit agents is challenging. Most institutions allow them to attend training on new topics two or three times a year. The training—usually involving two topics—must happen over a short period of four or five days—and in a location near the communities in which they work, places where electricity may be nonexistent and training space poor.

What: Content

Credit agents study the latest recommended practices and community views on each topic. Other important content includes selected principles and practices of dialogue education and facilitation skills. These content areas come together in the key skill they must learn: how to use scripted guides to teach and lead group discussions with clients.

What For: Achievement-Based Objectives

By the end of each training session, credit agents have analyzed key technical information, explored community attitudes and beliefs about the topic, and practiced teaching-learning sessions (with feedback) using scripted guides. In the Philippines, credit agents were amazed at how community attitudes compared with the technical information on breast-feeding. Having both sets of information—recommendations and local practice—better equips credit agents to engage clients in discussing new information while showing understanding of local practices.

How: Learning Tasks

Because of the geographical distances separating Freedom from Hunger from the field, learning needs and resource assessments of credit agents are designed into their training. During each training session, credit agents reflect on their own facilitation of previous topics, problems they faced, and specific facilitation and technical information needs. These issues can then be addressed in the current training. Other learning tasks in each credit agent training include these:

1. Critical assessment of research on the subject to be taught (for example, breast-feeding)

2. A community visit to discuss the topic area with village bank members

3. Analysis of national and local data to clarify the need for teaching the topic

4. Reflection on selected principles of dialogue education related to the topic (for example, respect, engagement, dialogue, safety, and relevance)

5. Most important, simulated practice of the learning sessions they will later use with groups of clients

Learning tasks that the credit agents do during their training create relevance for them; credit agents who analyze local data and learn from community members about their feelings on the topic gain confidence that the topic is relevant to clients' lives and important to them.

Learning tasks challenge credit agents to analyze session content and steps and to see things as clients see them. As a group *they* define the best ways to show respect for the learner and provide affirmation. *They* describe how to create safety in a learning environment by analyzing what safety means to them. *They* define their personal "rules" for creating safety to which they will hold themselves accountable. They also analyze in what ways the scripted learning sessions encourage engagement in learning, create relevance for learners, and promote dialogue.

Credit agents receive a full set of scripted learning session guides for the topic they will teach. Each guide provides the objectives of the session, the preparation they need in order to teach it, and a detailed description of the steps to follow. The steps include short presentations of new information, critical open questions to create dialogue among learners, and stories and other activities to use. Session guides also include all visual images that go with the steps. Microfinance institutions and credit agents prefer scripted guides because they reduce the preparation time needed to facilitate learning. The guides also provide a standardized way to facilitate sessions while allowing each group to explore specific points of interest to them. Thus, they ensure consistency in the presentation of recommended practices.

Freedom from Hunger promotes the use of "credit agent–centered management" principles with the local institutions with which it works. These principles focus attention on providing credit agents with the support (logistics and materials) and signaling (feedback on facilitation) to help them continually improve on the job. Credit agent–centered management focuses attention on supporting credit agents to teach learning sessions better. It requires supervisors to take part in training with the credit agents for whom they are responsible. In this way, they both understand the expectations for the credit agent and the supervisors can better support them and provide needed signals for improvement.

Assessing Credit Agents' Learning, Transfer, and Impact

Credit agents assess their learning during their training in two ways. First, they take short pre- and posttests on the technical content of the topic. The tests are also a critical part of the continuing dialogue with credit agents after the training because results allow trainers to identify areas of confusion and address them in staff meetings or through individual feedback. Second, learning session simulations assess learning. Credit agents facilitate these learning sessions for each other and immediately afterward provide feedback, decide about altering tasks, and clarify any areas of confusion.

Supervisors use a checklist when observing teaching in the field to assess transfer. The checklist assesses how well credit agents follow the steps in the guide, provide new content in a clear way, show respect, create safety, and praise clients. The guides used by the credit agents place particular emphasis on using small groups to engage their clients better. Experience shows that putting clients into small groups is difficult for credit agents. Therefore, the observation checklists pay particular attention to assessing the use and management of small groups. Use of the checklists encourages immediate feedback to the credit agent on her or his teaching and ways to improve it.

Local institutions assess evidence of impact not on changes in the organization but rather on changes in the lives of clients. Two tools are used to assess the impact of the learning sessions. The first is a mini-survey, which uses small samples to assess changes in knowledge and practice of clients. A less quantitative approach involves using participatory learning tools with clients during regular meetings. The tools have strong psychomotor and analytical elements to challenge clients to define if and to what extent the Credit with Education service is bringing about changes in their lives.

Principles and Practices of Dialogue Education

Freedom from Hunger takes primary responsibility for the design of both client learning sessions and credit agent training. In designing learning sessions and teaching credit agents to facilitate them, Freedom from Hunger staff draws on a broad array of dialogue education principles and practices. These are summarized in nine design and practice principles. *Design principles* cannot be modeled in a learning event; rather, they must be "designed into" the learning tasks themselves. *Practice principles*, in contrast, must be modeled while teaching a learning event—they must be "created" each time there is a learner-teacher interaction. Table 18.1 distinguishes the two.

Table 18.1   Selected Principles and Practices of Dialogue Education

Principles That Must Be Practiced	Principles That Must Be Designed into Learning Sessions
Respect: *Learners feel respected and like equals.*	Relevance: *Learners learn best by drawing on their own knowledge and experience. Learning must meet the real-life needs of the adult—for example, job and family life issues.* Dialogue: *Learning must be two-way to allow learners to interact with the teacher and other learners.*
Affirmation: *Learners need to receive praise for even small efforts.*	Engagement: *Learning must involve learners through discussion, small groups, and learning from peers.* Immediacy: *Learners must be able to apply the new learning immediately.*
Safety: *Learners need to feel that others value their ideas and contributions—that others will not ridicule or belittle them.*	20/40/80 rule: *Learners remember more when visual aids support verbal instruction. Adults remember best when they practice the new skill. (We remember 20 percent of what we hear, 40 percent of what we hear and see, and 80 percent of what we hear, see, and do.)* Cognitive, affective, and psychomotor interaction. *Learning should involve thinking and emotions as well as doing.*

The session guides are designed with open questions and learning tasks that engage learners' thoughts, feelings, and actions. The open questions open the door for dialogue between the credit agent and the clients and among clients. Because credit agents do not usually have time to decide how to create relevance or immediacy, they use a guide whose tasks and questions promote these principles.

Credit agents must critically analyze the session guide designs to determine if they follow the principles and they must suggest changes if not. They must also create an environment of safety, respect, and affirmation for learners. The design guides their teaching.

Freedom from Hunger developed a matrix to assess how well it has designed in the principles for each topic. This "accountability matrix" also defines the kind of learning task: tasks that connect learners to what they already know, help them examine new content, and help them do something with new content or integrate new content into their lives (Vella, 2000).

One Freedom from Hunger collaborator, CARD Bank Inc. (Center for Agriculture and Rural Development) in the Philippines, sees how life-changing exposure to these principles has been for its credit agents. Leaders have noted that credit agents trained in the principles display much more confidence and are more articulate and more creative in their problem solving. In addition, the credit agents who use Credit with Education have more satisfied clients and fewer dropouts. As a result, CARD Bank is expanding Credit with Education to all its branches—reaching over sixty-thousand female clients as of October 2002.

Local credit agent trainers (for example, in Haiti, Bolivia, Ghana, Uganda, the Philippines, and Madagascar) have expressed their satisfaction that the training materials follow selected principles of dialogue education. They also appreciate the use of the Seven Design Steps, which help them become more organized in their training and more effective in assessing learning. These steps are used to design both learning sessions and training materials to train credit agents.

Development of Theory

In addition to following the principles and practices of dialogue education, behavior change theory also influences Freedom from Hunger's design. One model—the Road to Behavior Change—provides a way of thinking about how change might occur for individual clients. Inspired by the Resistance to Change Continuum (Srinivasan, 1990), the model posits that each client is at a different place in relation to the behaviors discussed—for example, breast-feeding, use of family planning, and care of sick children. At any given time a client may be at any of the following "places" along the road to behavior change:

1. Does not recognize a problem requiring a change in behavior

2. Recognizes a problem requiring a change in behavior but fears change or her ability to change

3. Recognizes a problem and wishes to learn about solutions—actions she can take

4. Is ready to try some new behavior

5. Is willing to integrate the new behavior into her daily routine

6. Experiences obstacles in trying to change

7. Successfully integrates change into daily life

Learning sessions (and training of credit agents) must therefore allow people in different places to interact with content, analyze it, and consider how best to use it for themselves. The learning task must support them along a journey that can begin with no understanding of the recommended practice and lead to successful adaptation and use of a new habit or skill.

This view of "individual" behavior change is complemented by an education approach and design grounded in the theory of social capital. This theory recognizes that social change is not only a function of new knowledge of *individuals* but also of support structures and interpersonal means of managing change. *Social capital* here refers to how relationships enable individuals to take actions that they could not take otherwise. Village banks—in which members share both obligations to repay each other's loans (social collateral) and responsibilities to support each other to change child care and personal health practices—are a key location for social capital *creation*. Relationships of trust that develop through intimate sharing during education sessions provide mutual support for members. The literature on social capital is vast and growing (Coleman, 1988, 1990; Woolcock, 1998).

Conclusions

In this chapter we have seen the use of dialogue education in preparing credit agents to facilitate learning sessions with clients. This represents only one way in which Freedom from Hunger has internalized the principles of dialogue education and the Seven Design Steps planning process. Principles of dialogue education guide the design for technical assistance visits, management training, and negotiation with collaborators. Freedom from Hunger even uses these principles and approaches in engaging donors in dialogue about common expectations. In 2001, Freedom from Hunger provided training for *all* staff members in Global Learning Partners' Learning to Listen, Learning to Teach course. This reflects the commitment to integrate dialogue education as our way of doing business.

Because staff all "speak the same language" when it comes to the design of learning events, they are able to support each other and provide specific feedback. Learning needs and resource assessments are becoming a way to develop a better understanding of who is involved in learning events and why the events are occurring. Freedom from Hunger has helped some of its collaborators take part in the Learning to Listen, Learning to Teach course. In addition, it has shared principles of dialogue education with institutional and local trainers in nearly all the organizations with which it works. Thus, practitioners in over fifteen countries are now actively considering the role of dialogue, the importance of safety, how to engage learners, and how to create achievement-based objectives. The circle of users is widening.

References

Coleman, J. S. "Social Capital in the Creation of Human Capital." *American Journal of Sociology*, 1988, 94 (supplement S95-S120).

Coleman, J. S. *Foundations of Social Theory*. Cambridge, Mass.: Belknap Press, 1990.

Srinivasan, L. *Tools for Community Participation: A Manual for Training Trainers in Participatory Techniques*. New York: PROWWESS/UNDP, 1990.

Vella, J. *Taking Learning to Task: Creative Strategies for Teaching Adults*. San Francisco: Jossey-Bass, 2000.

Woolcock, M. "Social Capital and Economic Development: Toward a Theoretical Synthesis and Policy Framework." *Theory and Society*, 1998, *27*, 151–208.

Open Questions for Analysis and Synthesis

1. What did you see the Freedom from Hunger team do to make dialogue education work throughout the organization?

2. What principles and practices did you see working in this case?

3. What similarities do you see between this and the CASA case in Chapter Eight, where an organization takes on dialogue education?

19

Dialogue Education Goes to Primary School in Haiti

Linda Gershuny

This chapter describes the education of primary school teachers in Haiti, the first black republic, established in 1804. I was invited to consult with a group of Haitian educators about applying current research on learning to help improve formal education in primary schools there. Our aim was to help interested teachers render learning more effective and relevant in their classrooms, and to find alternatives to the usual severe methods of discipline by laying the foundations for a moral community in the classroom. The concept of capacity building for individual and social transformation (Anello and de Hernández, 1997) helped refine the beginnings of our approach.

During this time, members of the group of educators became acquainted with dialogue education when Jane Vella held a training session in Haiti for an AIDS prevention program. Her principles-based approach (Vella, 1995) provided an adaptable tool for developing a teacher-training curriculum designed to present new and appropriate methods through experimentation, critical reflection, and dialogue.

The Teacher-Training Program

Initially, we offered training sessions to teachers from ten primary schools. The teachers' positive response was encouraging. A mode of horizontal learning and reflection on action was established that continues to orient the training program. Our respect for these teachers grew as we became aware of their stressful working conditions. Despite very meager salaries and lack of training, they persevere. They work in stifling, crowded, dimly lit classrooms, where fifty to ninety children share an insufficient number of outdated textbooks and struggle to memorize lessons in a language they do not understand.

In 2000, PLAN International launched the Quality Learning Project with assistance from the government of The Netherlands. Our newly formed Haiti-based foundation, the Center for Learning, Training, and Transformation (CAFT, in French), was called on to design and implement a program of training for teacher coaches, school principals, and primary-level teachers in two departments of the country. Many of these teachers are secondary students themselves, trying to finish their own schooling at night classes.

Expected Impact

A concrete indicator of impact was set by PLAN: within the next three years the basic literacy skill level of the thousands of sponsored children and their classmates in these pilot schools would double. At the beginning of the project, only 14 percent of children completing grade two in the area could read and write in Haitian Creole and in French.

Design of the Program

At CAFT we plunged into the work of creating a learning experience with and for teachers that everyone hoped would begin a transformational process in these 360 classrooms. What strategy would provide the catalyst to reverse the deeply engrained trend of mindless rote learning and humiliating disciplinary methods—legacies of centuries of slavery, class discrimination, and dictatorship? We hypothesized that congruence between the dynamics of this teacher-training seminar and hoped-for classroom changes would be a key factor. In the absence of a uniform curriculum for children, seven *key elements* were gradually defined for beginning the process of change in the classroom.

An initial ten-day training seminar program was designed, using the framework for adult learning design provided by Global Learning Partners, Inc. In preparation, CAFT consulted every project school principal and teacher in person to assess interest, current practices, resources, and needs. By striving to apply the principles and practices of dialogue education, we ensured that the fundamental values of respect, participation, and cooperation would not only be talked about—as in traditional teacher training—but also experienced and practiced by the teachers.

As we emphasized with participating teachers, we were all scientists involved in an exciting experiment to discover how to improve the quality of education in Haiti. As training designer and facilitator, CAFT was responsible for listening to the teachers, observing their strengths and needs, and researching the most strategic and relevant concepts and methods we could find to bring as new input in their seminars. However, only the school principals and teachers themselves could reflect on their situations, grapple with the new input, and decide which aspects to integrate into their challenging work in the classroom. Through this dialogic process, the following course design has evolved over the last three years.

The Introductory Training Session

We used the Seven Design Steps to plan the training session.

Who: Participants and Facilitators

The participants were sixty schoolteachers of various ages and levels of experience. The facilitator had experience in formal and nonformal education in Haiti; this facilitator was assisted by eight coaches who were experienced schoolteachers recently trained as teacher mentors.

Why: The Situation

The school principals and teachers who participated in the program had expressed interest and commitment to improve classroom methods after meeting and exchanging views with PLAN and CAFT staff.

Where: Location and Setup

Training was to be held in three classrooms of a local school. School benches would be placed face-to-face to accommodate cooperative work in groups of four or six. A drum and battery-powered tape player and cassettes would be on hand. Everyday materials of all sorts would be available for creation of learning materials.

When: Dates and Duration

The course would take place over ten days during the summer school break, six hours per day, for a total of sixty hours.

What and What For: Content and Achievement-Based Objectives

By the end of the ten-day course, participants would have:

1. Named the *wisdom of Haitian proverbs* (a warm-up)

2. Examined course content, objectives, and schedule

3. Proposed *principles and practices of procedure* and participant interaction to be observed during the present seminar

4A. Reviewed the *project's key elements* and compared them to *Ministry of Education objectives*

4B. Conducted a *self-evaluation of their school's functioning* vis-à-vis Ministry of Education objectives, and shared at least one successful achievement with the other school teams

5. Proposed the *goals of education* to which their efforts would be devoted

6. Distinguished between two models of leadership

7. Visualized and analyzed the *capacities of a primary school graduate*

8. Predicted the *consequences of the presence of ten thousand leader-servants in their region*

9. Practiced *methods of active learning* and applied them to their grade level

10. Assessed *the importance of character education* and practiced a *sequence of daily values education activities*

11. Suggested and practiced *alternatives to punishment and humiliation as disciplinary measures*

12. Reviewed *ways of preventing discipline problems* through establishment of a moral community in the classroom

13. Practiced *positive techniques for engaging the cooperation of children*

14. Distinguished *open from closed questions* and practiced asking open questions

15. Identified *multiple forms of "intelligence"* and *named ways to diversify teaching* accordingly

How: Selected Learning Tasks and Principles

As is the tradition in Haiti, the introductory course began with devotions and singing. Teachers were invited to get to know one another in a warm-up learning task.

Learning task #1. The wisdom of the "old folks"— Haitian proverbs

Read the portion of a proverb that you have received and find three other participants to complete your proverb. Introduce one another, and discuss the relevance of this proverb to your work as educators. We'll hear from each group.

Amid laughter, the teachers visibly relaxed as they learned each other's names and shared ideas. Their insights and eloquence were impressive. These proverbs were put on the wall as a reminder to the participants that, heirs to a rich culture, they had not come as empty recipients to the course.

Without knowledge, a people dies (biblical).

Little by little the bird makes its nest.

Prevention is better than saying you're sorry.

With honey you attract the ant.

One finger cannot eat gumbo.

They shared expectations for the seminar after reviewing the content, objectives, and schedule (learning task #2). Next, consensus was established concerning session norms and procedures.

Learning task #3. Setting our standards

In groups of three, propose at least two principles to be honored in this course in order for everyone to learn and feel at ease. On a chart, write your principles in the left-hand column and a corresponding concrete action that you are committed to respect in the right-hand column.

In this task participants began to close the traditional gap between theory and practice, and to establish new norms for themselves. Many teachers subsequently applied this process of participatory rule-setting in their own classrooms, using symbols for the first grade.

The principle supported here was this: congruence between training methods and hoped-for change in teaching methods facilitates transfer of new knowledge and skills more effectively than simply telling participants how to improve.

Learning task #4. The seven A's and the six ministry objectives

4a. With your fellow teachers, review the six Ministry of Education progressive objectives for primary education: acquisition and application of various branches of knowledge, development of scientific observation, development of analytical thought, preparation for the active life, values education.

4b. Next, review the following project key elements— the seven A's in French—and compare them to the ministry objectives. What are your observations?

    Analysis: Asking and answering of questions by teachers and children, with emphasis on increasing understanding; reflecting on the social and moral aspects of new knowledge

    Attitude: Engaging the students in the establishment of a "moral community" in microcosm in the classroom through cooperative methods of organization and discipline and a daily activity of values education to develop leadership capacities

    Cooperative learning: Working in pairs or in small heterogeneous groups to foster individual and group progress and a spirit of collaboration

    Active learning: Learning through observation, discovery, and doing

    Atmosphere: Maintaining an ambiance of joy and harmonious interaction and inclusion; frequent use of educational games, music, and other arts to stimulate and channel the energy in the classroom

    Application: Orienting the learners to the immediate relevance and application of new learning in their homes and communities

Active collaboration of parents: Exploring with
parents their own collaborative role in helping
their children acquire useful knowledge, attitudes, and skills

4c. Identify which objectives have been addressed in
your school to date. Choose an accomplishment to
share with other teachers.

Having participants take the teacher's seat early on set in motion
dialogue between participants, and with facilitators. At the end of
the first day, despite the stifling heat, the energy level was high as
teachers realized that their experiences were contributing to the collective learning of the group.

The principle supported here was that dialogue engenders
engagement and energy. Connecting new learning to old increases
the capacity to learn effectively.

Learning task #5. Why educate our children?

5a. In groups of four, name reasons why we educate
children. Write on cards three to four reasons that
are most important to you. Attach them to the
board.

5b. Read this text, which ascribes a dual goal to education: individual and social transformation. Compare the goals you have stated to this perspective.
What are your insights?

"There exists a reciprocal relationship between the individual and society. Given the multitude of social problems that exist today, there is an evident need for an
education which prepares students to contribute to
the process of transformation, with the goal of forging a

society rooted in principles of unity and justice, and establishing an enduring peace" (Anello and de Hernández, 1997, p. 47).

Learning task #6. Two models of leadership

Compare two models of leadership: authoritarian and leader-servant. How do you interpret the role of the leader-servant with respect to his or her group? How do the models relate to the goals of education?

Learning task #7. Developing the capacities of the leader-servant

7a. Identify four characteristics that a child should have after six years of primary education. Discuss in groups of four. Present one of the characteristics in the form of a brief mime.

7b. Examine the list of capacities proposed for a Haitian primary school graduate that follows. What are your comments and questions? Which capacities do you feel should be given more attention in our primary schools? A Haitian primary school graduate is distinguished by:

> An understanding of physical, social, and spiritual reality, and an ability to apply adequately his knowledge of language, mathematics, and natural and social sciences
>
> A motivation, based on commitment to principle, to practice moral virtues and to engage in community service
>
> Academic and artistic capacities
>
> Leadership capacities for personal, interpersonal, and collective transformation

Learning task #8. Ten thousand leader-servants

Draw a web chart with the words "Ten Thousand Leader-Servants" in the central orb. Indicate the consequences in our locality over the next ten years if the ten thousand children in the thirty schools of our project begin to develop the intellectual and moral capacities of the leader-servant.

Discussing and drawing enthusiastically, the groups produced inspiring visions of changed conditions: more unified families, cleaner streets; integrity—less corruption—less crime; stronger governmental structures—continuity in government services; quality schooling.

The principle supported in the preceding four tasks was that creating a vision of the importance of their own work helps participants touch on generative themes. In this case, it lifted the seminar to a new level of engagement.

Learning task #9. Factors that foster learning

Search back in your memories and share something you learned well as a child (inductive work). Share the experience with a partner.

Examine research on the relative effectiveness of different modes of learning—from listening and reading (10 percent retention) to observing (50 percent) to learning through doing (70 to 90 percent retention) What strikes you (input)? Compare your own experience as a child to the results of this research (implementation).

Choose a lesson you will be teaching next month and state one way children can learn the new content by doing something (integration).

The principle supported here was that learning and understanding are increased when the sequence of tasks moves from simple to more complex, building on one another, and enabling participants to translate concepts into action.

The best antidote to discipline problems is good teaching. When children are engaged actively in interesting small group activities, they are much less likely to be disruptive. The next learning tasks allowed participants to practice active learning (learning task #9), examine a text on the importance of character education (learning task #10a), and practice a sequence of short daily activities including role-playing to help children understand and apply the virtues of justice, courtesy, patience, humility, and union (learning task #10b).

Learning task #11. Alternatives to severe disciplinary measures

11a. Recall an experience of severe punishment to which you were subjected as a child. What was your reaction? What alternative could have been applied? Share your suggestions in pairs.

11b. Examine these suggestions for encouraging good behavior in children. Underline those which you would like to emphasize in your classroom. We'll hear several responses.

> Establish rules and consequences with the students.
> Be firm and fair.
> Encourage the children to take responsibility.
> Teach good habits to the children; be an example.
> Show affection to your students; praise and encourage them; give them good counsel.
> Listen to your students and discuss with them; try to understand what they feel.
> Do not beat, denigrate, or otherwise humiliate children.

11c. Read these suggestions for creating a "just community" in the classroom. Propose a concrete action
for each suggestion that you find appropriate.

> Be a model of fairness in your treatment of all
> the students.
>
> Encourage and guide the students to be just to
> one another.
>
> Help your students to understand the balance
> between individual and group rights.
>
> Establish classroom norms and consequences
> with the students.
>
> Help the students recognize the benefits of
> working together in a spirit of cooperation.
>
> Stimulate a spirit of responsibility and initiative.
>
> Establish a "Contract of Shared Responsibilities"
> for students and teacher, based on cooperation,
> justice, and rectitude of conduct.
>
> Hold regular class meetings to discuss progress,
> deepen understanding, and solve problems.

The principle supported here was that when not only information but also ideas, feelings, and competencies are brought into play
through engagement in learning tasks, a process of learning and
transformation begins that allows teachers to return to their work
with new insights, attitudes, and skills.

Early Results

Although the main focus of our efforts was to support teacher learning and transfer of new skills, PLAN organized yearly testing to
establish an indicator of impact. To everyone's surprise, within less
than a year the three-year goal set by PLAN's learning adviser had
been met in the area of improving grade two Creole language skills
according to independent tests with control schools. A random

sample of grade two pupils in quality learning schools tested for Creole reading and writing ability scored at double the level of children in other matching schools.

Despite our joy at these early signs of positive change, we realized that there was plenty of work ahead: the children's level of language ability was still very low. Only 28 percent of children in project schools could read and write adequately in Creole at the end of grade two (14 percent in nonproject schools). The level was even lower in French literacy, although children in project schools again showed significantly better results than those in nonproject schools.

By the end of the second year of the project, testing of grade two children produced another surprise: a majority of children achieved passing grades in all categories of French and Creole literacy. These early successes seemed to confirm our hypothesis that a considerable margin of change could be achieved by introducing these key elements of classroom dynamics and accompanying teachers as they begin to modify curriculum accordingly. This was done without yet addressing other serious needs, such as improving teachers' academic level, developing appropriate textbooks for children, and alleviating physical conditions such as overcrowding.

In a country ridden with despair about its future, even more important to us was the enthusiastic feedback from coaches, principals, teachers, and children. Many said, "This is what Haiti needs. This approach should spread to all schools!" In at least two cases, principals gave free seminars to neighboring schools on their own initiative. One director told us that children liked working in groups so much that they did not want to go home at the end of the school day! An experienced grade six teacher admitted that he used to use corporal punishment, although he knew it was against the law. Since the seminar, however, he had put away his whip. He showed me his class of fifty students, working in pairs on mathematics problems. A low hum indicated engagement and concentration. He said, "Not only do students work well under the new approach but their schoolyard games are less violent."

We were thrilled to hear these examples of change, and made sure that abundant occasions were provided during follow-up training. Teacher feedback sessions, called quality circle meetings, were opportunities for teachers to share their successes, difficulties, and suggestions. This served as both stimulus and reassurance for those hesitant to abandon the security of authoritarian, teacher-centered methods.

The Power of Example

Our team of trainers and coaches worked hard to maintain their own unity through frequent consultation, and participants commented on the warm, supportive relations they observed. Singing, warm-ups, addressing participants by name, encouragement, and laughter helped establish an atmosphere strikingly different from most classrooms. We joyfully recognized the fruits of the practice of congruence when one teacher stood up spontaneously to announce: "These facilitators find something to appreciate in what we say, whatever it is. We can do the same with our students!"

How We Use Dialogue Education Now

To supplement the initial training, CAFT used the Seven Design Steps to design and conduct a total of ninety additional days of training for coaches, principals, and teachers that focused on reinforcing the key elements and strengthening literacy skills in all subject areas. Twenty-five sessions of values education were developed for children along with numerous session plans for active learning.

A three-stage program of parental meetings using visual learning tools, critical reflection, and popular theater methods is in process to explore ways to help their children learn effectively and develop good character. We also feel the need to pursue more actively the ongoing action-reflection process, and to form bonds with others working in the field to create a more synergistic effect. So far CAFT has organized four introductory Learning to Listen, Learning to Teach courses, one advanced course, one evaluation course, and a meeting of Global Learning Partners members to exchange methods and materials. It has also begun a database and resource library. We hope to establish a dialogue education institute in which themes can be explored in greater depth during two- or three-day retreats.

Conclusions

"Regard man as a mine rich in gems of inestimable value. Education alone can reveal these treasures and enable mankind to benefit therefrom" (Bahá'u'lláh, 1971).

We believe that we are only at the beginning of a long process of significant change in Haitian primary education. Our vision is that, just as educators came to observe what they called the miracle of Maria Montessori's work with disadvantaged children in nineteenth-century Italy, they will come to look at the miracle of effective learning occurring through dialogue, against many material and social odds. And perhaps these educators will reply, as did Montessori, that the miracle is not the method but the learners themselves, and their miraculous capacity to learn—each one a "mine rich in gems of inestimable value."

References

Anello, E., and de Hernández, J. *Educación Potencializadora*. Santa Cruz, Bolivia: Universidad Nur, 1997.

Bahá'u'lláh. *Gleanings from the Writings of Bahá'u'lláh*. Wilmette, Ill.: Bahá'i Publishing Trust, 1971. (Originally published 1939.)

Vella, J. *Training Through Dialogue*. San Francisco: Jossey-Bass, 1995.

Open Questions for Analysis and Synthesis

1. What did you see Linda Gershuny do in this case to share the principles and practices of dialogue education with Haitian teachers?

2. Look at all the learning tasks in this case. What do they tell you about how you yourself can structure learning in your work?

3. How does the issue of discipline figure into the use of dialogue education as you know it?

20

Taking Time for Praxis in Cambodia

Gail von Hahmann

This chapter describes how the World Education/Cambodia Non-Formal Maternal and Child Health Education Project used dialogue education to inform the design of a program funded by the United States Agency for International Development.

The Project Setting

Cambodia, 1994. The government was restructuring itself after four decades of regional and national upheaval and totalitarian, genocidal rule. On June 24, 1991, Prince Norodom Sihanouk, president of the Supreme National Council of Cambodia, requested humanitarian assistance from the United Nations. The resulting Declaration of Rehabilitation and Reconstruction adopted by the Paris Conference on Cambodia in October 1991 included plans for strengthening human resource development through on-the-job training of health workers (United Nations, 1991).

World Education, Inc., a Boston-based educational development organization, had designed a program it hoped would help strengthen and sustain Cambodian institutions. The program would also help rebuild trust and rekindle cooperative behavior through the transfer of the skills and principles of participatory education and development.

The Project Team

The World Education staff came from a variety of cultural backgrounds and had diverse professional skills. Staff members came from Nepal, Thailand, Ethiopia, the United States, Japan, and Cambodia. Some had expertise in public health, training, management, adult education, and information science. Some had survived the "three years, eight months, and twenty days" of the Pol Pot regime, sometimes being sent for training to Russia or another eastern bloc country. Some had survived by fleeing to camps across the border in Thailand, where they received training in nursing and medical technology.

The Project

The dialogue education project I describe here was designed to help rural mothers improve health practices in caring for their families, especially young children. Infant, child, and maternal mortality rates in Cambodia were among the highest in the world (Holcomb, Murakami, and Samnang, 1996). The strategy was to train government staff, who would then train frontline health workers in participatory, informal techniques and increase the effectiveness of the skills training that they, in turn, gave to rural mothers.

The project was planned to help the government staff acquire and practice skills needed to form an organization that could eventually offer fee-for-service training to the growing community of nongovernmental organizations (NGOs) and to newly reorganized government ministries. Underlying all the plans was an urgency to get services, education, and resources to people who had experienced decades of devastation and instability.

Starting at the Community Level

The project manager arrived in Cambodia during a confusing time. The United Nations Transitional Authority in Cambodia (UNTAC) was in town to help prepare for the May 1993 national elections. The Cambodian government, backed by Vietnam, was not yet officially recognized by the United States. Although the United States had authorized humanitarian assistance to be administered through World Education and ten other grantees, these groups were not allowed to spend funds directly through higher-level government structures. With painstaking, patient, participatory efforts, and lots of dialogue, the project manager decided to begin work at the community level.

With the help of two translators, local and regional health officers, and World Education staff from Boston, she was able to conduct two participatory method workshops in Prey Veng Province, a location deemed accessible and safe. Prey Veng had identified health education as a need. Cambodian health staff welcomed the proposed training, and local NGOs were willing to support it. These relationships, strengthened first at the local level, eventually led to formal collaboration with the Ministry of Health and its National Center for Health and Epidemiology (CNHE). The two workshops in Prey Veng marked the beginning of World Education's pilot project to train frontline health workers.

Engagement

During preparations for the third segment of the Prey Veng health worker training, the two translators were asked if they would be willing to facilitate the training with backup from the master trainers, none of whom spoke Khmer. They were familiar with the content, and they had translated every word of the previous training, observing and serving as co-facilitators in the previous two sessions. Still, it was a big jump from translating to facilitating, and the safety principle was teetering. The two-person team agreed to use this approach and set about preparing themselves to take on their new role.

Later, when the two had expanded to a training team of six, we were sitting together discussing the principle of engagement. After several attempts at defining this term, the team decided that "jumping into deep water" was an apt analogy. The third workshop in Prey Veng was a challenge and a success—thanks to the energy, commitment, and willingness of these two men to jump into deep water! Shifting from expatriate-delivered training to training services planned and delivered directly by Cambodian staff meant that more deep water awaited us.

Respect

As the Cambodian training team took on more responsibility, they shared concerns about potential problems during our weekly theory-into-practice discussions. "What do we do when a participant asks a question we trainers can't explain correctly?" "What do we do when trainees disagree with our explanation or with that of our resource people?" The group discussed this issue earnestly, and it reappeared in different forms over the next six months: How would these trainers gain the respect of the medical, educational, agricultural, and other professionals with more "experience" who were to be their trainees in this project? Would they succeed in helping these participants learn from less formally educated yet experienced local health workers?

We were sensitive to our trainers' concerns about validation in the eyes of those with more formal education. By conducting segments of the training-of-trainers (TOT) course in village settings we hoped to validate the knowledge and skills of frontline workers as well. Some of our trainees from government departments had higher degrees, including medical degrees. Their supervisors had agreed to our TOT plan. Yet when highly educated participants sat in the training room alongside village midwives, the tension was obvious. During a role-play in the Prey Veng training, a village midwife (our resource person—that is, session facilitator) described some advice she had given a patient. A young doctor, who was a trainee in this workshop, interrupted the role-play to tell her she had no business giving out such information. Our trainers had anticipated this kind of scene. They did not interfere. The midwife stood her ground, respectfully informing the young man she had simply done her job. Later, when it was time for the doctor to teach a health lesson to villagers who had joined us in the training room, he acknowledged the midwife's experience. A new kind of respect emerged in the sessions, and our trainers found the answer to their original question.

Immediacy

As the training team studied and practiced, demands for participatory training increased. Previously scheduled workshops were waiting to be designed and implemented by a training team that was still finding its way. One month after the "experiment" with the translator-trainers in Prey Veng, the World Education team was scheduled to provide a nine-day training program in Kandal Province for participants working on water and sanitation problems. This time the question came from the master trainer: "How can we safely and effectively train trainers as they simultaneously train others?"

Fortune smiled on us in the person of a young Cambodian woman who had training experience with UNICEF. Her supervisors allowed her to work with us. She became the mouth, eyes, and ears of the master trainers. With guidance from a public health specialist from Ethiopia, she worked tirelessly in the weeks before the training session, and each night during it, to review the design, explain details to the trainers, translate materials, and co-facilitate with the training team. Later, during a reflection on this workshop, a trainer described himself as "chirping" to the participants after having been "fed" the content the night before by mama and papa birds! The training team survived a number of close calls during those nine training days in Kandal. Safety teetered on its tiptoes again. But out of this risk-taking came lessons that we were able to apply immediately. We learned about humor, downtime, and stamina, and we identified three basic ground rules to guide World Education's delivery of training in the future:

- World Education workshops would now last a maximum of five days.

- The formula of three units of planning time for one unit of training would be built into our own schedule and emphasized in our training of trainers.

- Adequate time for follow-up with participants would also be part of our overall training designs.

Needs Dialogue

After the training session in Kandal had ended, reports of kidnappings, land mines along the road, and other violence by factional forces heralded several months of instability. Since we could not travel, we took this time to plan our next steps.

We designed what we called "needs dialogue" guide questions so that we could carry out a proper learning needs and resource assessment for subsequent workshops. World Education trainers could get to know participants and their context, give attention to participants, and gather the information they needed for a good design. In turn, participants could ask questions to make sure they understood the newly learned method and topics. Our questions were simple and direct: Tell us about your job. What is difficult? What would make your work easier? What training have you had? What skills do you need to practice?

When it was again safe to travel, our team members tried out the needs dialogue questions and brought home these issues: "When we go to conduct the needs dialogue, people are not in their offices. They are busy." "They think this is not an important task." "They don't know the reality in the field." "They want to know what we can provide before they tell us their needs."

It takes time and experience for people to recognize the intrinsic value of a learning needs and resource assessment. As time went on, the trainees' supervisors began to understand the importance of this early dialogue. They cooperated with the World Education trainers, allowing them the dialogue with future workshop participants.

It became clear to us and to clients that this two-way process is actually the start of the training. Training begins when the dialogue begins, before the first training event or workshop is even held. Trainees begin to think about their work through the lens of the survey questions before they attend the first session. They participate in design by engaging in dialogue with trainers ahead of time. Supervisors become familiar with the method and content their staff will be working with.

Praxis within Praxis

Action and reflection were daily fare for World Education trainers. As they prepared to deliver training sessions to clients, they planned sessions in pairs, read over each other's session designs, and gave feedback. Every session was practiced in front of the rest of the team (we called this a *dry run*), with time for feedback from the team. During workshops the training team met at the end of each day to look at what went well and what could be done differently. When the trainers returned from the field, further reflection meetings yielded redesign and improvement when needed.

Modeled on the Prey Veng pilot, the TOT course included six weeks of direct training conducted over a one-year period to allow participants time to develop their own training programs at the province, district, and community levels. The TOT curriculum covered approximately twenty-five topics in nonformal education (basic and TOT skills), community development, and management, with a focus on health education. These three topic areas presented the optimum information and skills that midlevel and frontline health, agricultural, and literacy workers would need.

Participants trained by World Education trainers were expected to return to their jobs after each segment of training, ready to conduct participatory training for their staff at the provincial and community levels. World Education also offered follow-up support on design and implementation to all TOT participants. These TOT participants would then return to World Education trainers for the following segment with experience gained from training their own staff as the raw material for the next TOT session.

A Formula for Praxis

When this concept of praxis was transferred to our clients' experience it took on a special value. We hoped to convey to clients that time spent in training design, implementation, evaluation, and follow-up should be calculated in proportion to each other to allow for maximum involvement of learners and to ensure adequate time for reflection and follow-up. For example, if the training workshop lasted one week, the proportion of all the segments would be three weeks of planning, one week of training, two weeks of reflect and record time, and one week of follow-up.

The three weeks of planning include time for learning needs and resource dialogues with appropriate people. Reflect and record time is the period when trainees return to work and begin to apply what they have learned on the job. It may mean reviewing notes, sharing information with other staff, or planning for a practice training with that participant's own trainees. The follow-up segment might involve World Education staff visiting the participant to review a training design or to observe a training session.

This segmented training also worked as a management tool. It helped us to be realistic about how many workshops could be accomplished in one year. It helped us realize that the training week of one workshop might be running simultaneously with the reflect and record portion of another. The World Education staff became adept at long-term planning. The proportioning of training segments also provided a way of costing the training and emphasizing the time and energy involved in educational endeavor, particularly in the planning stages.

Supervisory Commitment

When an organization came to World Education to request training, two points needed special emphasis. First, the supervisors needed to make a commitment to the follow-up segment of the training and to create a favorable work environment for encouraging participants to use what they learned in their everyday work. Second, they had to commit to a training schedule that allowed for practice and reflection time. Organizational representatives were asked to sign a document to formalize this agreement. Convincing busy, sometimes overwhelmed, supervisors and managers to allow their staff to attend three one-week sessions over a period of several months was truly a challenge. But once they began to see their staff use the new knowledge and skills at the worksite, they were more easily convinced to adjust to such a schedule. We also encouraged supervisors to participate in the training whenever possible, so that their commitment could be grounded in experience.

Accountability

The World Education training team eventually grew to eight, including six trainers and two translators who also could take on facilitator roles. This team received fourteen days of TOT and sixteen days of on-the-job training (OJT), during which they conducted actual workshops under the supervision of master trainers. The team received an additional twenty-two days of OJT in planning meetings and practice teaching sessions.

The World Education team also planned, designed, and implemented workshops for paying clients outside the project's regular target group. They took responsibility for meeting with client organizations, planning, designing, organizing, and managing logistics, and implementing and evaluating workshops and follow-up activities. In other words, they became accountable for delivering the "product." The management team still provided supervision, backup, and feedback when needed, and Cambodian administrative and logistics staff provided essential support. Beginning in mid-1995 and lasting for at least the next six years, Cambodian staff took charge of the delivery of training services.

Transfer and Impact

At the institutional level, impact has been recorded by formal evaluations. The key output of the project was the creation of a national training team. This Cambodian team, able to train directly in Khmer, has been the catalyst for capacity building in nonformal education. Partner organizations are replicating training received from World Education, multiplying the outreach of nonformal education approaches. The Cambodian team has trained twenty-two new trainers, who have trained seventy-five others. World Education trainees will, by project end, have trained more than a thousand health promoters who will have reached an estimated one hundred thousand people in more than 12,500 hours of lessons (Holcomb, Murakami, and Samnang, 1996). Cambodian government and NGO staff, in a multiplier effect, implemented vital training programs that were products of their own work plans, serving their constituencies.

At the community level, transfer was often dramatic. The first time the project manager asked trainees in Prey Veng what they wanted to learn, they said, after much prompting, "You are the trainers. We are the trainees. How can we tell you, the teachers, what we want to learn? You should know what we need to learn."

No one had ever asked the trainees, in any of their student experience, what they wanted from a teacher, topic, or course. We were turning things upside down and inside out. They allowed themselves to know that we needed their knowledge and experience in order for the training to proceed. In a recent interview, the project manager expressed her belief in the "process" of dialogue: "I am fully confident the program had a positive impact on World Education staff. We offered new possibilities: having all the answers is not imperative; asking questions is permissible, even preferable, and asking questions allows us to know how to teach."

Another management team member described how, for her, the project illustrated that participatory management and training can work even in a culture weary of participatory styles. It provided a foundation for the Cambodian trainers to become confident in the skills they had to offer their country in a time of rapid development (Youngwerth, 1995).

Conclusions

Gradually, most of the expatriate staff left the project for other positions or to return to their home countries. Cambodian staff also left to join other organizations, including United Nations–sponsored organizations. Learning had definitely taken place. The staff had grown professionally. They moved to other jobs using the skills that they had developed while with the World Education project. Six years later, a much smaller World Education training team still offers training to clients.

References

Holcomb, S., Murakami, H., and Samnang, P. *Evaluation Report on World Education/Cambodia Non-Formal Maternal and Child Health Education Project.* Boston: World Education, 1996.

United Nations. *Report of the U.N. Inter-Agency Humanitarian Mission to Cambodia.* New York: United Nations, Oct.-Nov. 1991.

Youngwerth, M. L. *Final Report and Recommendations.* Boston: World Education, Nov. 15, 1995.

Open Questions for Analysis and Synthesis

1. Gail von Hahmann names selected principles and practices she saw the World Education team using in the program. What other principles and practices do you see at work in this case?

2. What similarities and differences do you discern between this Cambodian case and other cases in this book that demonstrate teacher or trainer training?

3. What did the "needs dialogue" process described here teach you?

21

Educational Revolution
on the Volga River

Learning as a Personal Victory in the New Russia

Peter Perkins, Michaela B. Stickney

In September 1998, dialogue education was introduced to southern Russia through an important collaboration between a community-based environmental training center, the Volgograd Center for Environmental Training (CET), and Global Learning Partners, an international training group based in the United States. It was the most progressive approach to education encountered by this group of educators in the newly independent Russia. This chapter highlights the cross-cultural challenges that such an event presented and the uses of dialogue education in a demanding situation.

We begin by recalling a powerful moment that occurred at the end of that remarkable week. A warm September sun glistened across the wide expanse of the fabled Volga River. One riverbank is dominated by a robust industrial triangle of steel and iron manufacturers; the opposite bank is home to small dachas, where families and friends relax in flowering gardens. In the bow of an industrial riverboat, the gathering of people united in friendship celebrated. They exchanged songs expressing delight at completing a revolutionary week of learning about learning. The Russians offered songs about love for their country, the earth, the river; the Americans traded traditional folk tunes and spirituals. These songs about respect, heartfelt values, and meaningful connections reflected the learning concepts discovered during that groundbreaking week. By bridging cultural differences and uncovering shared values, this deep work allowed an educational awakening to occur.

The Collaboration: Volgograd Center for Environmental Training and Global Learning Partners

Volgograd, a city of one million people, lies on the Volga River, five hundred kilometers upstream from the Caspian Sea. During World War II, Volgograd was devastated; after the war it was rebuilt into a major industrial metropolis. The city's southern and northern districts are mixed residential-industrial neighborhoods that suffer great air pollution. The largest air pollution contributors in the city include an iron and steel mill, a diesel engine factory, a silica brickworks factory, and an aluminum plant (Institute for Sustainable Communities, 1998).

The Russian Air Management Program (RAMP) improved air quality by supporting new policies and industrial practices that influenced national institutions. Volgograd was selected as the site of a pilot study to test new methods and policies. The study was one of the first Russian collaborations between municipal and community leaders and businesses and national government ministries. A cornerstone of the project was the Volgograd Center for Environmental Training (CET), which was established to deliver training courses on managing natural resources and assessing environmental impact (United States Environmental Protection Agency, 1999; Institute for Sustainable Communities, 1998). CET was largely operated by women. It used training and partnering with industry and government to improve air quality, water quality, and human health.

CET cultivated a pool of talented course facilitators skilled in interactive, dialogue-based facilitation methods. This CET facilitation team was eager to learn techniques that would more actively engage participants in their courses and foster extensive group interaction. Their clientele ranged from regional and local government entities, industry and business organizations, scientists, and nongovernmental organizations (NGOs). They had already experimented with a "business game," a short role-playing activity that was a popular and stimulating part of several of their courses. This thought-provoking interface is where our educational revolution found its roots. As a new business in an emerging professional environmental field, the CET team needed to capture people's interest so that they would return to CET for additional training. Offering effective programs was the key to doing so. CET selected the Global Learning Partners approach as their guide to a new type of educational institution.

Twelve adult educators participated in the facilitator training program that Global Learning Partners offered. They represented three groups: academic lecturers from universities with expertise in fields of human health, agriculture, engineering, and jurisprudence; environmental permit and inspection specialists from the Volgograd City Environmental Services Administration; and staff members from CET, which hosted this event. Those of us from Global Learning Partners considered all these professionals to be respected peers.

Education as a Path to Self-Determination

Russian education at this point in time was usually guided by a top-down design. It followed the familiar process of lecturers presenting information as a monologue in a one-way flow from expert to learner. Tatiana S. Ananskikh, director of CET, was not familiar with other progressive education models in Russia. But she and her staff wanted to apply new knowledge and new methods in their educational program.

During our course, participants immersed themselves in the radical work that Jane Vella has developed during forty years of research and practice in adult education. Course content primarily involved concepts of adult learning theory and creating respect and safety in the learning environment. Content took on new names, such as dialogue, which became "polylogue," to delineate it as dialogue with many other people.

Principles and Practices That Inspire Dialogue

The use of dialogue was inspirational for the course participants because they were accustomed to the more formal lecture style of presentation. The Russian facilitators discovered that the concept of monologue did not result in as much retention as dialogue, practice, and action. Discussing, experiencing, and practicing elements of Knowles's theory on how adults learn with regard to respect, immediacy, and relevance helped them experience what it means to discover their own learning. These concepts represented a radical change in thinking for most participants. They discussed how experiential learning often was not directly linked to classroom lectures or technical presentations. What they learned in this course challenged the more traditional courses, which are designed for the teacher rather than for the learners. One participant wrote on the anonymous course evaluation form: "It helped to analyze and evaluate knowledge and to prioritize it. Analysis showed that this method is universal."

Dialogue-Based Learning Seems Less Professional

However, some participants expressed concern that a less formal method of teaching, which included so much dialogue, might appear unprofessional. Our challenge as course leaders was to make it clear that dialogue does not equate with a lack of professionalism. Rather, it is a means to deepen and diversify learning. The course became an exciting departure from the traditional Russian educational practice of disseminating information; it became a journey of learning that drew on the experiences of all participants. They saw more and more value in this discourse as the days went on; their level of analysis grew deeper and the application to their personal lives increased as well. The method not only felt professional but also felt important and even visionary to them.

How Adults Learn

One of the first memorable impressions we made, which related to the theory of how adults learn, was in the classroom configuration.

CET had permission to use a training room in the facility of its main sponsor, the Russian Ecological Academy. The room consisted of two rows of twenty small, paired desks neatly facing the front of the room. To create more intimacy and opportunity for dialogue, we asked permission to reconfigure the desks into groups of three to four.

At first our friends entering the reconfigured room seemed uncomfortable with the arrangement. We noted their somber facial expressions and quiet responses as they took their seats. After launching into the course, the comfort level grew. By the second day, the sound level rose to such a crescendo that it attracted members of the Russian Ecological Academy from other wings of the building. They heard laughter, saw dancing, and asked, "What is so funny? What are you doing?" They could tell by peering into the room that we were working hard, learning, and having fun. We felt that we had achieved success in creating a comfortable learning environment that facilitated the practice of substantive learning tasks.

Increased Energy in the Training Room

The transition from initial discomfort with informality to great enthusiasm occurred throughout the course. We recognized this shift when we compared responses to questions about what the Russians expected from this course with factors they identified in memorable learning experiences. The course expectations were fairly uniform, albeit valuable: "new knowledge," "new methods," "new practices," "new ties with people," and "new ideas." After beginning to experience the course, however, the language they used to describe learning factors became more personal and descriptive: "respect," "trust," "captures the mood of the group," and "the teacher is able to acknowledge mistakes" and "link teaching with the experience of the learners." This diverse and frank set of responses enlightened us about the needs of this group and helped us tailor learning tasks over the next few days. Olga Yurkyan, a science professor, roused the group when she remarked, "Learning is the personal victory of the student."

Moment of Awakening: Learners as Decision Makers

The learner-as-decision maker concept proved one of the most challenging to deliver, but once experienced became one of the most profound. Because the common process of education was largely a one-way street, recognizing their own dynamic role in a complete learning picture was liberating. Because Russia was at that time a newly independent state, people were discovering new freedoms and opportunities not previously enjoyed. Therefore, the ability to question and reflect on new information and practices was a new and necessary experience.

Translating the epistemological concept of learners as decision makers proved linguistically and culturally difficult. The difficulties reflected the depth of hierarchical thinking about education in Russia. The phrase itself had been translated from English by a Russian translator as "students as professionals." A supporting informational paragraph that accompanied the text described how the teacher "would allow the students to share their opinions with each other." But when Tatiana N. Galochkina, our interpreter, listened to us explain this concept during the course, she quickly clarified the confusing language. Smiles multiplied around the room. The awakening effect of truly understanding this concept rendered everyone momentarily speechless. For a few astonished moments, we were not sure quite how to reconnect to the course. In that flash of insight, we knew why we had chosen to be here together. We learned from overcoming this semantic difficulty that the ability to question authority—whether in government, media, or academia—was a radically new concept for our students. Brazilian educator Paulo Freire comes to mind when we think of cultural and governmental manipulation and the power of accessible and meaningful education. Freire (1972) wrote that posing problems where learners could apply their own knowledge and receive feedback gave them real power by expanding learning.

Feedback on Dialogue Education

Feedback from the group came in many forms, including their comments, some of which have already been mentioned.

The final written course evaluations were anonymous, which everyone liked very much; no names were associated with individual responses. One course participant wrote: "The analysis, evaluation, and priority-setting activities in the course represent how the concept of learners as decision makers was absorbed into the collective thinking and actions of the group."

Another course participant wrote how much she enjoyed "the practice!" She stated that "80 percent has been learned!" (rather than 20 percent) from the practice teaching sessions. The group continually demonstrated their proficiency with many of the principles. From learning task to learning task, they showed that they had absorbed course content by what they said to each other and how they applied these concepts to their own work. They articulated a shift in attitude centered on a growing acceptance of the concept that truly effective learning engages learners in the discovery of their own learning through events steeped in dialogue.

One participant was presenting her doctoral dissertation during the same week that our training course took place. She initially planned to attend only the first day and then return to her diligent preparations. But the activities of the first day captivated her imagination so much that she chose to come back. At first, she was distressed about preparing a practice teaching session because she thought it would take many hours in an already tight week. She started by preparing a lecture, but her team partners helped her see how using the Seven Design Steps would free her from focusing on facts to focusing on dynamic interaction with the other facilitators. Her relief was tangible.

Our interpreter, Tatiana Galochkina, found the learning process and experience so valuable that she invited us to visit her English language and interpretation school. There we met nearly seventy adolescents; we broke them up into two groups and met with them separately. The learning process was transferred to their classrooms as we asked *them* questions and engaged *them* in dialogue, instead of the reverse. They did not expect this approach and enjoyed it. Many said how different our method was, and that "we really liked this class." They wanted to know how to say it in the vernacular— "This was cool!"

What They Are Doing Now

We recently heard from our friend Tatiana Galochkina. She commented that the dialogue method has become quite popular in Volgograd and is being used in adult education classes at the Volgograd Pedagogical University. She added that the concept of "'echoing' for correcting mistakes works wonderfully for students of all ages." Another course participant, Sergei Ostroukhov, wrote to tell us that it was difficult to select which method or concept was most influential or useful: "All was so interesting and dynamic, that practically all the material was perceived as a unit." He added that the concepts have "become an integral part of my educational programs." He said that he likes the flexibility of the methods because they allow an awakening to occur in the classroom. Dialogue-based education has allowed him to "find common language with nearly all audiences, even the hardest" to reach. Olga Yurkyan described how the universal Seven Design Steps and open questions have been incorporated into her curricula, whether her audience is over one hundred people or only twenty people. Elena Vlasova finds working in small groups and using strong visual materials to be most helpful. She said that action-oriented activity in small groups "causes the students to focus on what is being learned, and not to be distracted by extraneous business!" Tatiana Ananskikh, director of CET, reported that the center is ready for advanced applications of dialogue education and invited us to come back.

Developmental Theory: Dialogue from Another Perspective

The Learning to Listen, Learning to Teach course that we taught to the Russian facilitators in Volgograd shares some themes with skilled inquiry, skilled listening, and skilled advocacy methods (Yellow Wood Associates, 2002; Brown, forthcoming; Senge, Kleiner, Roberts, Ross, and Smith, 1994).

The theory behind skilled inquiry is similar to that of asking open questions. Skilled inquiry uses open questions as a foundation for meaningful dialogue. As with open questions, skilled inquiry is a way to approach people and situations with the openness of a learner, rather than by playing the role of an expert. Questions asked elicit an individual's experiences, expectations, and interpretations. Use of open questions is one of the foundational principles of dialogue education, as experienced in Volgograd.

In skilled listening, the answers are not determinable through independent observation or interviews with others. Skilled listening is closely linked with identifying assumptions and expectations as factors in dialogue. To receive the overarching message is to discourage "overpersonalizing communications" so that expectations and assumptions are understood prior to taking action (Yellow Wood Associates, 2002, p. 58).

Skilled advocacy joins elements of skilled inquiry and listening into a direction of expressing assumptions behind personal or collective beliefs (Yellow Wood Associates, 2002; Brown, forthcoming; Senge, Kleiner, Roberts, Ross, and Smith, 1994), which is reminiscent of the process of listing expectations and learning factors in this Russian course. This process invites dialogue and leads to enhanced decision making "by allowing a group to access the full range of thought and creativity of its members" (Yellow Wood Associates, 2002, p. 60). Imagine how useful this could be to our Russian educators and community leaders as they help bring more people into the decision-making process in the new Russian society.

Skilled inquiry, listening, and advocacy translate well into the realm of problem solving and conflict resolution as a basis for meaningful dialogue. Because these skills, like those inherent in dialogue education, offer excellent ways for building trust and creating safety in dialogue, they are helpful in defusing potentially volatile situations. When conflict is minimized, it leads to positive exchange of dialogue and positive activity. We have often spoken of the power of safety as a means to build trust in dialogue-based education (Vella, 2002). We found that because we first built safety and trust with the Russian facilitators, it allowed them to open up to new ideas. A safe environment also led them to use some of these new ideas in their own work after they had completed our course.

Conclusions

Our complete experience in Russia included getting out of the classroom and coming together on the river. A transformation had occurred: we had moved from our separate roles as course leaders and course participants in the classroom to one interconnected group on the river as we celebrated the week's accomplishments. In a few short days, it seemed, we had learned several lifetimes worth of experience and knowledge from each other. By trading academic rigors for song, food, and joined hands, we transcended our different cultures in a community of learners and leaders.

As already noted, the course occurred at a time when Russians were experiencing greater individual freedom and opportunity. As members of a newly independent state, they needed their government and other established centers of authority to be open, accessible, and transparent. They wanted and had earned new respect, and were enjoying feeling empowered as decision makers. What they had learned and experienced in the Learning to Listen,

Learning to Teach course was being echoed in a much grander way in the new opportunities and freedoms they were gaining.

It was empowering to witness these positive changes and to realize that change was occurring not only in the classroom but throughout the entire country. The freedom and power that people discover when they truly learn are indications of how effective education can be and how it can change social context. The perception of possibilities among this group in Volgograd came primarily as a result of guided dialogue. Dialogue became the seat of power for the learners. Dialogue is the place where one grapples aloud with others to make sense of ideas and behaviors and construct them to fit their context. When people know that they know more, their confidence grows and matures over time. This development of confidence that was seen again and again translated into personal, social, and political change for these Russians from Volgograd. They know that we support them on their journey and that they are not alone. We are learning dialogue together.

References

Brown, J. S. *Learning Our Way Through Complexity at Work* (forthcoming).

Freire, P. *Pedagogy of the Oppressed*. New York: Herder & Herder, 1972.

Institute for Sustainable Communities (ISC). *Russian Air Management Program: Demonstrating Innovative Approaches to Improving Air Quality*. Montpelier, Vt.: ISC, 1998.

Senge, P., Kleiner, A., Roberts, C., Ross, R., and Smith, B. *The Fifth Discipline Field Book*. New York: Doubleday/Currency, 1994.

United States Environmental Protection Agency (USEPA). *Russian Air Management Program (RAMP) 1992–1999: Final Report*. Research Triangle Park, N.C.: USEPA, 1999.

Vella, J. *Learning to Listen, Learning to Teach: The Power of Dialogue in Educating Adults*. San Francisco: Jossey-Bass, 2002. (Originally published 1994.)

Yellow Wood Associates. *You Get What You Measure: Measurement Training Guide*. St. Albans, Vt.: Yellow Wood Associates, 2002.

Open Questions for Analysis and Synthesis

1. What did you see the Global Learning Partners team do to deal directly with the cross-cultural aspects of this situation?

2. How did you see the team recognize and celebrate that these Russian adult learners were decision makers throughout the training session?

3. What principles and practices did you see the Global Learning Partners team use throughout this case?

22

Using Dialogue Education to Transform Primary Health Care in Chile

Educacion Dialogante

Klaus Püschel

This chapter describes the influence of dialogue education on the development of a new residency program at the School of Medicine of the Catholic University of Chile for primary care physicians working in underserved areas in Santiago. The learning, transfer, impact, and meaning of dialogue education are analyzed by ten participants in the Learning to Listen, Learning to Teach course, which is used each year to open the residency program.

Reality Challenges the University

In 1993, a new medical residency program was started at the Catholic University medical school in Santiago, Chile. The new program aims at enhancing health care provided through community clinics to underserved urban populations in Santiago. A group of physicians already working in primary care realized that the seven years of medical training they had received in an academic hospital did not prepare them to meet the needs of the people who used community clinics. Health problems presented in community clinics were different from those seen at the university hospital. Interaction with patients and their families and the influence of social and psychological factors also differed greatly between the two settings. Primary care clinics were much closer to the everyday reality of the people, and therefore new skills were required to face that reality and to contribute to the improvement of the health of patients, families, and local communities.

A group of faculty at the Catholic University, led by Dr. Joaquín Montero, created the new residency program based mainly in community clinics. The program takes place in a nontraditional academic setting, close to the reality of the people whom these new physicians intend to serve. Montero worked with other faculty and the group of primary care physicians to design the new Family and Community Medicine Program.

The program had the key support of the academic authorities, who saw an opportunity to develop a new specialty that was unavailable in Chile. Authorities also perceived the importance of the program in contributing to the social responsiveness of the university by focusing the program in a highly underserved area.

The primary care physicians who entered the program faced a number of key questions: How were they going to learn in a "non-learning" environment—that is, in community clinics? These had been created only to provide services, not to provide learning. Who was going to "teach" these physicians if there were no "specialists" there? What did these new physicians need to learn, and who was going to define that curriculum?

A new educational model was needed to answer these important questions. Certainly, this new model should incorporate the critical reflection of reality by using four open questions: *What is happening here? Why is this happening? What problems will it cause in our situation? What can be done to improve such a situation?*

There was the essential need "to act on reality" but also to "get back from reality" a theory to understand the life that was going on there. The duality of the reflection-action had to be a key component of the educational model. Education in such a residency program must happen in permanent dialogue. The new residents and the medical school faculty had to find a way to interact with local reality, asking key questions, hearing possible answers, and learning.

In May 1993, the first cohort of seven family-practice residents started the new program. It began with the one-week course Learning to Listen, Learning to Teach" taught by Dr. Jane Vella in collaboration with Dr. Rosa Walker, one of the first faculty members in the program. Walker had studied with Vella at the University of North Carolina at Chapel Hill. Dr. Rodrigo Escalona, a Chilean psychiatrist trained at Duke University, collaborated in the teaching and translation of the course. Escalona decided to join us in developing the course for future residents. Dr. Joaquín Montero, the chief of the new program and also a former student of Vella's at UNC, decided to use this course to open the new program as a way to establish its learning model. We would have the principles and practices of dialogue education as a key component of the reflection-action strategy. Each activity of the residency—for example, clinical rounds, medical presentations, and community projects— would be based on dialogue education.

The Learning to Listen, Learning to Teach course (Vella, 1995) is now repeated each year. It is the first activity new residents have in their training. Ten generations of residents have participated in the course since 1993—seventy graduates and forty current residents. All program faculty, several other faculty members at the medical school, and many health professionals from the community clinics have also participated. Overall, about 250 people have participated in the course in Santiago since 1993.

To what extent have the principles and practices of adult education that were developed in the course affected the learning and action of the residents and graduates of the program? Are they applying these tools in their daily activities? What are their successes and failures? How has the course affected the teaching strategies used by faculty in the family practice program and at the medical school? These are the main questions that we ask after ten years of dialogue with dialogue education. This chapter presents the experiences of residents, graduates, and faculty members as it addresses these questions.

The Impact of Learning to Listen, Learning to Teach

A qualitative approach was used to gather information about the experiences and effects of the Learning to Listen, Learning to Teach course on residents, graduates, and faculty. Two researchers, Fernando Poblete, a family physician from the program who participated in the course in 1998, and Daniel Diaz, a research psychologist who has not yet participated in the course, conducted key interviews. They were in charge of conducting the "dialogue about education" with ten representatives who had participated in the course since 1993. The group of ten included two residents from the Family and Community Medicine Program, three graduates working in primary care, three faculty members (including two former residents), and two medical educators who are now working at the recently created faculty development program of the medical school.

A semistructured questionnaire was created to guide the conversation. Topics were chosen based on the three evaluation principles used in dialogue education: learning, transfer, and impact. These three principles were complemented by a fourth concept in the analysis: meaning. *Meaning* was a common key word used by many of the participants as a very first way to connect their current reality with the experience they had in the course. Therefore, we decided to incorporate this concept with the three evaluation principles in the analysis.

Several content areas were addressed. The significance participants give to the course was addressed by asking them to choose a symbol they related to the course and explain its meaning. Participants were also invited to describe a recent "educational experience" and to name the most useful educational principles and practices involved. They were asked to describe an educational principle or practice they now frequently apply to their work. They were invited to describe what principles they do not use or find difficult to apply. Finally, they were asked to share their ideas of the concept and practice of dialogue education, or in Spanish *educación dialogante*.

Interviews were tape-recorded, interviewers took field notes, and transcriptions were made based on the tape recording. Oral consent was obtained before interviewing each participant. The analysis of the information was made using traditional standards for qualitative research (Pope and Mays, 1999). Common themes and key words of the main ideas were found in the conversations and presented in this evaluation.

All participants selected for the interviews agreed to collaborate in this evaluation. The average interview lasted about forty-five minutes. The two main environments participants referred to were the academic environment and the community setting where many of them developed their practice. Both are important for our evaluation, and therefore are considered in the present analysis.

The Meaning of Learning Through Dialogue

Three main ideas emerged when participants explained the significance of the course on their current practice. First, all said that the course represented a landmark in their careers. Second, it meant a way to systematize intuition. Third, many participants said that the course allowed them to build a new synthesis of theory and practice based on the experience and knowledge of teachers and students.

New Perspectives

"From receiving the information teachers have to give me, I have gone to choosing the knowledge I need to use." This is how one young resident of the program expressed the shift that happened in her mind after the course. The banking approach (Freire, 1972) that she experienced "at school and during the seven years at the university" was replaced by a new way of learning. Now, she says, she will choose the knowledge she feels she needs to improve her practice, and moreover she knows "how to do that."

A graduate from the program said he realized why the course was presented at the very beginning of the program: "It was a landmark in my career; it set the tone for the way we will face problems and learn from them. It is the axis of the methodology we used to learn from reality."

Many participants highlighted the importance of the first week of their residency program when they took the course. They noted how it changed their interaction with their reality. Many remarked on the new "praxis" of reflecting and acting on reality.

One professor represented his experience in the course as a circle. The image of a circle captures dialogue education, where everyone can see each other and all have the same opportunity to participate. In contrast, in the traditional approach the teacher confronts the audience in a linear relationship. A circle is a great symbol to capture the ideas of inclusion of all learners as subjects (decision makers) of their own learning.

Systematizing Intuition

"It was always there but now I can see it and can share it as a gift." Most participants in the course expressed the idea that it built on their unconscious knowledge. As one of the faculty members working in medical education said, the course allowed her to "name" things she already had within her but was not conscious of. Now that she can name them, she is able to share them, to give them as a gift. This recognition of things that were already there is the essence of dialogue education, the *metanoia* (Vella, 2000). It involves a deeper awareness of oneself produced by the right dialogue between one's own spirit and the reality.

New Creations

A strong theme among participants was that dialogue education has the beauty of combining the experience and knowledge of students and teachers. From this process emerges a new creation, a co-construction, a synthesis. One of the graduates working in primary care chose clay as the symbol that connected him with the course. Shaping the knowledge of the community and health professionals to improve health was like molding the clay to produce a new vessel.

One of the residents mentioned that with dialogue education she learned "during" the class and not "before or after" the class, as was her experience with her former educational experiences. In dialogue education she was able to build on her knowledge and create new meaning. She had not previously heard about the concept of quantum learning. She delighted in the idea of the movement of the content beyond itself in order to make new significant meaning for her context (Vella, 2002). This resident felt she already "knew" it when she heard it. She recognized the concept: "It was always there."

Principles and Practices

Participants mentioned a number of relevant principles and practices of dialogue education when talking about their recent educational experience, such as generative themes and the importance of the *who* (learners, safety, and respect). Other principles, such as working in small groups, the seven steps for designing an educational session, immediacy, and engagement were also frequently named.

The Importance of the *Who*

Participants offered many examples illustrating the importance of their considering *who:* the learners. One professor, when describing a difficult situation in a course he was teaching at the time of the interview, mentioned that things were not flowing as well as in the previous course with the same residents. He had to go back ten years to review his original notes about principles and practices of adult education. "We realized that at this time we had not carefully considered the needs and expectations of the residents, or their generative themes. Yes, I think we forgot the *who!*"

How could we discover the generative themes of a group to produce effective dialogue education? A graduate gave some important
clues for perceiving the generative themes of the community in the
primary care setting where he works. He highlighted the importance
"of always having your eyes wide open to see what is going on with
people, your ears in constant alert to hear what they are talking
about, and your nose always cleared to 'smell' what people really
care about." That was his description of how to discern generative
themes and achieve engagement in the health promotion activities
conducted with the community.

Safety

A safe environment in which to teach and to learn was a key component of dialogue education for most participants. Some associated this safe environment with freedom: freedom to speak, feel,
and do, all essential elements for effective learning. A resident who
described her experience teaching a group of adolescent mothers
how to take care of their babies went back to the idea of safety and
freedom. She felt "lighter" using dialogue; she could remove her
given label as an expert. She realized that some of the mothers knew
things that she did not know, and she realized that she, as physician, had permission not to know everything.

One faculty member noted the difficulty he had in achieving
safety, a key principle for learning. It requires changing personal
styles in the interaction with people, especially if we believe they
are subjects of their own learning. He was recognizing with Paulo
Freire that teaching is certainly a *human act* (Freire, 1972), a real
interaction between minds and souls.

Transfer: The Effect of Dialogue Education on Practice

The university and the community were the two environments
where the group of participants applied the principles and practices
of dialogue education. In the academic setting, they described many

experiences using dialogue with undergraduates, graduate students, and teachers. They also reflected on the link between dialogue education and evidence-based medical strategy. This approach has gained strong support among faculty as a way to apply the most recent scientific evidence to their teaching and practice. In the community setting many experiences were described where doctors used the principles and practices of dialogue education in interactions with patients, community groups, and other health professionals.

Many participants mentioned the importance of using dialogue education to teach the principles of evidence-based medicine (EBM) effectively. One faculty member had named the risk that existed of transforming EBM into merely a technocratic tool. He noticed that using dialogue education to teach EBM puts the focus on the person. He saw that dialogue education allows EBM to start with the person's needs and finish with the person's options, an effective learning cycle. This prevents the oppression of a complex technology.

Another faculty member described her experience using the "found objects" task (Vella, 1995, p. 171) to engage a group of faculty members during a workshop for improving teamwork. One of the faculty members, Joaquín Montero, arrived late and was invited to choose his symbol. He immediately recognized the task and laughed. "I know where this is from." The teacher conducting the session had taken the Learning to Listen, Learning to Teach course in May 2002, ten years after Montero had invited Jane Vella to Chile to conduct the first version of this same course. This instructor was now applying the dialogue education principles and using them to teach Montero and the other faculty members. As she said in the interview, "The word is spreading, people are using the principles, and now we are hearing back from them. Dialogue education has come full circle!"

Vella described the new role of the professor as a resource person in the learning process during the course she conducted in Chile in 1993 (Vella, 1995). Ten years later a resident from the Family and Community Medicine Program working with a group of young pregnant women in a poor neighborhood in Santiago applied that same principle. She designed a task for women working in small groups. There, they spoke of better ways of taking care of their new babies: "I sat straight and saw how they were talking in their own language, learning from each other, sharing what they knew. I was happy not being 'the professor'; I almost didn't have to talk at all!"

Impact: Changing Reality by Using Dialogue Education

The "significant meaning" that participants of the course have given to the principles and practices of dialogue education, the "learning" they have achieved, and the "transfer" they are applying in many settings—all have started to affect a variety of environments.

"Thinking with Your Toes" to Improve Health Care in the Community

The energy shown in the rippling leg muscles of Rodin's *Thinker* was used by Vella (2002) as an example of quanta, a measure of energy in the language of physics and also a measure of the energy of learning in the language of dialogue education. She invited us to use the same energy, to "think with our toes" when using dialogue education. A graduate of the program offered the same invitation to a group of elderly people who participated in a diabetic care workshop. The workshop focused on improving foot care in diabetic persons and preventing complications of the disease. Participants were involved in the design, implementation, and evaluation of the workshop. It grew from twenty participants to fifty. They had to increase the number of trainers from three to six, and had to find a bigger place to do the training.

After the workshop, the group of elderly people not only knew how to take care of their feet but also demanded that the primary care clinic hire a podiatrist to check their feet at least once a year. Currently they are building a foot care clinic for the whole community. The elders called this workshop *la revolución de los pies* (the revolution of the feet). The full power of dialogue education emerged in this experience. The group was clearly thinking with their toes to take care of their feet. The content of the workshop moved beyond itself and into the context and lives of the group. Physicians witnessed quantum learning in urban Santiago.

Faculty Education at the University

One of the features that now distinguishes the Family and Community Medicine Program is the dialogue education methodology used for learning and teaching. Many faculty members inside and outside the program have taken the dialogue education course that is offered yearly. Despite this, the shift in the educational paradigm is not easy because, as one resident stated, there are "established canons, authorized models of teaching and learning that are hard to change." However, this resident also said: "I feel strongly that dialogue education is effective. Now we have the tools it is our job to continue the change."

Conclusions

In 1997, the Catholic University's School of Medicine was accredited by the American Association of Medical Colleges. One of the main recommendations of the evaluation team that participated in the accreditation process was that the medical school needed to improve the training of its faculty in teaching strategies. A new Center for Clinical Teaching Training was created with the funding of the Chilean Ministry of Education and the World Bank. In 2002, the center decided to incorporate the Learning to Listen, Learning to Teach course in the obligatory curriculum for earning a faculty development program teaching certificate. About fifteen faculty members from the medical school will take the course annually. This will be an opportunity to reflect about education, and certainly a big step to continue the change. This university is engaging in a fruitful dialogue with reality.

References

Freire, P. *Pedagogy of the Oppressed*. New York: Herder & Herder, 1972.

Pope, C., and Mays, N. *Qualitative Research in Health Care* (rev. ed.). London: BMJ Publishing Group, 1999.

Vella, J. *Training Through Dialogue*. San Francisco: Jossey-Bass, 1995.

Vella, J. *Taking Learning to Task: Creative Strategies for Teaching Adults*. San Francisco: Jossey-Bass, 2000.

Vella, J. "Quantum Learning: Teaching as Dialogue." In J. Ross-Gordon (ed.), *Contemporary Viewpoints on Teaching Adults Effectively*. San Francisco: Jossey Bass, 2002.

Open Questions for Analysis and Synthesis

1. Why do you think Dr. Montero of the medical school proposed doing a week of dialogue education as the first part of the residency in family and community medicine?

2. What surprised you most about this case?

3. Where do you see dialogue education going in Chile?

23

Organizing to Undo Racism in Canada

Designing for Safety in an Antiracism Program

Peter Noteboom

This chapter describes the design of a Canadian antiracism education program. I have found antiracism work to be one of the most challenging areas in education: the topic is potentially explosive, it is deeply felt at a gut level, and the destructive power of racism is rampant.

The Opening to Diversity Program

I was recently invited by the race relations committee of a group of local churches in Toronto to work with them to design and implement an antiracism education program in their communities. This committee is part of the area churches association, or classis, of the Christian Reformed Church in North America, a Protestant denomination in the Reformed tradition.

These churches are largely immigrant and second-generation churches from single ethnic groups. Over the past fifty years, these churches have created successful communities, tending to relationships among their members and in the surrounding community and maintaining a strong, distinctive worship tradition. But lately the

---

Note: The "we" in this chapter, who deserve credit for the learning documented here, are Tim Nguyen, Steve Kabetu, Fred Witteveen, Nick Overduin, Ben Vanderlugt, Henrietta Verbaan, Chris Pullenayagem, Shiao Chang, Esther deGroot, and Faye Dundas

surrounding neighborhoods have begun to change, with many new ethnic groups represented and occasionally attending these churches. Many have not become members of the churches, however, and there has been a persistent feeling that they did not feel welcome. As part of the larger denominational effort, the race relations committee received financial support to begin its Opening to Diversity Antiracism Program for Toronto-area churches.

In this project I was working through Unfolding, Ltd. Connie Kuipers, from Global Learning Partners, was co-facilitator. The thirty-hour course that we gave to facilitators derived from Global Learning Partners' Learning to Listen, Learning to Teach course.

A Multiple Stage Process

Together we made plans to develop antiracism education materials and train future facilitators. Before launching into implementation of these plans, wise committee members suggested that we offer them as a series of awareness-raising and information-sharing evenings in three different church settings. These sessions became an important part of our learning needs and resource assessment (LNRA). They were carefully designed and facilitated using dialogue education techniques.

I suggested that we keep the principle of safety foremost in our mind while designing these sessions because I personally have had the experience of antiracism training where I did not feel safe and therefore not free to take risks to learn. So as designers and facilitators, we avoided imposing content on our audience but rather presented it as something to be critically reviewed or added to. We did not pose questions that put participants in the spotlight in the large group without the prerequisite sequence of simpler content. We designed learning tasks so that participants had the occasion to test their thoughts with a partner first. We did not rush through content or agenda items that we had planned without sharing the reasons why they were included in the program. As contributions to a safe learning environment, here are some of the choices we made:

- Sharing the purpose for the sessions in some detail

- Telling the history of the project

- Asking for clarifications, and inviting others to share what they knew

- Offering occasions for partner work so that all voices could be heard

- Checking frequently where we were in our agenda,

- Sharing where we were going with our process

Stage One: Information-Sharing and Awareness-Raising Evenings

After considering the participants (who), the situation that called for the learning event (why), the parameters of time (when), and the location (where), we decided on three content topics (what): the antiracism-diversity dialogue project, stories of race and culture, and how to get involved with the project. Here is a selection from the agenda for one of the evenings:

Learning task #1. The antiracism-diversity dialogue project

1A. Listen to this brief presentation on the early stages of this project. Circle on the handout what interests you.

1B. What did you circle? What excites you about this history? What phrases represent items you want to learn more about?

Learning task #2. Stories of race-culture

2A. In groups of three, analyze this definition of racism that has been adopted by some agencies of our denomination: *Racism = Race Prejudice + Systemic Misuse of Power*. What is new for you in this definition? How does it fit with your experience? We'll hear a sample of your responses.

2B. In your same groups of three describe a situation where you have experienced or observed racism in your congregation or in another religious or faith-based group. We'll hear a sample of your responses.

Learning task #3. Getting involved with the project

Listen to this brief outline of upcoming events and opportunities to get involved.

They read an outline of scheduled activities.

Name ways you see your church engaging with this program. Name ways you see yourself personally engaging with this program. Jot down your responses on Post-it notes and post them for all to see.

As we reviewed the results of our evening sessions, we were confirmed that this was a relevant topic, with a strong sense of immediacy in some churches, and none at all in others. This helped us narrow our target churches in the first phase to three that were already experiencing a necessity for this kind of learning. The strongest message we heard was about the pace of our scheduled activities: "Slow down!" This helped us move out of our project-management time orientation and join them in their "church time." We adjusted our own expectations and time lines. These evenings also turned out to be important occasions for talent hunting: identifying potential antiracism facilitators to be recruited later on.

Stage Two: Planning the Content Together

The second stage of our learning needs and resource assessment was a weekend planning workshop. We jointly took the next steps in designing our training program. We named what we knew about educating for change, pooling what we knew about all the possible topics in the area of antiracism, and then narrowing down that list to five core topics that could be learned over a sequence of five one-hour workshop sessions. Once again we designed with safety in mind. We began with a cooperative learning experience of pooling what we know about educating for change.

Learning task #4. Honoring our own experiences

4A. Think of a time when your own involvement in a conversation or learning event contributed to a positive experience in educating for change. *Share* that experience in groups of three. Then, *analyze* your stories. What were the factors that contributed to making that a positive experience? *Write* down your factors on the cards provided, and *post* them.

4B. *Analyze* and *synthesize* our factors. What are the common themes that you see emerging from our factors? What consequences do you see for our own work? Together, *note* some guidelines for our planning, learning, and teaching.

The results of this learning task on naming the factors and guidelines that contribute to a positive experience in educating for change also demonstrate the importance of safety and sound relationships to learners. Here are some of the factors that participants named: safety in the context of relationship, acceptance, respect, understanding, love, safe environment, affirmation, creating a safe space for sharing, safe setting, honesty, engagement, sharing stories (giving of yourself, hearing stories, listening), being open, skilled teacher.

After honoring the kind of learning we wanted to facilitate, we named and collected the universe of possibilities for antiracism issues. However, before we could take the crucial step of deciding on the content of the first five antiracism modules, a crisis occurred. We entered what I call the "groan zone"—we left the discussion of design in order to debate and dialogue about the necessity of the program, the role of the race relations committee, and just who the modules were for. This is where the participants asserted ownership over the program, shared their doubts about its place in Toronto churches and its feasibility, and finally took the risk of agreeing to move forward. During the balance of the morning's activities, which included a leisurely outside walk built into the learning tasks, the antiracism program was born.

These are the topics that the participants named for study:

Exploring our experience in diversity and racism—Learn how we see each other; discover what we have in common; discover how we are different; tell stories

Faith and culture: our true identity—How culture shapes us; what it means to be "one in Christ"; what the Bible says about "differences"

Exploring brokenness: historical background and cultures—Canadian context: history of racism and resistance; history of the church and its theology; acculturation, worldview, visible-invisible culture, ethnocentrism; structures and systems

Exploring self-awareness, structures—Prejudice, tokenism, discrimination; what racism is, ethnicity-race; elements and levels of racism; power and structures

Steps to wholeness—Building relationships; action steps; hospitality; friendship; how to organize

Once again, safety was the key principle in the design and facilitation of this session. Here are some of the decisions we intentionally took about safety:

- Provide less content; focus on the essentials.

- Reassure participants by not backing down when the outcome is uncertain.

- Mix small group and large group work.

- Build in physical activity as part of the learning tasks.

The multiple-stage learning needs and resource assessment process, which involved planning, developing, and designing the antiracism program together, has contributed significantly to the program's relevance for the community it intends to serve.

Deepening Our Learning Together

After we had decided on our themes or topics, we recruited facilitators. The committee and the facilitators decided together that we needed more depth, more content in the topics covered to build confidence and increase the safety level. We adopted a twofold strategy.

First, we invited in a team of resource persons to offer us antiracism training, and the antiracism facilitators formed teams in groups of two to do research on their chosen themes and document their findings before the next stage. Then we offered the facilitators a thirty-hour course during which they learned and practiced how to design and facilitate classes on their own theme or content area based on the principles and practices of dialogue education.

The principle of safety also played an important role in choosing a time frame for the thirty-hour course that worked for the facilitators. They were all volunteers. It was clear that a four- or five-day sequence during the workweek would not be feasible. My own preference for four consecutive Saturdays was also ruled out. To allow for family time and minimize the effect on the weekend, the participants unanimously chose four sessions including 7:00 to 9:30 on Friday nights and 8:00 to 1:00 on Saturday mornings.

Widening the Circle

Finally, the design work of the antiracism facilitators was shared with the support community, and future learners. The design, called Widening the Circle: Opening to Diversity and Undoing Racism, is extensive and detailed. Here is a sample workshop design for the section on Exploring Brokenness: The Canadian Context of Racism and Resistance to Racism. (It should be noted that the learning tasks shown here are offered with the permission of the Race Relations Committee of Classis, Toronto, Christian Reformed Church.)

Learning task #1. Program review

1A. *Listen* to this brief description of the purpose of this learning session and the learning objectives for the next hour.

Learning objectives: By the end of this session, we will have:

Described the architecture of racism and resistance

Contrasted and compared the commonalities and differences in racism and resistance in Dresden, Ontario

Named reasons why we fail to see racism

1B. Images of racism

Close your eyes. Take silent prayer time to prepare for this learning session. Relax your body. Identify a visual image that represents racism for you. Inspect that picture in your imagination. What about that image represents racism? When you are ready, describe your image in the large group, and listen to the images of your fellow learners. What image was most commonly mentioned? What image of racism did you find unexpected? Which responses represent images of racism that you'd like to learn more about?

Learning task #2. A story of racism and resistance in Dresden, Ontario

2A. Listen to this brief description of the details of the video *Journey to Justice* (National Film Board of Canada, 2000). What do you already know about Dresden and racism in Dresden?

2B. Watch this video clip. As you watch, jot down the components you see of both racism and resistance to racism.

2C. In groups of three, share the components of racism that you've written, and brainstorm additional ones together. Write your components of racism down on the cards provided, one component per card. Then call them out and post them on the chart provided.

2D. In your same small group, share the components of resistance to racism that you noted down, and brainstorm additional ones together. Write your components of resistance to racism down on the cards provided, again one component per card. Call them out and post them on the chart provided.

2E. Examine our chart on the architecture of racism and resistance to racism in Dresden from that video clip. Together, what would you add to our two lists?

2F. Now, compare and contrast the two lists: What differences do you see between the two lists? What similarities do you see? Arrange the cards on the chart in a way that best represents the relationship between the two lists.

2G. How would you summarize what we've learned so far?

Learning task #3. Video replay

3A. Watch this replay of the panel discussion in the video clip. This time, ask yourself this question as you watch the video: Why did the white community in Dresden fail to see racism in their community in the 1950s?

3B. Share your answer to that question in pairs. Then, share your responses with the larger group. We will jot down your responses on the flip chart as we go. Which of these responses can help illuminate our own ability to recognize racism in 2002?

Learning task #4. Images of resistance to racism

4A. Recall a (recent) situation where you recognized racism, then share that situation with a partner. What means do you see to resist racism in that situation?

4B. Once again, close your eyes. On your own, identify a visual image that represents resistance to racism

for you. Inspect that picture in your imagination.
What about that image represents resistance to
racism?

4C. Stand and rearrange yourselves to form a circle.
After a moment, call out your symbol of resistance
to racism in the group.

Notice how the antiracism facilitators designed for safety. They
designed a sequence of simple to complex questions, small groups,
and *respect* for the golden rule of safety: "Far enough away to be safe,
close enough to be relevant." This design makes the personal experience of the participants more relevant with each new task, at an
appropriate pace, respectfully moving toward ever more critical
thinking and acting.

We enthusiastically adopted a principle from antiracism work: we
cannot teach racism away; we need to organize. All our sequencing of
content and learning tasks build toward this complexity: organize and
commit to personal and community praxis—action with reflection.

Conclusions

As evidence of the success of the Toronto antiracism team, I include
excerpts from some participants' reports:

"They created a safe antiracist environment in both tone
and tenor. There was no racialized anger or hostility observed or
encouraged."

"The format and process was consciously participant-centered.
Learning was designed to actively and creatively engage participants
at the emotional, cognitive, and behavioral levels. Instructional
techniques were appealing to effectively engage participants in both
small groups and plenary discussions."

"Facilitators were appropriately low-key but they showed high
commitment and enthusiasm. They created a learning environment
that was more content-driven than personality-focused."

"From beginning to end a spirit of humility and grace filled the room. The facilitators wisely used integrity to engage participants and to diffuse potential opposition or angst. I found the participatory ambience inviting compared to a conflict or purely didactic approach."

We have discovered that safety is created by design in the learning environment through an atmosphere of welcome and belonging.

Reference

National Film Board of Canada. *Journey to Justice*. Toronto: National Film Board of Canada, 2000.

Open Questions for Analysis and Synthesis

1. What do you see as the implications of a dialogue education program on racism in churches?

2. This case focused on *safety*, a vital principle of dialogue education. What other principles and practices do you discern here?

3. Name one thing you have learned from the learning tasks in this case that you can implement in your work situation.

Conclusion: The Future
of Dialogue Education

Jane Vella

Both the lessons learned in this research and the questions raised by it can move us with clarity and deeper consciousness into our work tomorrow.

Lessons Learned

I was touched by Sarah Gravett's discovery that although learners do construct their own meaning, they need a sure, firm model to practice from in order to reach autonomous, skilled use of what they have learned. Many of the cases point out the need for adequate, professional, aesthetically attractive materials to support learning and ensure transfer. More than one case dealt with the preparation of a dialogue education curriculum that was translated into written materials.

I also read again and again about the need to start at the top of an organization if patterns of learning and teaching are to change. Dr. Montero, who supported Klaus Püschel in Chile, was a dean of the medical school; the entire leadership team of the Volgograd Center for Environmental Training took part in the program described by Peter Perkins and Michaela Stickney. When we do program planning, this recognition of the need for decision makers' endorsement and enthusiasm can be useful.

Concern about the *who* informed all the designs described in this case book. In the Canadian antiracism program, the planners spent time deciding who would be the most appropriate participants for their educational event. Using the Seven Design Steps made a difference in the design of NETWORK's national workshop and in CASA and EFNEP's curricula designs. When the *who* and the *why* were made clear and explicit, educators could select appropriate content and design effective learning tasks. Learning tasks are the heart of dialogue education, as this case book shows. Every story included their implicit or explicit use. This put the focus of each program on the work of the learners. The work of the VISMT team reminds us that the purpose is not dialogue; the purpose is learning.

That is a political stance: power is shared in this form of adult learning. Sometimes the political stance is explicit, as with Michael Culliton's work for NETWORK and Gail von Hahmann and World Education's warm concern for the village leaders of Cambodia. Sometimes the political stance is implicit, as with Meredith Pearson and Jean Anliker working in federally funded programs for women, and Klaus Püschel teaching physicians to care for the poor in Chile.

As the educators who wrote in this volume became more conscious of indicators of learning, transfer, and impact, they were able to adjust their designs. "How do they know they know?" became an operative question for Barbara Gassner in her work with welfare recipients in Vermont; individual learning and the collective learning of the group were distinguished and celebrated. Marianne Reiff saw transfer into the work life of her "weekend college" students, and Elena Carbone saw her undergraduate nutrition students use in later professional training what she had taught them. Transfer was obvious in Greg Walker-Wilson's work with the Mountain Microenterprise Fund as students put their new business plans into action. The impact was visible in the work of the physicians at the residency program in Santiago, Chile, and in Linda Gershuny's work with teachers in Haiti.

Questions Raised

The questions raised in these cases point to a present and future research agenda for dialogue education. How can we resolve the dilemma of material to be "covered" and the use of learning tasks? How can we get enough time to support people in the hard work of learning? How can we get support for design time? How can we win the support and enthusiasm of executives who say they do not have time to take a course or even read a book?

Dialogue education tomorrow must address these research questions. Many of them deal not with the immediate design but rather with the social environment and roles and relationships. From my peaceful porch in North Carolina, I urge all of you who are concerned with the advance of effective education to do two things: *celebrate* and *document*. First, celebrate. Name the successes and the obstacles overcome. Affirm the hard work of people like Cynthia Bizzell, who spent years redesigning the CASA curriculum, Jane Connor, who dares to offer effective undergraduate learning to large numbers of students, and Robb Davis and friends, who have made dialogue education standard practice worldwide in Freedom from Hunger. Then, document. Write for research journals, present at conferences and seminars, produce more case books and records of institutes. Celebrate to keep the energy up; document to spread the energy around the globe.

Quantum thinking assures us that the work of NOJI and CA/WIC, the teaching and learning at the Wisconsin Union and in VISMT, the innovations of EFNEP and CASA, are all affecting educational practice. Distance learning is affected by the video-conferenced undergraduate training programs offered by Steve Stahl and the weekend college format used by Marianne Reiff. Nonprofit organizations have not been the same since the board training of Darlene Goetzman and Karen Ridout: the energy is different now! The whole is more than the sum of its parts.

I am moved by letters from graduate students in adult education who say: "We are using your books as our texts. I am delighted with what I read because it is what I always knew education was meant to be." It is a sign of hope that a generation of adult educators is studying the power of dialogue.

When I invited educators to contribute to this case book I made it plain that this was meant not as a eulogy but as a statement of how challenging it is to design and lead effective learning. Malcolm Knowles ended his 1984 case book with this conclusion: "What a world of infinite potential we are entering" (p. 422). A generation later we can say that we live in that world and are ready to make it one "in which it is easier to love" (Freire, 1972, p. 24).

References

Freire, P. *Pedagogy of the Oppressed*. New York: Herder & Herder, 1972.
Knowles, M. *Andragogy in Action: Applying Modern Principles of Adult Learning*. San Francisco Jossey-Bass, 1984.

Appendix: Selected Principles and Practices of Dialogue Education

Training Through Dialogue (Vella, 1995) offers a summary of selected principles and practices known and named at the time it was published. This appendix reviews in greater depth many of those named in 1996 and also adds a few more learned since then from our ongoing action research. We begin with the all-important Seven Design Steps and Four I's, then continue in alphabetical order.

The Seven Design Steps

This is a tried-and-true program-planning instrument that is congruent with the principles of dialogue education.

First we consider *who*: the participants in the educational event. We name the leaders. We tell how many participants, and as much about them as we know from *the learning needs and resource assessment*. Then we name the *why*: the situation that calls for this educational event. I like to phrase it: the named *who* need to. . . . Then we name the time frame, *when*, and the site of the event, *where*. The more detail here the better. You cannot name what the content of an educational program is if you do not know how much time you have to do it, or all the details of the learning place. *What* is named next: the specific content the *who* needs to learn to meet the *why*. A cautionary note is useful here: most educators write too much *what* for their *when*. The content is laid out as a set of nouns or verbal nouns: for example, a time line of all of the operas of Verdi, the composer's development ending in *Falstaff*, four familiar arias from *Nabucco, Rigoletto, La Traviata,* how to recognize themes in Verdi's operas. Achievement-based objectives (*what for*) are written to parallel the content, so that the learning tasks can be set up as *what the learners do to learn the what.* In this case the achievement-based objectives might be: By the end of this two-hour session, all learners will have:

> *Examined* a time line with the titles of all Verdi's operas and where they were written and first produced
>
> *Read and responded to* an essay on Verdi's development over time
>
> *Heard and responded to* three arias, one from *Nabucco, Rigoletto,* and *La Traviata*
>
> Heard those arias again, naming the recurring themes in each aria

The seventh step is *how,* which names the learning tasks and materials. Once the achievement-based objectives (*what for*) are congruent with the content (*what*), the learning tasks are virtually given. In this case, one learning task would be as follows:

> Learning task #1. *Examine* this time line that shows the titles of all Verdi's operas and where they were written and first produced. *Circle* any names you already know. *Underline* operas you hope to see and hear soon. *Share* your time line with one other student. What are your questions about this time line? We'll hear and respond to all.

Are the Seven Design Steps essential to dialogue education? No. However, now that you know them and once you use them, you will discover for yourself how deeply they enhance and focus the process.

The Four I's: Inductive Work, Input, Implementation, Integration

This is a sequence of learning tasks that is effective. Inductive work connects the new content to this set of learners, evoking prior knowledge and their generative themes. For example, as you design to teach a group of young adults the science around the issue of tobacco addiction, you can begin with an inductive learning task that invites them to (1) identify common addictions, (2) name addictions they have had in their lives, (3) describe a film or book that showed a character with a serious addiction. The input task offers available and current data on addiction in the form of charts, or handouts, posters, a video or documentary film, a chapter in a book. Learners are asked to interact and engage with that input and report on that interaction. In this way, the teacher is aware of their grasp of the input. For example, read this page from [book title] on signs of addictions. Circle those you have actually seen, in life or in film, and share what you circled in your small group. What are your questions?

Every set of learning tasks must have substantive input. Dialogue education is research-based. How the data or information is offered is what is unique. Any trivializing of input is counterproductive. Learning does not take place when the content is trivialized. Input tasks lead to implementation tasks, where the learners do something substantive with the input. For example, an implementation task would be this: as a team, make a poster that you will share with a teenage friend, with one data-based message about addiction. An integration task is one that moves learners from the session back to their workaday world. For example: in your team, compose a letter to teachers in your local high school, offering them a workshop on the dangers of addiction. Describe what content you will share in that workshop.

Using the Four I's in the design of courses and educational programs ensures that learning tasks flow in an appropriate sequence toward measurable learning.

Accountability

This is the principle that assures us that the design is appropriate for the groups of learners, the content fits the time frame, the learning tasks evoke products that are documented in a personal portfolio. Careful use of the Seven Design Steps moves us toward accountability.

This is such a transcendent principle in that all the other principles are at its service. If our design is not accountable, it is worthless. Who is accountable to whom? The educator is accountable to learners, the learners are accountable to one another in their small groups and to the educator. No one escapes the sweet burden of this principle.

Affirmation

Arthur Miller put it so well in *Death of a Salesman*: "Attention must be paid!" (Miller, 1949, p. 56). I have often said that that phrase is vital to the success of adult learning. I invite teachers to offer *lavish* affirmation. Be generous with praise and see what results you get in terms of learning. In high school, I wrote an essay entitled "A Walk in the Woods." Since my high school was on Forty-Second Street in New York City, this was quite an imaginative effort. I wrote: *The path stretched like a leafy Champs Elysees into the trees.* The teacher wrote on that essay: I have never read anything quite as lovely! That occurred fifty-seven years ago. I am still writing! Lavish affirmation is powerful. I have noticed that those who most strenuously resist this practice are almost always folks who need affirmation the most. "Thank you!" is lavish affirmation at the appropriate time.

Analysis-Synthesis

We take apart a situation (analysis) and then put it back together (synthesis). We name what we perceive, offer our suggestions as to why a situation occurs, consider the implications for our own life, and then draw conclusions. This involves using a focused case study with the four open questions:

1. What do you see happening here?
2. Why do you think it happens?
3. When it happens in your work, what issues does it raise?
4. What can we together do about it?

When this becomes an implementation learning task, after some significant input it can bring meaningful learning. For example, teaching young people the hard facts of tobacco addiction, you follow up the input with a story of a man who is dying of emphysema, dragging around a tank so he can breathe. Those four open questions invite analysis and lead to a personal synthesis. The open questions for analysis and synthesis that follow each of the cases presented in this volume are intended to move the reader to learning.

Authenticity

Those who wish to take up the profession of counselor or psychotherapist must themselves undergo personal therapy. Being a teacher of adults demands the same discipline. Few adults will put up with anything false in a class or program. If they have the option to object or leave, they will. Dialogue education, these principles and practices, demand a great deal of the teacher. The first demand is for authenticity: *You get what you see!* When the teacher rings true, from the first moments of the learning needs and resource assessment to the final impact evaluation, the learners echo that authenticity.

Autonomy

Learning tasks and dialogue education in general demand that learners act with autonomy throughout the course or program. That is, they decide the meaning of what they are learning, how they will use it, and when. This happens quite naturally. It can be celebrated by educators' naming the behaviors that show autonomy and affirming them, and by educators' never deciding what learners can decide and never doing what learners can do for themselves.

This is another "heart of the matter" principle. Dialogue education cannot work in an environment where a teacher makes decisions for adult learners. Such behavior is not congruent to the purpose of dialogue.

Congruence

In this model, the design and implementation of adult learning must be congruent throughout. That is, the materials show respect, the time is appropriate for this set of learners, the challenge is at a level that fits the group. The educator consistently does what he or she is teaching. These principles and practices apply not only to learners but to all involved in a dialogue education program. We saw this congruence in the stories of Sarah Gravett's work with colleges, and in Marianne Reiff's description of her work with adults in a weekend college. They had to do what they were teaching.

Consultative-Deliberative Voices

We have a consultative voice when we offer suggestions. We have a deliberative voice when we make decisions. In a feedback session, for example, learners offer suggestions to the designers-teachers in a consultative voice. What is vital is for us to know clearly what voice we are in at any time. Feedback is always given in a consultative voice. The teacher uses a deliberative voice to decide what the content of a program will be and invites the consultative voice of learners to corroborate or amend her decision. Being unclear about this principle leads to serious trouble in program planning and teaching.

Design

I love this word. It speaks to all the aspects of an educational experience. When I revised *Learning to Listen, Learning to Teach* in 2002, I went through the manuscript and removed the word "planning" in favor of the term "design." We design for learning and can be surprised at the results. The Seven Design Steps inform what we will do, not as a unilateral plan toward a preconceived objective but as a design that can be contextualized.

Dialogue

This is the prime principle. Remember, it is a means, not the end. The end of this structured approach to adult education is *learning*. Dialogue is the principle that informs every decision, every learning task, every relationship, every piece of learning material. We do not do this work in order to enter into dialogue. We do this work in order to learn and to support the learning of others.

Echoing and Paraphrasing

In dialogue, we listen to learners. They know they have been heard when we can echo their responses or arguments—that is, say what we heard them say. Or we can paraphrase what we heard, using our own words. These are practices directly related to respect and accountability.

Energy

This is a quantum thinking term that speaks to what occurs among a group of learners when a well-formed design of dialogue education is offered. The room sparks with ideas, dialogue, objections and differences of perception, and laughter. I can tell when learning is taking place by the level of energy in the room. Sometimes, as we know, energy is silent and somber, smoldering. At other times, the paint is coming off the walls. An introvert shows her energy differently from an extrovert. In any case, we need that energy in a learning situation.

Sarah Gravett has done a study (Gravett and Geyser, 2003) of what occurs in the brain when a professor is talking and students are passive listeners. As she says: "The professor is getting a high!" We can share that energy by designing relevant, appropriate learning tasks that share the high as synapses fire in all brains, not just in one.

Engagement

The engagement of the learners in their own learning is essential. Kurt Lewin (Johnson and Johnson, 1991) taught that such engagement was cognitive, affective, and physical. Always! Gravett (Gravett and Geyser, 2003) shows that a university lecturer is deeply engaged and gets a "high" from his own lecture as a result of what is occurring in his brain, in his body. Dialogue education is simply designed to share that "high" to engage learners deeply in the process of making theory on any subject. Lack of physical engagement means no learning, or worse, learning that it is our role to be passive, to listen quietly, not to be engaged.

Evaluation: Indicators of Learning, Transfer, and Impact

Evaluation is the measure of quantitative and qualitative indicators of learning completed in a learning session: a conference, seminar, course, program. When the Seven Design Steps have been used, the specific, explicit content (what) and the achievement-based objectives (what for) so control the learning tasks that learners are moved to do the work involved in learning. Indicators are behavioral: *wrote two short, focused learning tasks in an hour; led a feedback session asking open questions.* Indicators are specific and the verbs used are not unrelated to the verbs named for learning tasks and achievement-based objectives (Vella, 2000).

Transfer is the use of a skill or a knowledge set or behavior in a work site or at home, outside the classroom or seminar room. Skills, knowledge, attitudes are transferred when they are used, not when they are tested. In that use, the learned content is often improved by fitting into the context of the learner. Transfer is also measured by products and actions: *designed a curriculum using dialogue education; led a Boy Scout Troop safely on an overnight camping trip.* Transfer can also occur in the learning event: Is that an indicator of learning or of transfer? What a lovely dilemma for a teacher to face!

Impact is the personal or organizational change manifest as a result of the educational event. It is not always possible to see a direct correlation from event to impact. The case of the Family and Community Medicine residency program in Chile described in this volume is a rare example of almost direct correlation of impact to learning.

Feedback

Feedback is not evaluation. Feedback is the response of a group of learners to an event, or to a program. A force-field analysis is a useful instrument for feedback, inviting learners to name what was useful and what they would suggest be changed. The feedback task is a learning task: name what you found most useful in this session. Then offer your suggestions for what might be changed. As learners do this task in their small groups, they get the courage from one another to say things they could not say alone. As they hear their colleagues' responses, they are reminded of their own implicit feelings. It is vital for the educator to welcome all feedback, and to avoid defending the program or actions of leaders. In this format, negative feedback is offered as suggestions for changes—in a consultative voice. The response to feedback is always either "Thanks!" or "Can you clarify what you mean by that?"

The feedback process used for teams when they complete their practice teaching in the Learning to Listen, Learning to Teach training course is invaluable. There are two compound parts. The designers-teachers are invited to say what they liked about their design and teaching. The "students" are then invited to name what they liked about this design and teaching. The team is then asked: What will you do differently next time? And the students are asked: What are your suggestions to this team?

The first time this process is used, everyone involved wants to defend and reply: "Well, I did that because. . . ." We invite them to say: "Thanks!" This is a critical implementation of the social revolution that dialogue education demands: this is not an adversarial relationship! We all need practice in living in such a new system.

Force-Field Analysis

This is a useful tool for feedback or for the analysis of any situation. Using a T format, learners are invited to name what was most useful to them in a session or program, and to put that on one side of the T. Then they offer suggestions about how the session can be improved, and write that on the other side of the T. This is a visible presentation of feedback or any analysis.

Found Objects

The practice of using found objects (anything that one can put one's hands on) brings to life the principle that learning involves ideas, feelings, and actions. It is an amazing move from the abstract to the concrete, from the general to the specific. A found object used as a symbol moves the creative imagination into uncharted waters. Learning task: find an object that symbolizes dialogue education for you!

Gallery Walk

I find that the most fruitful learning tasks involve products. For example, in that class on tobacco addiction, learners can produce one-message billboards on poster paper. As each team presents its message, team members are invited to put them on the walls of the room. All learners get a synthesis learning task: in pairs, move about the room, examining all posters. Select the one message that you would take home to your teenager.

Such a gallery walk could be a way to learn from poster displays at conferences. When small groups are armed with a learning task, they can make the most of a poster display or whatever the gallery has to offer.

Generative Themes

Paulo Freire used this term (1972) to guide those educators who wanted to use dialogue in their listening to learners and their use of what they heard. The learning needs and resource assessment shown at work in this casebook illustrates one way of hearing generative themes of learners. Themes are called generative because they generate energy for learning.

Humility

Humility is seen as the stance of the confident, well-prepared educator who recognizes that he has something to learn from learners and from their new configuration of the content he is teaching. Without a modicum of such humility, this design for dialogue is not possible.

Humor

"I am not laughing at you," said Robin Williams to the nervous adolescent in his literature class in the film *Dead Poets Society*. "I am laughing near you!" No laughing, no learning. This practice (or is it a principle?) is directly related to authenticity and autonomy. And to humility!

Ideas, Actions, Feelings

The fact that all learning is cognitive, affective, and physical is a principle that becomes a practice. It is related to Kurt Lewin's research (Johnson and Johnson, 1991) and also to our good common sense. We know we did not learn to ride a bicycle by watching our brother ride, or learn the table of the elements by memorizing it, or gain self-confidence by reading a book. We did what we needed to do to learn these skills, concepts, and attitudes. We were engaged with the ideas, physically and emotionally. Lewin was right. The challenge to us all is to design learning tasks that involve all three: ideas, actions, and feeling.

Immediacy

This was early on named an essential element of adult learning. That is, adults come to learning for their self-directed purpose, which the educator has to honor. The design, informed by a clear understanding of the situation (why) and the who, is aimed at the bull's-eye of immediacy. This learning has to work for them here and now. When the content is immediately useful, you know it is relevant and the energy in the learning group will be high. When energy falls, it is a clear sign that there is little or no immediacy. Adult learners bring their context to the classroom; they will be quick to test the immediacy of what they are learning as they try to fit it into their context. Again, this is a good reason to do an effective learning needs and resource assessment.

Inclusion

The best way to examine the meaning of this principle is to consider its opposite. If a learner is not included, she feels *excluded*.

That is a great way to stop learning. This means welcoming the most difficult student, the one whose position is furthest from yours. This is the work of equity: all are not equal, but all get the same attention, the same chance, the same opportunity to learn. It may be the principle and practice at the heart of dialogue.

Inductive-Deductive

Inductive work occurs when we begin with a life experience, a story or a case study, a film or a program for review. Then we move to theory that explains why the event represented took place as it did. Inductive = action to theory. Deductive work occurs when we begin with a theory and then experiment with an implementation of that theory. Deductive = theory to action. Notice that the Four I's proposed for a learning task (Vella, 2000) include inductive and deductive work. Moving back and forth between these two is how learning occurs.

Learners as Subjects or Decision Makers

This is another principle at the heart of dialogue education. The philosophical distinction between subject (that which acts) and object (that which is acted upon) is being used here. In dialogue, all are subjects. All are actors. The design of education is an invitation to subjects to deal with content as decision makers, not as clay pots to be filled (objects). How many other principles and practices does this one influence?

Learning Needs and Resource Assessment

This practice is an essential part of the dialogue education protocol. It is a simple step where the educator invites the opinion of learners on the program, their sense of their own needs as learners, and the resources they bring to the event. In the appendix to *Taking Learning to Task* (Vella, 2000) there is a list of suggested ways to do an LNRA.

Learning Tasks

Learning tasks are the heart of this structured approach to dialogue education (Vella, 2002). A learning task is an open question put to a small group who have all the resources they need to respond. A learning task is a task for the learner, not for the professor or leader. This shift of the locus of energy from the lectern to the learners in small groups is a quantum leap toward learning and the construction of theory that fits a context. Making this shift is never easy. I once heard Paulo Freire say: "Only the student can name the moment of the death of the professor." I suggest that the "professor" names his own death as "professor" when he acknowledges that he too is learning.

Open Questions

The practice at the heart of dialogue is the design of open questions. A learning task is an open question put to a small group with all the resources they need to respond. I dare say that this is the practice that moves stumbling efforts into dialogue, and that transforms roles, and evokes critical thinking and constructed learning. Closed questions: *What's the capital of Maryland?* and fishing questions: *Who's buried in Grant's tomb?* sound the death knell to learning. If one asked me what drives sixteen-year-olds on their birthday to clean out their high school locker, go directly to the DMV for their license, and then go to McDonald's for a minimum-wage job, I would say it is a lack of open questions. Open questions invite dialogue. A corollary to the practice of open questions is the difficult practice of quiet on the part of the teacher. A learning task is a task for the learner.

Praxis

This is a Greek word that means action and reflection. When a learning task is well designed, it demands praxis, not practice. Learners use new theory in a deductive task, examine their use of that theory, and shape the theory to fit their context. Action without reflection is not good practice, of course. These cases show how they became praxis in the telling of them.

Preparation

The cases in this book show the quality of preparation needed to design an effective dialogue education program. Preparation is intimately related to the principle of *time*. My own experience has been that I need two hours of preparation for each hour of "teaching." Without this quality of preparation, teaching is not what it can be. The use of a learning needs and resource assessment, the Seven Design Steps, and learning tasks and appropriate materials usually ensures this two-to-one ratio or shows it to be conservative. In any case, preparation is both a principle related to respect and a necessary practice. Notice that preparation is not only of content but also of process.

Reinforcement

How often do I need to reinforce a concept or a skill with a group of adult learners? We repeated the adage "Twenty-two times to habituate" in *How Do They Know They Know?* (Vella, Berardinelli, and Burrow, 1998). However, that seems a small number for learners like me. In any case, educators must recognize the principle of reinforcement, doing innovative and diverse learning tasks again and again so that learners do indeed know that they know. The implementation and integration learning tasks indicated in the Four I's are a form of reinforcement. Documentation of transfer is another way for a learner to reinforce a skill or new set of knowledge.

Relevance

Consider how the relevance of what you are teaching relates to generative themes, to the Seven Design Steps that begin with *who* and *why*, to ensure relevance of the *what*. Relevance means that what is being learned has meaning to the learners. This relates also to the principle of immediacy: adults want and need assurance that what they are learning is immediately applicable in their lives.

Respect

Respect for the learner and for colleagues is operative at every level. An open question is a sign of respect. Designing and preparing learning tasks in an appropriate sequence so that learning takes place is evidence of respect. Offering the right amount of learning in the time given, without crowding, is respectful. As learners are treated with respect, we see them acting differently with one another. The "natural" adversarial relationships prevalent in our social structures give way to collaboration and laughter, evoking confirmation of the assumptions of dialogue education.

Role-Plays and Sociodramas

One practice I use with some reluctance is a role-play or sociodrama to present a case for the implementation learning task. My concern is that I am not a therapist, and a role-play or sociodrama, with exquisite immediacy, can evoke responses from learners that are at a level I cannot serve. Role-play and sociodrama are valuable practices in the hands of a talented educator; however, because they are delicate, they are not essential to this model of dialogue education.

Safety

Safety in a learning situation must be created by the teacher. Peter Noteboom's study of the design of an antiracism workshop in Canada shows how the principle and practice of safety can inform a program. Adults often come to learning events with some temerity. All of the cases show how the creation of safety was one of the first tasks of the teachers or program directors. Safety is not the absence of challenge or of work. The Canadians said: "We have discovered that safety is created, by design, in the learning environment, by an atmosphere of welcome and belonging." Again, it is part of a whole learning fabric: challenge is offered with the promise of support in printed materials, reinforcement, and a sensible sequence of learning tasks. No one of these principles and practices acts alone.

Sample

When a learning task has been completed, it is not necessary for every team to report on their results. Hearing from a small sample provides the necessary closure to the task, and enough confirmation so that the leader knows the task has been well done, and the learning has occurred. Using a sample prevents the tedium of a "round robin" response and still allows for comprehensive reporting.

Sequence

Sequence is such a valuable principle that it often feels like a practice. As I examine a set of learning tasks, or a list of achievement-based objectives or content, I now always look at the sequence: small to large, simple to complex, single to many, familiar to unfamiliar. That practice comes from honoring the abstract principle of sequence. When the sequence is off, you can watch the learners' self-confidence and energy fall. The sequence of the Seven Design Steps, for example, is vital to effective program planning.

Small Groups

Because learning tasks are often done in a small group, this is a central practice of dialogue education. In a paper entitled "Taking Socrates to Task" (Vella, 2001), I wrote that the dialogue we speak of is not between teacher and student but among learners, of whom the teacher is one. It is not vertical but horizontal dialogue, accomplished in the midst of a learning task. What occurs in the small group is learning, not only of the content being taught but also of the context and culture of colleagues. Different perceptions of content can be examined, argued, and a synthesis occurs. The report of a small group can reflect differences or some level of consensus. This is reality. The small group is another essential element of dialogue education.

Stories and Case Studies

You have seen a use of case studies with open questions to guide learning in this book. Learners telling their own stories can be part of the inductive learning task. Input can be provided through stories or case studies shaped to a particular format. Implementation learning tasks can afford learners the opportunity to do something with that input. They could, for example, say how the original story they told might be changed by application of the new data. Everybody loves a story. In *Learning to Listen, Learning to Teach* (Vella, 2002) I taught twelve principles and practices of dialogue through stories. Stories and case studies in dialogue education are used not only to illustrate but also to teach a concept. The interpretation involved when a story is told invites learners immediately to use their context, and make the content theirs.

Time

Respect for the value of time for preparation and for learning is essential in dialogue education. We have come to a point today where we will not do a session without enough time. When teachers are not using dialogue education, they can cover as much as they wish in a given amount of time. They can speed up the presentation or slow it down. Dialogue education takes time because learning takes time. We have an axiom. Three things are necessary for effective dialogue education, in this order: time, time, and time.

Titles

Everything in the materials used for dialogue education has a title: programs, booklets, LNRA, individual learning tasks. Being faithful to this principle is closely related to respect, to accountability, and to congruence. We do what we teach.

Warm-Ups

A warm-up is a learning task used as the first in a session for a number of purposes: to bring learners together, to focus on the subject at hand, and to create an atmosphere of seriousness and safety. It is a learning task. There is no such thing as a "little warm-up." We cannot ever trivialize the process or the content without losing both. The title of a warm-up learning task might be: Learning task #1. Warm-up: our experience with lasers. This relates to stories, to respect for the participants' experience, to relevance, and to focus on the topic.

References

Freire, P. *Pedagogy of the Oppressed*. New York: Herder & Herder, 1972.

Gravett, S., and Geyser, H. (eds.). *Teaching and Learning in Higher Education*. Pretoria, South Africa: Van Schaik Publishers, 2003.

Johnson, D., and Johnson, L. *Joining Together: Group Theory and Group Skills*. Englewood Cliffs, N.J.: Prentice Hall, 1991.

Miller, A. *Death of a Salesman*. New York: Viking, 1949.

Vella, J. *Training Through Dialogue: Promoting Effective Learning and Change with Adults*. San Francisco: Jossey-Bass, 1995.

Vella, J. *Taking Learning to Task: Creative Strategies for Teaching Adults*. San Francisco: Jossey-Bass, 2000.

Vella, J. "Taking Socrates to Task." [www.janevella.com/archives]. 2001.

Vella, J. *Learning to Listen, Learning to Teach: The Power of Dialogue in Educating Adults*. San Francisco: Jossey-Bass, 2002. (Originally published 1994.)

Vella, J., Berardinelli, P., and Burrow, J. *How Do They Know They Know? Evaluating Adult Learning*. San Francisco: Jossey-Bass, 1998.

Index

Please remember that this is a library book,
and that it belongs only temporarily to each
person who uses it. Be considerate. Do
not write in this, or any, library book.